Selected and Edited by

Christopher Cerf

and

Marina Albee

with Lev Gushchin

Consulting Editor: Lynn Visson

Translator: Hans Fenstermacher

With an Introduction by

Vitaly Korotich

Editor in Chief of Ogonyok

SMALL FIRES

Letters from
the Soviet People
to *Ogonyok* Magazine
1987 – 1990

SUMMIT BOOKS
New York   London   Toronto   Sydney   Tokyo   Singapore

Summit Books
Simon & Schuster Building
Rockefeller Center
1230 Avenue of the Americas
New York, New York 10020

Designed by Levavi & Levavi/Carla Weise
Manufactured in the United States of America

1   3   5   7   9   10   8   6   4   2

Library of Congress Cataloging in Publication Data

Small fires : letters from the Soviet people to *Ogonyok* magazine
1987–1990 / selected and edited by Christopher Cerf and Marina Albee
with Lev Gushchin ; consulting editor, Lynn Visson ; chief
translator, Hans Fenstermacher ; with an introduction by Vitaly
Korotich.
p.   cm.
Includes index.
1.Soviet Union—Social life and customs—1970– 2.Public
opinion—Soviet Union.   3.Soviet Union—Politics and
government—1985– 4.Russian newspapers—Sections, columns, etc.—
Letters to the editor.   I. Cerf, Christopher.   II. Albee, Marina.
III. Gushchin, L. N.   IV. Visson, Lynn.   V. Ogonek.
DK287.S53   1990
947.0854—dc20   90-44472
CIP

ISBN 0-671-69397-2
ISBN 0-671-72876-8 (pbk)

CONTENTS

ACKNOWLEDGMENTS

"Before the era of Mikhail S. Gorbachev," *The New York Times* reported in a 1988 front-page story, "readers' letters were regarded as fit to print only if they made a point the authorities wanted to make, and they were severely edited for that purpose."

But that situation changed abruptly in 1987 when *Ogonyok*, a popular Soviet weekly whose name means "a small fire," became the first magazine in the USSR to publish a regular, broad-based "Letters to the Editors" column. The Letters section of *Ogonyok* was immediately recognized as the first national forum of open political and social dialogue available to Soviet citizens, and, from the very beginning, it attracted an unprecedented outpouring of opinion and passion from people all over the country.

Credit for this astonishing development belongs principally to three men—Vitaly Korotich, the Ukrainian poet who took over as editor-in-chief of *Ogonyok* soon after Gorbachev's ascension to power and immediately began using the hitherto pallid feature magazine (Korotich claims he "used to buy it only for the crossword puzzle") to test the limits of the newly declared policy of *glasnost;* Lev Gushchin, whom Korotich brought to the magazine as his deputy editor-in-chief; and Valentin Yumashev, editor of "A Word from the Reader," *Ogonyok*'s Letters column. We admire each of them greatly (it must be remembered that they had no guarantee they would be spared should Gorbachev's reforms fail), just as we admire the hundreds of thousands of ordinary citizens who responded to *Ogonyok*'s bold invitation to state their feelings and opinions in writing. Without their courage this book, of course, would have been impossible.

We are grateful, too, to Korotich, Gushchin, and Yumashev for embracing so enthusiastically our notion that readers' letters to *Ogonyok* could provide Westerners with a unique, first-person look at everyday life in the Soviet Union, and for their unflagging help in putting the manuscript together. In particular, we wish to thank

Lev Gushchin for his inventiveness, for his organizational efforts, and for the many patient hours he spent with us—in Moscow and New York—sifting through piles of reader mail and providing invaluable background information. We are also profoundly grateful to Valentin Yumashev and the staff of the Letters Department, who carefully copied and FAXed to us in New York the "best of" each week's new mail—no small accomplishment in a country where duplicating and FAX machines and phone lines are at a premium. Even more important, they searched tirelessly through the hundreds of thousands of unpublished letters in *Ogonyok*'s files to find additional material to enrich and balance our presentation.

Lynn Visson, our consulting editor, used her remarkable skills as an interpreter and her impressive knowledge of the Soviet scene to dictate on audiocassette summaries of the thousands of letters— all in Russian—that crossed our desks. Our debt to her—for her services and for her wonderfully supportive advice—is incalculable. And thanks, too, to the others who helped with summaries and preliminary translations of the *Ogonyok* letters: in particular, Vladimir Zheleznikov and Ruthanne Kasday Williams.

We also wish to express our deepest gratitude to Gavriil Popov, Olzhas Suleimenov, Sergei Khrushchev, and the late Andrei Sakharov—distinguished Soviets who somehow found the time to contribute notes and special commentaries to our book.

Hans Fenstermacher, our translator, worked gallantly around the clock to keep up with the flow of letters while events in the Soviet Union continued to unfold at breakneck speed, even as our deadline approached. His independent research on the victims of Stalin's repressions also proved a priceless resource.

We extend our special thanks also to Victor Khrolenko and Cynthia Rosenberger of Belka International, whose hospitality knew no bounds, and whose interpreting skills, knowledge of the Moscow bureaucracy—and FAX machine—rescued our project time and again; and to Igor Menzelintsev and Andrei Menshikov, who made our visits to the Soviet Union so much more productive and pleasant.

We are also grateful to Ed Victor and Andrew Nurnberg, our agents, for their friendship, encouragement, and support; and to Jim Silberman and Anne Freedgood of Summit Books; Florence Falkow, and Eve and Frank Metz of Simon & Schuster; Kyle Cathie of Kyle Cathie Limited; and Dieter Curths and Gerald

Trageiser of Paul List Verlag for their creativity, advice, patience persistence, and faith in our project.

Others whose help, advice, and hard work proved invaluable include Edgar Cheporov, Inge Cheporova, Julia Ede, Margaret Foley, Seva Gakkel, Vladimir Kovalyov, Ina Meibach, Boris Rabbot, Scott Robb, Jonathan Sanders, and Kenny Schaffer.

Thanks, too, to Trude Flynn and her fellow transcribers—Kenneth Lo, Virginia MacVeigh, Quisqueya Meyreles, Barbara Pressman, Kirk Walsh, and Andrew Zack—who somehow managed to transfer Lynn Visson's small mountain of taped letter summaries into our Macintosh computers and our file cabinets. And finally, a very special thank you to Jill Rabon, who, day in and day out, kept everything from falling apart.

Christopher Cerf
Marina Albee
July 1990

ОГОНЁК (o-´gon-yok),
m., a light,
a spark, a small fire.

Ogonyok.

Vitaly Korotich, editor-in-chief of *Ogonyok.*

INTRODUCTION
by Vitaly Korotich

Only in a country where the government is ineffective can the editors of a weekly magazine receive so many letters. People are turning to us because they want to change their lives, and they see us journalists, whom they trust, as their main ally in that battle. When people became disillusioned with the previous corrupt leadership, they discovered freedom in discussing the actions of those who had brought this tragedy upon the country, and they used that freedom to the fullest. Their letters became fearless, and our correspondents were so accurate and courageous in presenting their views that one could only rejoice at such widespread sophisticated political thinking.

I believe that M. S. Gorbachev has found allies in the majority of the people who write letters to our magazine. Allies, but also overseers. People are demanding changes. Many letters are like manifestos, and most of them are calling the system and its leaders to account. The time has come to pay up. Today we are paying for all the merrymaking of our bemedaled leaders. The bills of many decades are collecting on M. S. Gorbachev's desk, and he must pay every one of them. Such are the times. Many letters to our editorial office are just such bills. We, too, have to pay.

Someday, after life returns to normal (but when?), we will receive fewer letters. When people begin to believe the leadership again, they will turn to it more often, and they will discuss and insist on changes for the better. But for the time being they write and complain to us. They do so because of our reputation, because we have not yet been caught in a lie. They do so because our readers feel we are part of their lives; we are with them in their struggle and in their pain. It is no accident that during the past four years subscriptions to *Ogonyok* have gone from a few hundred thousand to four million. I think this surge is unique and unparalleled— worthy of inclusion in the *Guinness Book of World Records*.

Our country turns out to have a remarkably high tolerance for pain. Perhaps that is because for so many years we were obliged to be happy. We were granted permission to marvel at how wonderful our country's government was; after every more or less formal meeting it was customary to compose a collective letter to our leadership. These letters were never sent; they symbolized our loyalty to the system and its leaders, nothing more. In this culture of universal exaltation, when grieving was permitted only in solitude, people mastered the art of writing letters resembling internal monologues, where they recorded confessions, and expressed their deepest thoughts.

The art of pain—I have written and thought about this many times—is higher than the art of happiness. Pain is always concrete. Whether it is a tooth, arm, leg or back that hurts, you understand the root of your suffering; you feel it not in some abstract way, but precisely, concretely. Most of our letters are about pain. And about how to overcome the pain. Soon, there will be some 200,000 of them a year. At the beginning of 1986 there were barely twenty a day. Everything is different now. The openness of our society, its desire to have its say after decades of censorship, is stunning. People are writing letters, asking questions, and providing their own answers.

For too long our basic laws, even our Constitution, explained to us only what we were obliged to do. We had rights, but they were sometimes ephemeral ones, like a hen's right to soar above the clouds. Now people have begun to understand the meaning of the major prohibitions (without obeying them in any way) and the meaning of the fact that many things are allowed. People are hurrying to have their say, like a stutterer who has just been cured and is hastening to prove to himself that he can talk as well as everyone else.

Sometimes, too, those who know no other language than threats are rushing to speak out. We constantly receive letters with promises to kill, humiliate, destroy. They are like tidings from the past. I do not know about your laws, but ours do not prohibit writing and sending such letters. These threats are all the more horrifying because the newfound storm troopers are not merely threatening to act, they fully intend to do so. And people who are angry at the shocking things going on around them are becoming frightened and at the same time tempted by the prospect of a return to a strong authority, and by the hope of punishing the trouble-makers.

This is not as simple as it seems. In a country where fifty years ago tens of millions of citizens fell victim to repressions, and where a careless letter calling for democracy could become the basis for a death sentence, one has to make many internal changes to keep from being afraid. And people *are* changing. They are becoming more trusting, braver, purer. Everyone understands that in a country where millions went through prisons and labor camps there had to be and are hundreds of thousands, if not millions, of jailers and informers. Informers also write letters, but rarely to us; if they do, it is with threats. Informers write to the government, warning it that the agents of capitalism are seeking to destroy the foundation of our marvelous society. And these letters are studied very seriously, and respectfully answered. This situation is understandable if one realizes that for too long yesterday's all-powerful citizens of the Soviet Union were told that they, in fact, *were* socialism. And so today they perceive a threat to themselves as a threat to the socialism they built.

If only you could see those people who have so often been called your capitalist agents! More often than not, they are people who are waking up, or have already awakened, to political activity. They are separated from capitalism by the entire history of their personal experience. But they have gotten tired of the lies and are fully prepared to overcome them at any price. In a democracy, you come to understand certain things are more important than your own life. *We* were told that it was especially fulfilling to give our lives for a dictator. . . . And thousands of people have written about that in millions of letters.

Perestroika has not yet given birth to its own great literature. It is still only in the process of breaking down people's consciousness. It has yet to create its own theater and cinema, but it has already spawned its very own "epistolary novel"; it is already assembling the letters of those who believe in it, and it draws hope from those letters. They are like the notes left in Christian churches next to the icons, like the bundles of pleas to God near Moslem shrines, or like the messages placed in the cracks of the Wailing Wall in Jerusalem. The people have begun to speak; they are turning to truth, and nothing can stop them. Our new "letter" culture is part of the breakthrough to freedom sweeping the country, part of our attempt to return in rejuvenated form to the fold of world history and mankind.

In today's Russia, which yearns for democratic changes, letters have broken through all the postal inspections and censorship and triumphed. People are taking the responsibility for society's development upon themselves; they are becoming its creators and chroniclers. Perhaps we will never again write such despairing and magnificent letters as we do now. It is most unfortunate that for the past two years we at *Ogonyok* have published only a small fraction of our mail—about one thousand letters, or more accurately, excerpts from them.

Our people is experiencing a renewal. Through our confessions we are becoming different, more courageous, more open. Please, keep your eyes on us as we enter our new life. Give us more time and freedom—we will do everything we have planned, no matter how painful it is for us.

Airplanes have a so-called black box, which records the communication between the crew and the ground. Whatever happens to the airplane, the black box preserves all the words that were spoken. Our Letters Department is *Ogonyok*'s black box. Whether we make it or crash to the ground, it should be very interesting for you in America to read all of this. After all, our roots are intertwined in the soil of our shared planet, and our branches share its air.

Vitaly Korotich
Editor in chief, *Ogonyok* magazine

A WORD ABOUT
"A WORD FROM THE READER"

At *Ogonyok,* early every morning a courier named Volodya brings in a huge bag filled with letters. It is one day's mail to "A Word From the Reader," *Ogonyok*'s letters column. Politicians and homeless people, collective farm workers and scholars, crazies and geniuses, soldiers and schoolchildren, students and pensioners, the voices of the entire country are in that bag. There is not a single town in the Soviet Union, not even the smallest village, from which we haven't received at least one letter.

In 1986 there was a total of 12,000 letters; in 1987, 46,000; in 1988, 102,000; in 1989, 150,000. People used to write hardly at all; now there is an avalanche of letters. And that means they trust us, they want to say something important and valuable. . . . This can only make us glad. And we are glad. But it also almost makes us cry. Opening every letter, reading it, and sending the answer off to the author, putting it in our files . . . all of that involves tears the world never sees. When the magazine was bad, nobody read it, and nobody wrote to it; those were happy times, too, because we didn't have to work, we could just sit around and relax. Now the staff of the Letters Department takes shopping bags of letters home, because they can't finish reading the mail at the office. They read about leaky roofs, a director's pilfering, nature, the collapse of the Party, the helpless government, Stalin and Lenin, good capitalism and bad socialism and the opposite, bad capitalism and good socialism, Jews and "kike Freemasons," nationalists and extremists . . . everything. It isn't easy to take. But for some reason no one from the department wants to leave; on the contrary, everybody wants to work in *Ogonyok* magazine's Letters Department. Why? Probably because it is a remarkable feeling—to find yourself on the tip of a pen which, right at that second, at that moment, is writing history.

Three years ago, most of the letters that had negative words

Ogonyok.

Lev Gushchin, deputy editor-in-chief of *Ogonyok,* and Valentin Yumashev, editor of the magazine's weekly letters column, "A Word From the Reader."

for the regime were unsigned. A year later there were practically no anonymous letters, no matter how treasonous (according to the standards of the recent past) the thought they offered was. Three years ago, we just read the letters ourselves and rejoiced at how intelligent our subscribers were. Suddenly, we understood that we couldn't go on this way: why should only the department staff enjoy those wise and controversial ideas?

Let us be very immodest: Thanks to *Ogonyok,* our country has discovered a new genre—readers' mail. Just a few weeks after we started our "A Word From the Reader" column, it was already obvious that the ten or twelve letters on two pages of *Ogonyok* had an audience of millions—an audience as dedicated as the one for the articles by academicians and specialists. A short letter from someone involved in the Chernobyl cleanup often said more about the tragedy than the most probing journalistic reports.

Today practically every Soviet newspaper—from *Pravda* and *Sovetskaya Rossiya* to *Literaturnaya Gazeta* and *Moscow News,* from *Izvestia* to *Sovetskaya Kultura*—has borrowed the idea of a "readers' letters" column from us. We welcome this imitation, especially since it has turned out that the *Ogonyok* letters are consistently the most sincere and revealing.

Now what almost everyone who knows something about our work tries to figure out is, What are our criteria for selection? How, out of that bulging bag, do we choose the ten or fifteen letters to fill two pages of the magazine? In actual fact, it's very easy. From the beginning, we've set out to make *Ogonyok* that place where you can express any opinion, even if it does not match the Party's, or government's, or, it goes without saying, the magazine's point of view. The important thing is for that opinion to make people think, argue and take another, even a very small, step toward truth.

And so, we publish a letter by a Stalinist who wants to send the entire editorial staff of *Ogonyok* to Siberia immediately, before, like Trotsky, we manage to escape from the country, where we will be much harder to catch and eliminate. We print the letter because every person today should know that these people, for whom the decisive argument in any discussion is still the commissar's revolver, do exist.

And then there is this letter: An attentive television viewer watched a deputy in the Supreme Soviet voting and saw him push two buttons at the same time—he was casting his own vote, and his friend's, too. And the very next day after the viewer's account was published there were hot debates about it in the Supreme Soviet.

People hate the cooperatives. We publish some letters defending the cooperatives and literally, before our very eyes, public opinion, warped by shortages, long lines, hatred and envy of the large sums of money other people have (which they may even have earned legitimately), changes ever so slowly, into a normal, civilized view of the cooperative movement.

Today ministers and generals, politicians and social scientists refer to readers' letters in *Ogonyok;* the magazine's mail has become a unique barometer of public opinion and a cross-section of society in all its contradictions.

There is, of course, censorship—of two kinds. The external, political, state one is terrifying in its absolute power. But because it is understandable, it isn't so insidious. Internal censorship, which abides in almost every person who writes, is far more horrible. It keeps us from breathing free, from holding up our heads.

The state censors suppress letters for simple, obvious reasons: If a reader curses the Party—the letter goes out; curses the KGB— out; curses a Politburo member—out; curses the Army—out again. . . . Out, out, out.

But our own censorship is more sophisticated. A reader curses the Soviet Peace Committee for bureaucratism, formalism and all kinds of other shortcomings. Well, why put in that letter? Our friends and colleagues work over there, and the Committee is headed by essayist Genrikh Borovik; why fight with them? Or there is a letter in defense of Yeltsin. Well, why publish that one? Yeltsin is supported by the people anyway, but Mikhail Gorbachev will read it and get upset again that *Ogonyok* is siding with his main opponent. The list goes on.

This letter won't get through anyway—so why put it in? That's the internal censor speaking. But why did that internal debate over whether to include a letter even get started? Because the number of reprimands, warnings, criticisms and other administrative punishments leveled against the Letters Department staff at *Ogonyok* is equal to the number of reprimands for all the other departments combined. Every time we publish a stinging letter, we feel some trepidation—are we getting into another scandal or did we miss it this time? A journalist who writes his own article is personally responsible for every fact, every word. But when we publish a letter, we rely only on the reader himself, who could always be wrong or mix up dates and facts. And that's why we get those familiar phone calls from the Central Committee of the Communist Party of the Soviet Union—a commission has been set up to investigate the letter published in issue so-and-so. But it is getting much easier to breathe; recently the Central Committee's problems with us have been fewer and fewer.

Soon the censors will be done away with completely. Discussion of a press law is now in full swing. But the internal censor will stay in every one of us for a long time to come. We can only hope that our children will grow up to be different.

Letters Department
Ogonyok magazine

PERESTROIKA

❀

Ogonyok: Marat.

"Bread . . . milk . . . meat."

POTEMKIN SAUSAGES

I want to share with you my thoughts about the anniversary exhibit called "The Omsk *Oblast*[1] Over Seventy Years." The exhibit is impressive. Indeed, it demonstrates how the *oblast,* and the country as a whole, progressed from sandals and old wooden ploughs to spaceships and "Don-1500" combines.

But there are a couple of things that are puzzling and upsetting to me. In the agricultural industry section I noticed that there was no price given for two kinds of "cervelat"-type smoked sausage, although the boiled sausage and all the other meat products had their prices clearly marked. I asked the person on duty in the hall (who was an employee of the enterprise that manufactured the sausages), "Why doesn't the smoked sausage have a price?" The woman answered, "Oh, we don't make that sausage for sale. We only made a small amount for this exhibit."

Smoked sausage made only for exhibits, and not for people, is an infuriating farce. I have absolutely nothing against smoked sausage. It's just that if sausage is displayed at an exhibit, it should be available in the stores, too. Why, that's obvious!

A. PODOLSKY
Engineer
Omsk
Published December 1987

[1] An *oblast* is an administrative region, or province, within the Soviet Union.

THE ECONOMIC EFFECT OF STANDING IN LINE

UPI/Bettman Newsphotos.

Soviets lined up to buy boots outside a Moscow shoe store.

Standing in line has its own "moral" effect.

Time spent waiting in line is directly deducted from our free time. It results in additional fatigue, sometimes in aggressiveness, and prevents people from engaging in activities that would fulfill their cultural needs.

Based on material collected in extensive observations in Leningrad, conducted by the Investigative Laboratory of Regional Economic Research at the N. A. Voznesensky Institute of Finance and Economics, the economic "effect" of standing in line has been calculated: the annual expenditure of time by Leningraders waiting for commercial, household and medical services exceeds 850 million hours.

We have also been able to deduce a kind of "coefficient of effectiveness," from the point of view of the consumer, for each branch of the service sector. For enterprises performing household services, the figure is 60 percent; for food stores, 46 percent, for industrial goods stores, just over 42 percent. In last place is health services—25 percent. As these data clearly demonstrate, there is enormous room for improvement.

It seems to me that lost time should be taken into account as an integral part of economic and social planning.

V. PROKOFIEV
Candidate[1] in Economic Sciences
Leningrad
Published December 1987

A LINE OF ANTS

When I was an eighteen-year-old girl, I went to work in a sugar factory. And I was amazed at the massive stealing that went on. At first, I got really angry, but three days later at the end of the shift, the other girls poured out a whole bag of sugar for me, so I wouldn't be the "odd man out." Since then they've tried to pour some out for me every day. You may ask, why didn't I resist? How could I? During the lunch break, when the bosses went out to drink tea, the whole shift would attack the drying machine to get their "allotment."

To cut down on the stealing, they put in Party members to keep watch, along with the regular guards. But all they had to do was go on break, and that line of ants would be right back there again, stretching out into the corridor.

That's how it was for many years. And even now, in the time of *glasnost* and *perestroika,* some things are the same as they used to be. There are too many passive people. Some are biding their

---

[1] A Soviet "Candidate" Degree is approximately equivalent to an American Ph.D.

time; others are scared of losing the place they've been sitting in for so long. But who's going to tell the truth?

O. I. YERYUKOVA
Venev, Tula *oblast*
Published March 1988

HOW TO SOLVE
THE NATION'S FOOD PROBLEM
(AND GET TIRES FOR YOURSELF
IN THE BARGAIN)

In recent years, state stores have made a practice of bartering goods that are in short supply for agricultural products—for example, wool, meat, butter, etc. It's not for me to judge the usefulness of this practice, but these buying and selling deals sometimes take a very perverse form.

More than once I've witnessed scenes like this: A buyer needs tires for his car. They aren't for sale anywhere, but one of the state stores has them. In exchange for each tire, one is required to present eighteen kilograms of butter. That's only for one tire, so if the buyer needs four, well, you can imagine. . . .[1]

But that isn't the point. Naturally, the owner of a Zhiguli[2] doesn't own that much butter and, besides, the market is very far away. So, by mutual agreement between the seller and the buyer, the buyer—on paper—purchases eighteen kilos of butter from the seller, at seven rubles a kilo, and—again, on paper—sells it to a previously agreed-upon state wholesaler for six rubles. He is given a receipt for the butter he allegedly sold, in exchange for which he receives the desired tire. (In reality, he has "only" had to pay eighteen rubles extra—one ruble for each kilo.) The wholesaler

---

[1] The seventy-two kilograms needed to buy four tires would be equivalent to almost 160 pounds of butter.

[2] A popular Soviet automobile.

then "sells" the butter back to the store. It seems to return to its rightful place. In all of this, it isn't important whether there really is butter in the store or not; the documentation says everything is clean. Nobody will figure it out. Hocus-pocus? Oh, yes, and hardly as harmless as it seems at first glance.

Suppose a store has sold, let's say, ten or twelve of these tires; the records show that 200 kilos of butter have been sold to the people. But where is it? The same kind of machinations go on with meat and honey. And if this happens in many stores, you can imagine how many tons of first-class grocery products show up in the state accounting figures, which somebody somewhere then analyzes and draws general conclusions from.

If this method were used widely enough, it wouldn't take much effort to solve our food problem. On paper, of course. And the important thing is that everybody wins, except the consumer.

L. T. MAKAROV
Shmyki, Syumsin region
Udmurt ASSR
Published March 1988

EVERYTHING BUT HOUSING . . .

I am a builder by training, and I have spent my entire long adult life doing all kinds of construction work. I was a manual laborer, a mason, a plumber, a carpenter, an electrician, a handyman, a foreman, an area chief, an engineer and, for the last few years, a technical engineering supervisor for the district. I have built four village schools for 320 people, a feed factory for the *oblast,* a professional-technical school, a trade depot, a building materials plant, more than fifteen residential buildings around the *oblast* . . . I can't even list everything.

I built a children's hospital with 120 beds, and along with it a heating system, a laundry, a garage and a pharmacy, but not a single square foot of residential space. There are patients, but no one to treat or care for them, no one to heat the building or do the laundry. In the village of Ynyrga I built a shed for 400 cows, and once again not a single square foot of housing. People are living in ramshackle housing left over from Tsar Nikolai's time. Aren't they as much human beings as the people in Moscow and Leningrad?

I have seen cows that went unmilked for weeks at a time. They stand up to their knees in dung. They are surrounded by drafts. In November and December about 150 cattle died of respiratory infections. Do you think anyone lost the slightest bit of sleep over that? Not a chance. For 200 milk cows there are only two milkers and some schoolchildren. Go ahead and try to fulfill the state plan with that! Incidentally, the plan will, of course, be met, but only on paper. The lying starts with the milkmaid and the cowherd and, I imagine, goes all the way up to the minister himself, with all of them assuring anyone who will listen that the plan was fulfilled.

As horrible as this picture is, it satisfies the district, *oblast, krai*[1] and the Ministry itself. Everybody keeps quiet and waits it out. Our disgusting attitude toward people has made them lose all faith. They don't express any dissatisfaction but just sit there silently, nodding their heads.

Let me make a suggestion. Not a single construction project should be built without housing. Then we'll always have the workers we need and a totally honest attitude toward our labor duties, a healthy moral climate and faith that our productivity can genuinely be improved.

Viktor Ivanovich BOGOMOLOV
Village of Maima
Gorno-Altai *oblast*
Published March 1988

HOPING FOR A MIRACLE

Recently, I noticed a curious fact. Different pages of the statistical manual *The Economy of the USSR in 1985* cite different data about how much the national income of this country increased in 1985 as compared to the previous year. If you believe page 40, it increased

---

[1] A Soviet administrative region, larger than an *oblast*.

3.1 percent, that is, 15 billion rubles. But farther on in the text, we read that the increase was only 4 billion, that is, 0.8 percent.

That's an almost fourfold difference: 11 billion rubles! It boggles my mind: how could there be such contradictory information in one and the same publication of the official statistical agency? This is all the more significant since 1985 was the final year of the eleventh Five-Year Plan. If the size of the national income in 1985 was defined incorrectly, then all the calculations of the growth rates for this indicator in the *twelfth* Five-Year Plan are also in doubt.

In such a situation, it would be natural to expect a clarification from the State Committee on Statistics of the USSR, or for them to admit that they made a mistake. But the agency is saying nothing and is hoping stubbornly for a miracle: Maybe nobody—neither our own readers nor foreign ones—will notice. Instead of clarifications, we get the usual manipulation of information. In the statistical annuals for 1986 and 1987, the data on the size of the national income (in billions of rubles) have disappeared completely. All they publish is the percentage indicators, the growth rate indexes.

Perhaps the time has come to break the statistical agency's customary monopoly on access to socioeconomic information and its analysis and interpretation. We need to be able to verify the calculations of the indicators that are so important for the economy and for every citizen. And the methodology of the calculations should be discussed in open forums. We must be certain that we have the right not only to know everything about the country we live in, but to know it without distortions in this or that direction.

M. A. IVANOV
Candidate in economics
Senior professor
Department of Price Formation
N. A. Voznesensky Institute of Finance and Economics
Leningrad
Published September 1988

SHAVING OUT OF "SHEER GRIEF"

I am writing to you in amazement at the August television broad-cast, "*Perestroika:* Problems and Solutions." The entire course of the roundtable discussion demonstrated with crystal clarity that centralized administrative management of the country's economy shows no promise, and that the organizations trying to carry out this function are helpless. The broadcast, contrary to the partici-pants' intent, ended up being glaring propaganda for radical eco-nomic reform. In their discussions about people's vital concerns, the participants revealed a remarkable lack of understanding of these concerns and of the mechanisms connecting events in our daily lives.

For example, the viewers asked, "Why have cookies and candy disappeared from store shelves?" They were told: "In recent times, a large amount of baked goods are not being used for their primary purpose." What's the implication, that cookies and chocolates are being used to make moonshine? Somehow that's hard to believe.[1] Another question: "What happened to all the safety razor blades?" There was a ready answer: "We have started to sell less vodka, and people have millions of rubles left unspent, so they've started spend-ing them on household items other than food." What does that mean? Have people who can't get vodka started shaving more often out of sheer grief? Yet another question: "What is being done to eliminate lines in stores?" Answer: "The important thing is to ex-pand self-service and introduce prepackaged goods."

I am writing this letter from Archangel. There are no lines here for butter or for sausage. Butter is for sale here freely in neat little packages; and there just plain isn't any sausage at all in the stores. As you can see, there can be various reasons for a lack of lines.

In the discussion about what measures are being taken to increase quality, the participants went on and on about state quality controls, and about bringing representatives of trade organizations into the production process. No matter that one of the panelists was talking about television sets and another about tuber plants.

---

[1] One of Mikhail Gorbachev's earliest reforms was a stepped-up national campaign against alcoholism. Severe limits were placed on the sale of liquor, and, because it was being used by home distillers, sugar was rationed.

Are the participants in this roundtable—all responsible comrades—really unaware that problems of selection, quality, lines, speculation and service will be solved automatically if supply exceeds demand? And that in the opposite case, such problems are simply unavoidable?

Yu. S. VARSHAVSKY
Leningrad
Published September 1988

GLORIOUSLY LAGGING

On July 28 of this year, in the Kremlin, a group of state and Party officials received awards. In addressing the recipients, A. A. Gromyko said, "They [the medals] are granted to people in this country for glorious deeds, for successes that noticeably affect the area in which those people work." N. V. Gorshkov, the Chairman of the State Committee of the USSR on Computer Technology and Data Processing, was awarded the Order of the Red Banner of Labor (*Pravda,* July 29).

Two weeks later at a regular meeting of the commission of the Supreme Soviet of the USSR on science and technology, the activities of the agency headed by N. V. Gorshkov were evaluated, and "the Deputies came to the conclusion that our country's lag behind the world level of production and use of computer technology has reached a critical, strategically dangerous level, and this lag, despite measures . . . that are being taken, is continuing to grow. . . . The Deputies noted that the efforts of the Committee are at present directed primarily toward drawing up guidelines, but it has shown little initiative in carrying out its assigned tasks and has had no noticeable influence on the technical level and quality of products" (*Izvestia,* August 14).

So, where are the "glorious deeds," those "successes that noticeably affect the area" in which N. V. Gorshkov is working?

M. PUTIVLSKY
Zelenograd
Published September 1988

WHAT'S IN A NAME?

For several years now there have been polemics in the major newspapers about changing the names of cities, giving them back their original names, and renaming avenues, squares, streets, city parks, etc.

I decided to write you to point out yet another side to this issue.

Many of our *kolkhozes* and *sovkhozes*[1]—how should I put it?—have names that don't correspond with real life and that discredit our ideas, hopes and aspirations.

I am referring to *kolkhozes* and *sovkhozes* that have for many decades not been doing the job assigned to them by the state—debtor collective farms that exist only through subsidies, or state-owned collective farms that are ruining the state—while at the same time carrying bold names like "Lenin's Path," "Will of the Proletariat," "Victory," "Fifty Years of the USSR," "Such-and-such Party Congress," "October Revolution," "Lenin's Behests," etc. Very often it's just absurd: there is a huge sign on the main road of the collective farm with the rousing name "Road to Communism," but the only way you can go down that road to the main collective-farm building is on an all-terrain vehicle or by tractor. . . .

This kind of collective farm (or state-owned farm) would more appropriately be named "Forty Years Without a Harvest" or "Thirty Years of Padded Figures."

A. MIKHNO
Zheleznogorsk
Stavropol *krai*
Published September 1988

---

[1] *Kolkhozes* are Soviet collective farms, and *sovkhozes* are state farms. In theory, a *kolkhoz* is a collective venture belonging to the peasants who live and work on it, while a *sovkhoz* is owned and managed entirely by the state. In practice, there is virtually no difference between the two.

KNITTING AND TAXES

My letter will, of course, change absolutely nothing in the fates of those people who want to do private work on the side. I am referring to people whose income is less than 100 rubles a month. But still I would like it to be published.

The major obstacle is the District Finance Office, which discourages any interest in this kind of activity. That is what happened to me.

My wife and I knit woolen hats and give them to a store at a price of eleven rubles apiece. We buy the wool in Bashkiria at six rubles for 100 grams. I am an invalid, and my wife has had ten children. Together, we can knit only about ten to fifteen hats a month. You can figure out whether we make a lot of money or not.

Today I was called into the District Finance Office and listened to a decree on the tax system and on the completion of numerous forms. As a result, I came home, and my wife and I decided not to knit any more hats. It isn't advantageous to us anymore and gives us no profit or benefits.

Ya. PANKRATS
Orenburg *oblast*
Published April 1989

JOY, ECONOMIC DIGNITY
AND CARBURETORS

Against the background of shortages of so many necessities, it's somehow awkward to talk about the lack of spare parts for cars. But still. . . .

Our family Zhiguli isn't young anymore. According to its passport, it is already fifteen years old. But it has spent almost half its life in repairs, or, rather, waiting for spare parts. For a long time (one and one-half years), I couldn't get a cam shaft, then a right rear door (eight months), tires (one year), the right-colored paint, a windshield or battery. Now the car is standing still again—there are no front clutch disks for sale anywhere.

About ten years ago they wrote that there weren't enough spare parts because the economic planners assumed a "standard period of use" of about five to six years for a passenger car. Meaning what—that we, the car owners, are the ones to blame because we rarely trade in our old models for new ones? Do the planning authorities really not know that people are on waiting lists for cars for fifteen to twenty years?

The lack of spare parts is sometimes explained by the shortage of metal in the country. But we produce twice as much as the USA. What is more, out of every one hundred people there, fifty-five have their own car; here, it's only four. And how much metal do you need anyway to make a carburetor pin, which I haven't been able to get for two years now? Even the technical repair stations don't sell the tiniest metal handles for the car's heating system or the thin steel supports that raise the hood, or electrical safety fuses that cost pennies (instead of them I put in "plugs" made of copper wire that I find lying around).

Okay, fine, there's no metal. But then, why are there no wind-shields or rubber or plastic parts for cars? (Good thing they don't have any wooden parts, or there'd be a shortage of them, too.) What we do have enough of is decrees on economics, including the problem of spare parts (the problem we created ourselves). Let's admit it, finally,· neither *Gosplan*[1] nor the Ministry of the Automobile Industry is capable of balancing supply and demand for spare parts. Our hopes are on the new system of independent cost-accounting.[2] Recently, I have heard that it isn't profitable for factories to make spare parts for which low prices are set by the "higher-ups." Well, let's raise them, then. On the black market I paid eight times the state price for a cam shaft, ten times more for a handle for the heating system, and five times more for a little metal support. Do the Price Institutes at the State Committee on Prices of the USSR really need to do theoretical research to come to the obvious con-clusion: to get rid of the unprofitability of a high-demand product,

[1] The state planning agency.

[2] Under the new system of "cost accounting," state enterprises are no longer 100 percent subsidized, and are responsible for their own losses and profits.

all you have to do is raise the price. I, personally, would be only too grateful if I could buy a new carburetor easily in a store and pay, let's say, one and one-half or even two times as much for it, instead of having to get it, with a lot of difficulty, from a speculator and pay five times as much.

With a reasonable increase in the wholesale and retail prices for spare parts, many of the automobile plants, I'm sure, would be interested in producing them and would find the extra resources and manpower to do so. Why *not* find them if this would guarantee high profitability?!

Vladimir Grigoryevich CHIRKOV
Kiev
Received by *Ogonyok* April 1989
Unpublished

"WHATEVER'S IN THE STORE MUST BE IN THE WINDOW"

People who work in the retail trade are supporting "artificial shortages" and earning tens, if not hundreds, of thousands of rubles. And the ones who suffer from this are the working class and the state. These crooks aren't afraid of anybody, and nobody scares them; they buy everything and everyone.

It seems to me that we have to adopt severe, even harsh laws to punish those who are guilty of creating artificial shortages. The old capitalist principle, "Whatever's in the window must be in the store," should be changed to a new, socialist one: "Whatever's in the store must be in the window." For those who disobey—harsh punishment. Then, maybe, the number of cases of hiding away foodstuffs and household goods, and of their spoilage, will decrease by at least half.

P. P. KIRSAN
Kharkov
Received by *Ogonyok* May 1989
Unpublished

Ogonyok.

Empty shelves in a state store in Minsk.

UNEMPLOYMENT:
A NECESSARY EVIL?

I always read the writings of Otto Latsis[1] with extraordinary interest. I can't remember an instance when I didn't agree with him.

But now there is his article in *Sovetskaya Kultura* [*Soviet Culture*] of 13 December 1988, entitled "Unemployment—the Price is Too High." As far as future price reform is concerned, I agree with the author completely. But as for unemployment . . .

Mr. Latsis writes correctly, "In developed capitalist countries they have unemployment only because they want it."

Ah, but there's a good reason why they "want it"! The history of mankind shows that, aside from coercion, there are only three

---

[1] A progressive Soviet writer and editor, currently deputy editor of *Kommunist*.

stimuli for successful work: need, profit and fear—the fear of being left without a source of livelihood.

In this country, not a single one of these stimuli is operative. There is no need to work; everybody knows that even if he does nothing, he will somehow manage, especially with the catastrophically low needs of the Soviet people. Profit is a fiction: whether you work well or badly, your minimum living wage is guaranteed. There's no point even talking about the third stimulus: a loafer will just laugh in response to the demand that he work honestly. Any other enterprise would be glad to take him.

Unemployment, as sad as it sounds, is necessary! It is one of the signs of a healthy, flourishing society. And a division of property is inevitable. Incidentally, the labor market could be a remarkable weapon in the fight against the forces trying to slow down *perestroika*. How wonderful it would be to see the labor market brimming with a line of eighteen million of our bureaucrats, who weren't able to become the managers we so badly need today. If push comes to shove, they could work as clerks, farmers, janitors, doormen or post office employees. After all, we really have a hard time finding people for those jobs.

We absolutely must "compromise our principles." There is no other way.

Aleksander IVANOV
Writer
Moscow
Received by *Ogonyok* Spring 1989
Unpublished

NO SOAP?

On September 12–15 of this year I participated in the State Control Commission's inspection of goods being stored in the port of Ilichevsk.[1]

The situation on September 14, 1989 was as follows: All of the warehouses in the port were completely full of goods in very short supply. The port was storing 8,931 tons of imported industrial goods, including 1,401 tons of soap, 1,385 tons of soap powder and detergents, as well as clothing, footwear and fabric purchased abroad. The port warehouses held 8,935 tons of imported food products, including 6,663 tons of tea and 1,218 tons of coffee. And the number of imported goods in the port is growing because of the constant lack of railroad cars for transportation.

We all understand that the situation with the railroads cannot improve with so many tracks and so much rolling stock in disrepair. But how can you explain to the people why there is no coffee or tea in the stores in Kiev and Odessa, where the tea could be shipped by truck? And the absence of those goods in the city of Ilichevsk, which lies literally 500 meters from the supplies of tea and coffee, is completely inexplicable.

It is very upsetting that the Supreme Soviet and Council of Ministers of the USSR stubbornly refuse to see this.

D. A. PAVLOVSKY
Freelance inspector
Oblast Control Commission
Odessa
Received by *Ogonyok* September 1989
Unpublished

---

[1] A port city on the Black Sea, near Odessa.

WITH FRIENDS LIKE YOU . . .

Issue no. 27 of *Ogonyok* magazine (July 1989), included an article by Professor I. Gorelov, a doctor of philology, entitled "Will a Professor Champion the Workers' Interests?" In that article, Professor Gorelov tries to show that the workers do not need to worry because all scholars in general, and he in particular, are fully backing their interests. Gorelov writes, "I am on your side. I have been, in particular, ever since I visited the mines of the Krasnodanugol Association several times in 1955–1956. Believe me, I am defending your interests."

Fine, Comrade Gorelov, you are on our side. But more than thirty years have passed since 1955, and what has happened? Nothing. But as soon as the miners in the Kuzbass[1] announced a strike, immediately there was hope that things would get moving. And this fact is convincing proof that if the working class doesn't do it, who will? There were a lot of supporters, but no action. And the system that the professor outlined and called absurd is, in fact, completely workable. Professor Gorelov writes, "If one accepts your point of view, our situation will apparently not be straightened out until we split up into various parties: the party of the workers will see to the interests of its members, the party of the peasants, to its own. . . . No, you cannot agree to something so absurd."

Well, that is exactly what we need, only it would not be parties, but independent trade-union organizations. And the Congress of Deputies of the Supreme Soviet is the sole authority that can act as an arbiter and judge on disputes that come up. Why haven't the miners' jobs been mechanized and their daily conditions improved? Because we do not have independent trade unions, in particular mining trade unions. Only an independent trade union with its severe economic demands is capable of raising a worker's wages. High wages must absolutely be linked to high productivity. Now our workers' wages are so low that it isn't profitable to replace them with machines.

If the workers are incapable of defending their own interests, no one else will. I have never heard or read of scholars anywhere on

[1] The USSR's richest coal-mining region; a major center of strike activity during the summer of 1989.

our planet striking to demand higher wages . . . for workers. The workers don't need someone else's patronage to keep from being humiliated. Nor should they have to thank some benefactor for their "happy" life. Reliable benefits are not ones that "someone gave us once"—after all, if they were given to us, they can be taken away. But we won't have to thank anybody for ones that we have taken ourselves.

K. CHERNYAEV
Skilled worker
Borer, sixth class
Leningrad
Published October 1989

GIVE US BACK OUR LAND!

All of my ancestors, since time immemorial, have been peasant farmers. I myself did not become one—only because of collectivization—but until I was twelve I lived in the village of Trudnikov that was once in the Rostov *oblast*. From very early on I worked with the soil and grew grain along with the adults. I know a lot about that kind of work, and not from hearsay either.

Maybe it sounds banal, but I really can't keep silent any longer, because I am sick and tired of the chatter of dilettantes and demagogues about the so-called food problem. There is no such problem! There is a Stalinist disrespect for peasants. No, not disrespect, but sheer malice and contempt, covered up by a hypocritical concern for their welfare.

There are no difficulties with food production! There is a basic cowardice about the prospect of losing power over the peasants, of losing one's warm, cozy little position.

Give the peasants the land and end the prohibitions[1]—and

---

[1] The writer is referring to restrictions on land ownership and on the sale of privately grown food.

this "problem" will disappear and our long-suffering people will forget that word "hunger."

A unique situation has now developed: Russia can immediately have civilized, intelligent peasant farmers who are capable of managing their homesteads and creatively applying science's newest achievements.

Remove the bans and the descendants of those very independent farmers who were destroyed as a class will return to the soil. The pull of the land is still in their genes, and they don't have to be taught how to work.

Our descendants will never forgive us if we pass up this chance. In ten or fifteen years it will be impossible; there will be a shift of generations, and the last generation raised on the land will be gone.

V. BRAGINTSEV
Moscow
Published October 1989

DOCTORS . . . NOT VETERINARIANS!

In the weekly *Argumenty i Fakty* [*Arguments and Facts*] (no. 42), I read an interview with Politburo member Yegor K. Ligachev, a Secretary of the Central Committee of the CPSU. I will not go into the contents of the interview and Ligachev's views because as a retired locomotive engineer I am in no position to argue with a Secretary of the Central Committee.

I am worried about something completely different. As the interview makes clear, Yegor Ligachev graduated from the Moscow Aviation Institute and the Higher Party School of the Central Committee of the CPSU. If you look at Ligachev's age, you will note that he received his education not today or even yesterday, but, figuratively speaking, the day before yesterday, when many things, including the methods of building socialism and even "Communism in one country,"[1] were viewed differently than they are today. We have rejected many unshakable dogmas of those times because they interfered with the normal development of the country. This raises the question, how can the esteemed Mr. Ligachev, with his aviation/technical training and a political education not up to today's level, be in charge of agriculture in the Central Committee, and use the authority of the Central Committee to determine the course of development in such an important area? Even the untrained eye can see where we stand now. It turns out that only in words are we in favor of highly educated professionals who can lead us out of this crisis; either that, or agriculture is such a primitive field that anyone who feels like it is entitled to give advice. Why is it that when we are sick, we turn to the most qualified doctor possible, and don't run to the veterinarian—even though they both write prescriptions in Latin?

A. Ya. DISHLERS
Member of the CPSU since 1958,
retiree, former railroad engineer
Valmiera, Latvian SSR
25 October 1989
Unpublished

GUNS FOR SOAP?

In an October issue of *Argumenty i Fakty* (no. 39) an interview was published with the Deputy Director of the Central Institute of Economics and Mathematics of the Academy of Sciences of the USSR, N. Petrakov. In response to the question "Is it now possible for us to produce military hardware for export?" the interviewee, without batting an eyelash, said, "Why shouldn't we? . . . Why not

---

[1] "Socialism in one country" was Stalin's theory that Communism could be built in the Soviet Union alone, even if revolution in the rest of the world failed to keep pace. This slogan became Stalin's rallying cry in his ideological struggle with Trotsky.

sell what there is demand for? We sell our military technology, and with the money we receive we buy the household goods we need." So there! Take that!

In the recent past, we were always told that we were supplying arms only to our allies, and only for their defense against treacherous neighbors. But many people, I think, remember the dispute between the leaders of South Yemen, with whom we were friendly in the mid-1980s, which ended in a battle in which both sides used artillery and tanks "made in the USSR."

Now the right to trade arms is defended with the hypothesis that "everybody does it." Unfortunately, this "everybody" is still a harsh reality of our small world, a reality left over from the past. All of us are responsible for putting an end to arms proliferation, but someone has to be the first to stop. Who will that be? Us? The USA? Israel? . . .

Perhaps I shouldn't be paying such close attention to Comrade Petrakov's statements, but one circumstance forces me to do so: N. Petrakov, along with everything else, is a People's Deputy of the USSR. And it is hardly dignified for a statesman to encourage the trade of Soviet machine guns for laundry detergent, and to characterize this kind of transaction as one of *perestroika*'s great achievements.

A. UTKIN
Ivanovo
Published November 1989

"ONE LAST CHANCE TO STAY AFLOAT"

I recently read about the creation here in Leningrad of the United Workers' Front. As I understand it (I was at meetings and listened to speakers from workers' political clubs), the major ideological postulate of this front is that the working class is the most progressive and revolutionary one in our society, and is therefore entitled to be the guide for other classes and groups. This role for the working class was defined by Marx's theory and supposedly exists independent of historical or current events and conditions, and even of the level of consciousness or education of the mass of workers.

In short, the United Workers' Front is proposing to turn us around 180 degrees from *perestroika,* and to have us go back half a century from a nation of all the people to a dictatorship of the proletariat; from general human values to "class" values; from pluralism cut this to avoid longer reset to ideological monopoly; from a uniting of society's healthy forces to a division into one legitimate force (that is, the workers) and the "companions" to be led by them. That is why it is so logical that such major figures as Nina Andreyeva[1] and Mikhail Popov, the main ideologue of the workers' political clubs and the watchful guardian of our socialism against "petit bourgeois erosion," should appear in this movement.

Let us take a look at who needs the United Workers' Front.

The Party *apparatchiks* from Brezhnev's "socialism" of yesteryear, whose very ship is sinking under their feet, have one last chance to stay afloat. They suddenly remembered that—all their special stores, and special hunting privileges and freedom from laws and lines notwithstanding—they are the "flesh of the flesh" of the working class. Incidentally, they have always needed not only their "special" dachas and "special" girls, but also "special" workers, who would eat food from the lord's table and read out speeches composed in the lord's own offices: "We, the workers, are used to speaking frankly. . . ."

But this is a different time. The mass democratic movement for a determined renewal of society has become a reality in the form of the recently created Leningrad Popular Front.

This movement, which is so dangerous to the "stagnation"[2] bureaucracy, can obviously be neutralized only by a sufficiently massive countermovement. And it is not so important whether this

---

[1] A rigidly pro-Stalinist teacher of chemistry at the Leningrad Council Institute of Technology, whose letter, "I Cannot Compromise My Principles," sent tremors through the ranks of the adherents of *perestroika* when it was published in *Sovietskaya Rossiya* in March 1988. At first, it was feared that the publication of Andreyeva's letter indicated that conservatives were regaining the upper hand in the Party. But in early April, an editorial in *Pravda* strongly condemning Andreyeva's ideas helped restore the confidence of the reformers.

[2] The period of Brezhnev's rule, from 1964 to 1982, is widely known as the "Period of Stagnation."

is based on the idea of nationalist exclusivity (like Pamyat[3]) or class exclusivity, as in this case. Just so long as it is a *counter*movement, so long as its appeal is as far as possible from reason and as close as possible to the instinct of aggressive solidarity inherent in the politically immature masses. It is no accident that at the meetings of the workers' political clubs one can hear socially provocative ideas like "On that black day of March 26,[4] the workers were quietly pushed out of power"; "The intelligentsia is performing yet another experiment on the workers"; "No one but a worker can defend the interests of the workers"; "Up with workers' control over trade, the service sector and the creative unions." [I personally heard this (the last time) at a meeting at the Gorkovskaya metro station on the eve of the second round of elections.]

The point is that the secret opposition to *perestroika* is ready to do anything to preserve its power and privileges. One can only hope that the United Workers' Front will succeed in attracting only the extremist elements of the workers in the political clubs and that the more "aware" workers will have the good sense to entrust the country's tasks to honest, competent, creative people.

Is Russia really capable only of dividing, destroying and marching in formation?

Yu. A. BIROV
Metalworker, age 57
Leningrad
21 June 1989
Unpublished

---

[3] A nationalist organization whose stated purpose is the preservation and restoration of artifacts of ethnic Russian culture, Pamyat is actually a virulently antisemitic paramilitary group, many of whose members sport black T-shirts emblazoned with anti-Jewish slogans (see pages 212–215).

[4] March 26, 1989 was the date of the opening round of national elections for the first Congress of People's Deputies.

THE COOPERATIVE MOVEMENT

One of the most radical—and controversial—reforms of the Gorbachev era has been the Law on Individual Labor Activity, which, within limits, permits groups of individuals to join together voluntarily to form, run and profit from their own business enterprises. As Stephen F. Cohen has written in Voices of Glasnost,[1] *one of the "crucial battlefields" in the struggle for perestroika pits "the fledgling cooperative economic movement against hostile local authorities and popular suspicions of even this 'socialist' form of private enterprise."*

According to Cohen, "the number of registered cooperatives grew dramatically between January 1988 and January 1989, from 13,921 firms employing 155,880 people to 77,548 with 1.4 million employees, but they remain a tiny fraction of the economy. In the more congenial environment of Moscow, for example, in April 1989 they provided only 2.2 percent of the city's consumer goods and services." Unless the cooperatives can overcome the reactionary forces arrayed against them, contends Cohen, "there will be no flourishing Soviet marketplace, substantial nonstate property, or economic reformation."

Now that we are doing all we can to encourage and promote individual work initiatives (and that's proper!), I would like to share my impressions of the "work" activities flourishing near the Byelorussian Railroad Station in Moscow.

I'm not revealing any secrets by saying that we used to see the same thing before: at the train stations in the capital shameless women openly hawked a suspicious-looking "cotton candy" or sweet candies, or an invalid with no legs would be pushing "mousy-mouse, the children's toy," in the underpass below the street. Then, that kind of activity was considered illegal and was stopped by the police.

But today, now that the Law on Individual Labor Activity has been adopted, the number of train station traders (read "parasites") has increased tenfold! And they are much younger now, too.

Now it is fashionably dressed young men between twenty and thirty-five. Their little three-legged table holds a sign saying: "The Such-and-Such Cooperative." But it would be naive to think that

[1] Stephen Cohen and Katrina vanden Heuvel, *Voices of Glasnost* (New York: W. W. Norton & Co., 1989), page 31.

they raise cows or pigs in their own backyards and therefore make a considerable contribution to the agricultural program of the country, or that they wallpaper apartments or repair televisions or refrigerators. Young "cooperators" sell photo-maps of the "Stores of Moscow," which cost one ruble! And there are photographs with "Dream Books" for interpreting dreams, Eastern and other horoscopes, calendars with Vladimir Vysotsky[1] or the rock duo Modern Talking on them.

Beyond the subway entrance, between the rows of flower sellers, an attractive girl is walking around with an ostrich hanging on strings, made from brightly colored balls taken from a baby's rattle. But that bird goes for five rubles! Her companion, a young man with a beard, is standing to one side with a box of unsold items, smoking nervously.

[1] Vysotsky was a very popular Soviet singer, poet, and actor.

Ogonyok: Anatoly Bochinin.

A "cooperator," wearing a Brezhnev mask, sells novelty items in a Moscow park.

The "decorative aquarium-vases," with little swans swimming inside, are even more expensive: a little one goes for seven rubles; a big one for ten!

Of course, some might point out to me that serious people go right past these hawkers without stopping, and that all of their products are for people who don't know what to do with their money. I doubt it. A bad example is contagious, and once people see how easy it is to "earn" a lot of money completely legally, those masquerading parasites will quickly have followers. Only, who will benefit if tomorrow there are peddlers of ostriches and aquarium-vases not only at the Byelorussian train station, but at all the stations from Moscow to Vladivostok?

Oleg GONOZOV
Artistic director of the City Park
Ishnya, Yaroslavl *oblast*
Published January 1988

Quite recently I read a memorandum, entitled "On the Problems of the Development of Cooperative Forms of Activity in Cities" (I am sending a copy to the editors), addressed to the Presidium of the Executive Committee of the Kiev City Council of People's Deputies. It was signed (under the number 007-415) on December 16 of last year by the deputy chairman of the Kiev City Committee, V. Savchuk. The document speaks about the organization and work of cooperatives, mentions some positive things, but mostly talks about the negative, including, and I quote, "Also alarming is the fact that over 30 percent of the heads of cooperatives are people under the age of thirty, each of whom has been in the labor force no more than ten years. There are many of Jewish nationality and people with no specialized training, and few retirees or members of the CPSU."[1] And farther on: "The shortcomings and errors pointed out above are a consequence of weak organizational work on the part of Regional Executive Committees and economic leaders in guaranteeing that Party and governmental decrees on the development of cooperatives be carried out."

I personally know of no decrees on the Party or governmental level that prohibit or limit the participation of young people and

[1] The Communist Party of the Soviet Union.

representatives of various nationalities in the organization of cooperatives and their work. What we have here is a local initiative. But
the abovementioned document was not written by a member of
some informal group, like Pamyat ["Memory"], but by the deputy
chairman of the City Committee, who sent it around to the various
city agencies. It is doubly offensive when this sort of prejudice is
propagated by someone in an official position.

G. Ya. SHKLYAREVSKY
Filmmaker at Ukrkinokhronika
Member of the Union of Cinematographers of the USSR
Kiev
Published April 1988

At the meeting between the representatives of the working class and
the Central Committee of the CPSU, the brigadier of the metal-
workers and pipe fitters of the "Leningrad Metal Factory" production association, V. S. Chicherov, expressed his dissatisfaction with
the "undeservedly large incomes" of cooperatives.

People are particularly indignant at the notorious three-
million-ruble profits of one of them, and they are demanding that
something be done about this sort of thing.

At the same time, a metalworker from the Cherepovetsk met-
allurgical plant, Yu. V. Arkhipov, is unhappy with the ration system for buying groceries, under which a worker gets only half a kilo
of sausage per month.

It's no secret to anyone that there are underground millionaires in this country, who made their fortunes through thievery,
bribes and speculation on shortages. A lot is being written about
that now.

But when an enterprising person with initiative is able to sell
a product made in the USSR—a product that nobody here needs—
to the West, get badly needed consumer goods for hard currency,
sell these goods in this country *at the state price* (I emphasize this)
and earn millions—that makes people mad.

If there were about 200,000 such people, our stores would be
swamped with consumer goods. Let those inventive and energetic
people go ahead and become millionaires (even billionaires), but let

us be able to buy any item, including—believe it or not—sausage, and the kind that even the cat will eat.

V. V. GUREVICH
Candidate in technological sciences,
Senior researcher of a Scientific Research Institute
Who lives only on his salary, does not want to become an under-
    ground or legal millionaire, but wants his children to live in a
    flourishing country
Published March 1989

AN OPEN LETTER
TO THE CHAIRMAN
OF THE ALL-UNION COUNCIL
OF TRADE UNIONS, S. A. SHALAEV

Dear Stepan Alekseyevich:

No doubt I should have written to you earlier, immediately after the Plenum of the All-Union Council of Trade Unions, which was held a month and a half ago. But I wanted to speak with figures on hand, and it took time to get them. Let me say right away that the directors of cooperatives in Moscow, whom I represent, followed the Plenum with great interest and paid particular attention to your speech. Our interest is understandable: even before then we could feel the social atmosphere growing heavy with dissatisfaction. The cooperatives have had opposition from the very start, but because the government announced that it wholeheartedly supports the cooperative movement, the battle against them has been conducted in a secret, one might even say unfair way. People have had to become very sophisticated—like racists in the USA. There, in an effort to discredit the black population, people use this kind of device: If a white man, say, steals a coat, they say "John Smith stole a coat." But if it's a black man, they say "A black man stole a coat." The same thing is true for cooperatives here. If a man does something wrong, and he is in a cooperative, that fact will invariably be emphasized.

The leaders of the trade unions who have entered the ring to do battle with the cooperatives have rejected such sophisticated methods. What do they need them for? Your kindred spirit and colleague in running the trade unions, the chairman of the Moscow City Council of Trade Unions, V. P. Shcherbakov, gave a speech at the Congress of People's Deputies and asserted with Bolshevik directness that the activities of the cooperatives are "heightening the shortage of goods, emptying store shelves, increasing corruption, bribery, speculation and the growth of organized crime." How were people expected to react to the portrait of such a monster? They reacted as intended.

True enough, cooperatives have their sins. But can a mother with AIDS give birth to a healthy baby? In the same way, our economic and political system was hardly capable of producing an ideal child. Are you seriously convinced that it is the *cooperatives* that are to blame for the empty shelves in the stores? The same cooperatives whose share of the goods produced in the country totals 1 percent? And are you convinced that it is *we* who have corrupted young people, whose involvement in crime, as we've all observed, is growing? Perhaps the cooperatives are the most convenient target today for people looking for an answer to the age-old Russian question: who is to blame? At one time, they blamed the aristocrats, then the intelligentsia, the peasants, the "cosmopolitans," the dissidents, the Jews and foreigners. . . . Interesting—if cooperatives did not exist, whom would you blame?

I am not in the slightest upset with people who were told for decades that being rich was immoral, that commerce and stealing were the same thing, that wearing out the seat of your pants at work and receiving your little kopecks was a worthy activity, but earning a good living was shameful. People were psychologically unprepared for the cooperative phenomenon; what kind of attitude could you expect? But you, the leaders of the trade unions—when you found yourself in the fifth year of *perestroika,* didn't you decide to play upon people's feelings? It was very convenient to arouse people's anti-cooperative sentiments in order to demonstrate to them your concern for their interests and well-being.

You showered an already well-prepared and surly public not only with empty accusations, but with figures, too. Referring to data from the Moscow Trade Union Council, you said directly at the Plenum that in only seven months of this year, Moscow cooperatives withdrew 1.602 billion rubles from their accounts in the city's banks and deposited only 58.5 million. How were people to

understand those figures? There was only one way. We took out a
lot and returned very little; in other words, the difference ended up
in the cooperatives' pockets. (Incidentally, the Moscow Cooperative Council conducted an opinion poll at several enterprises, and
that is exactly how people interpreted your remark: the cooperatives made off with one and a half billion rubles.)

Now let me ask you, Stepan Alekseyevich, what did you have
in mind when you spoke of the "cooperatives withdrawing money
from their own accounts"? I admit, we thought about it and tried to
guess what you meant, but we could not understand. If it was from
our own accounts, then why did we withdraw it? If the accounts
were our own, doesn't that mean that the money belonged to the
cooperatives? And what does that "withdrawal" figure mean? If you
meant the earnings of Moscow cooperatives over seven months,
then your figure—forgive me—is simply incorrect. Actually, it was
almost one billion rubles higher, namely 2,522,100 rubles. In economic parlance, that figure is called revenue, or the income from
the sales of goods and services.

Let me give you a little pleasure, Stepan Alekseyevich: after
all, counting someone else's money, in someone else's pocket, is so
much fun. Do a little arithmetic, and you'll see whose pockets the
money the cooperatives withdrew from their bank accounts ended
up in. First, let's recall that figure: two and a half billion rubles.

Now, let's begin: 1,107,300 rubles went for material
expenses—raw materials and equipment, state social-security payments, payments to various outside organizations for services without which production is impossible, expenses for transportation and
business trips, interest for the use of credit—and, also, amounts
donated for charitable purposes. I will not burden you with a figure
for each item; if you wish, you can find out the figures from the
appropriate agencies yourself.

Now about real income—the amount which is, in fact, tax-
able. For Moscow, this amount was 1,414,800 rubles. The city
received about 48 million in taxes. That is not very much, of course,
but are we the ones who make tax policy? Are we the ones responsible for the qualifications of the financial specialists, who at first
determined that all cooperatives should pay a 3 percent, 5 percent
or 10 percent tax, but today, because they've become frightened,
have decided on 20 percent, 40 percent or 60 percent?

The income was used as follows: 257,600 rubles went to the
fund for development: enterprises need to expand, to build, and to

buy new equipment—I think that is understandable. I myself am already tired of the figures, so I will be brief: Approximately 99 million went to the insurance fund and for repayment of credit. In other words, this money was not taken in but given back. Are you counting?

So, now we have come to the most interesting figure: wages. This amounts to 845,900 rubles. First we added it all up, and now we are going to divide. We're going to divide by 7—that is, by the number of months in which the money was earned. And again by 300,000 (which, according to the statistics of the Moscow Soviet, is the number of people working in cooperatives in Moscow). What is the average figure? Just over 400 rubles per person per month. That is not so little, of course, but, God knows, it isn't all that much, considering the times we live in. Not to mention the 1 percent given to the trade unions, which adds up to some 8.5 million rubles.

In any case, the figures are hardly as overwhelming as those in your speech. Incidentally, in that speech you also added that 384 million rubles, "the money earned by the cooperatives in the month of July, is equal to one third of the wages of the entire Moscow work force." What is the point of that comparison? Perhaps we did even a kopeck's worth of damage to the wages of the Moscow work force? But why, despite the obvious inaccuracy of that comparison, is it still impressive? Perhaps because it contains a glaring juxtaposition: it seems that everyone else in Moscow is in the work force, but those in the cooperatives are not. There is only one conclusion: ordinary people work, but the cooperatives cheat, speculate and live off the misfortunes of the motherland. How should people like that be treated?

Here, Stepan Alekseyevich, I must give you your due. One month after your speech defending the population against the co-operatives, I was at a meeting organized at Luzhniki Stadium by your kindred spirits in the Moscow Trade Union Council. And I understood that many people (not without the help of the trade union bureaucrats) have found their answer to the question, who is to blame? You, of course, know the slogans from the meeting: "Down with the rip-off cooperatives!" "It's time to deal with those who dreamed up cooperatives!" "We don't need a government that supports speculative cooperatives!" I counted 362 signs like that.

Oh, excuse me, I left out one more figure, and I can see that I need to be accurate with you. The last item in my financial statement is the amount of available funds in the cooperatives, which equals 171 million rubles. The cooperatives, fearing the forcible closure of their accounts in the various banks, placed the main portion of this money in personal accounts in savings banks, thereby increasing by 140 million rubles the sum of money with which there is nothing to buy. If we count carefully, we will get a remainder of available funds of 31 million. Where is it? Well, that money does not exist, Stepan Alekseyevich. Please excuse my bluntness, but it went to bribe various government and private individuals. And you can well imagine that the cooperatives did not volunteer these funds.

So much for my income and expense statement. Now, I'm thinking to myself, why did you have to use false figures at the national rostrum if you could have contacted the agencies you know so well and found out the real ones? Perhaps it was a mistake? Or perhaps you trusted too much the information you received from the Moscow Trade Union Council?

Continuing to think about it, I've come to the conclusion that no, probably we're not dealing here with a mistake or a matter of excessive trust. But what then *is* the problem, my esteemed Stepan Alekseyevich?

A. FYODOROV
Chairman of the Board of the Moscow Cooperative Union
Published October 1989

"ONE HUGE LINE"

The impetus for writing this letter came from what, in today's times, must be considered a completely banal incident. Here in Grozny, as in many cities in the country, the coupon-rationing system has been introduced for soap and detergent. This is really an

ordinary occurrence (and that is frightening!), although dumping
the blame for the lack of soap and laundry detergent on the prolif-
erating bootleggers, as happened when sugar coupons were introduced, is pretty difficult.

Literally the day after the rationing system was introduced,
the widest selection of soap and other detergents appeared in all the
stores. And I . . . I was, frankly, gripped by a feeling very close to
fear.

In other words, it was all lying around somewhere. And that
"somewhere" was not in Boston or even in Moscow, but right here
in Grozny. You should have seen the faces of the women calmly
putting the coveted "coupon" soap in their bags. There was a kind
of cosmic weariness and anguish in their eyes, but no hatred. That
had disappeared in the wild pre-coupon "soap powder" battles.

I suddenly had the feeling that I was witnessing a murder. A
quiet, anonymous and irreversible murder of *perestroika.*

The point is not only and not so much the soap powders. The
point is that there are limits beyond which you cannot safely go.

I have the deepest respect for the fighters for *perestroika,* the
writers and economists, journalists and theater directors. I am
wholeheartedly with them. And I'll never exchange *glasnost* for a
piece of sausage. But I just can't understand how a woman who
gives ten hours at work, including the trip there and back, can be
expected to stand another two or three hours in lines. For what?
Nowadays, for practically anything at all. . . .

The revolutionary or even the reformist spark of any society is
not unlimited. It can muster up its strength and lift even a heavy
burden, but it can't keep holding it up forever. The society could
run out of breath. At best, there will be social apathy. But at worst
. . . God forbid.

When the entire country is becoming one huge line, there
comes a time when the line decides a great deal, if not everything.
And the line is already quite clearly linking the catastrophic disap-
pearance of whole groups of goods with *perestroika.* Yes, that's
right! And no numbers, not even the most terrifying—the millions
of victims of Stalinism—will frighten the line and convince it that
it was worse under Stalin. No, things were better, the line claims;
more stable.

And never mind Stalinism! They are even prepared to forgive
Brezhnev his five stars. Is it political shortsightedness?

Somehow this view is getting more understandable. In the

morning people want to wash up—with soap—and eat breakfast,
preferably with some protein. I don't know about anyone else, but
my tongue has trouble saying that edifying phrase, "Man does not
live by bread alone." It is true. But he lives by bread, too.

M. VERSHOVSKY
Grozny
Published May 1989

GLASNOST

Ogonyok: Vitaly Peskov.

"AIRING DIRTY LINEN"

I work as a teacher in a school. As a member of the "Knowledge" Society and a deputy to the local soviet, I was asked to prepare a speech for the evening in honor of the Seventieth Anniversary of the October Revolution. I studied M. S. Gorbachev's speech, "The October Revolution and *Perestroika:* The Revolution Continues," thoroughly and collected material about exemplary production workers in our village. In my speech I pointed out not only the successes, but also the shortcomings of our village, district and school. I gave the speech on November 6, and a week later I was called into the Executive Committee of the village soviet. I was accused of being apolitical and told that I would not be allowed onto the podium at the House of Culture anymore. They said I just was not ready to speak to the entire village because I was airing dirty linen in public.

I did not agree with the accusations by the Executive Committee, and I think I am right. But after a rebuke like that I have lost my desire to tell the truth, especially since the Party organization of the Cheremkhovsky collective farm and the chairman of the village soviet have suffered because of me. They were both reprimanded for not checking my speech, and for letting me onto the podium. Apparently, *glasnost* and *perestroika* have not reached us yet.

Z. I. KUPRIYANOVA
Village of Cherenkhovo, Chitin *oblast*
Published January 1988

WHITHER THE REVOLUTION?

At the end of October, Central Television announced the broadcast of a four-part film called *The Revolution Continues.* The first two episodes were shown, and they were truly very interesting. But the third episode, which was scheduled to be shown on October 28, suddenly disappeared without a trace. Just like the "good old days" of stagnation. Do you remember? When a story printed in several parts would suddenly be stopped at the most interesting point and the continuation would never follow.

V. P. GUBAREV
Kustanai

SPIRITUAL FOOD SHORTAGE

At the corner of our building is newspaper stand no. 99. On the average, it gets only about fifty-six copies of various newspapers and magazines, including four of *Sovetskaya Rossiya,* not a single copy of the newspaper *Trud,* and six *Ogonyoks* a week.

To buy any newspaper at all, a huge crowd gathers long before the stand even opens. For lack of anything to do, they chatter and complain about the district and city leaders and the heads of the newspaper printing agency. They say, "You can't even buy a newspaper without standing in line and making a giant fuss." They cut back the sale of vodka and there isn't enough spiritual food. *Glasnost* and *perestroika* have been coming to us mainly through the press so far, and there isn't enough of either of them to go around.

A. E. TYUGAEV
War veteran
Omsk
Published April 1988

XEROXING EAST AND WEST

There is no doubt that when it comes to manual typewriters we are "ahead" of the whole world—as we are in steel and metal production—as long as you take into account that industrially developed countries have stopped making them and switched to electric ones.

Typewriters have something in common with another area we are "ahead" in—carbon paper. In the West, it is hardly used any more. As a rule, one copy is typed on the typewriter, and the necessary number of copies are Xeroxed. Copying machines are not kept behind steel doors with a sign, "No Admittance to Unauthorized Personnel"; rather, they are located in any convenient spot. . . .

The situation regarding copying technology in this country is completely different. Copiers are tangled up in the darkness of prohibitions and instructions. Such bans used to be explained by the need to combat ideological diversions and the dissemination of pornography. Sinister stories circulated about what spies would do if they got hold of our Xerox machines. . . .

And now, in developed countries, the personal computer is starting to replace the typewriter. The PC can be considered the perfection of the typewriter, rendering such routine work as retyping totally obsolete. All you have to do is type the text once, and then make corrections in the computer's memory to create a new version. And the computer has a printing device, called a printer. What does fate have in store for the personal computer? What will the bureaucrat's creative genius come up with for *it?* What has it *already* come up with?

A. TRAKHTMAN
Sverdlovsk
Published 1988

THE (NOT QUITE) COMPLETE
WORKS OF DOSTOYEVSKY, ETC.

I was very pleased to learn in issue no. 3 of the magazine *In the World of Books* for 1987 that the State Publishing Committee is planning an unlimited edition of the works of Fyodor Dostoyevsky in six volumes. Finally, every Soviet citizen will be able to have the collected works of this remarkable Russian writer.

But when I saw a list of the contents of this edition, I found out that the editors had not included in it one of the greatest novels of world literature, *The Possessed!* Are we really, even now, still afraid to make this novel universally available?

In the years of the Cult of Personality,[1] an attempt was made to remove Dostoyevsky, and most of all *The Possessed,* from our culture. During the struggle against cosmopolitanism,[2] the writer was, for all practical purposes, banned, and for excessive interest in him, people could even be sent off to "places that were not so far away."[3] In 1935 the type had already been set for a marvelous individual edition of *The Possessed* at Academia publishers, but even Maxim Gorky's attempt to save the edition from destruction was fruitless (see his "Notes From a Reader—On the Publication of the Novel *The Possessed"—Pravda,* January 24, 1935).

But this isn't 1935! Since then *The Possessed* has come out three times in the collected works of Dostoyevsky; indeed, it received a wide circulation in a twelve-volume appendix to *Ogonyok* in 1981.

This opus should not only definitely be included in the new unlimited edition of Dostoyevsky's collected works, but it should be published separately, too. It is the only novel by the writer that, over the past seventy years, has not appeared once as a separate book. Everybody should read *The Possessed.* It is a timeless appeal to human conscience and a timeless condemnation of human baseness.

S. V. BELOV
Member of the Union of Writers of the USSR
Candidate in philology
Leningrad
Published April 1988

Where can you buy M. S. Gorbachev's book on *perestroika?* And how many copies have been printed? Why haven't I seen it for sale? Why can't I get it in the library? I am angry that many Soviet

[1] The "years of the Cult of Personality" is a phrase referring to Stalin's reign.

[2] "Cosmopolitan" is a label of disparagement that came into vogue during the 1930s. It was used to imply an undesirable interest in, or loyalty to, external rather than Russian influences. Often, although not always, the word was used as a euphemism referring to the Jews.

[3] i.e., Siberia.

citizens, as opposed, for example, to the citizens of Great Britain—
in whose hands I saw the book during one of the Moscow–London
televised "space bridges"—don't have the opportunity to read a
book by the leader of their own country.

Natalya Sergeyevna MIKHAILOVA
Candidate in geological and mineralogical sciences
Leningrad
Published May 1988

Today, in the period of *glasnost,* works whose publication we
couldn't even dream about until recently are coming out in large
printings. But here's something surprising: why, with today's freedoms, does a book whose publication has been promised repeatedly, and whose author has apparently not been subject to state
criticism in this country for seventy years, remain forgotten? I'm
referring to Karl Marx's book *The Secret Diplomatic History of the
Eighteenth Century.*

Finally, toward the fourth year of *perestroika,* they've begun
to publish *The Secret Diplomatic History of the Eighteenth Century.*
Not in a large printing, not on the pages of a generally available
popular magazine and not in a special edition, but in a limited
edition of the journal *Questions of History* magazine.

But somehow I don't feel like jumping for joy. It makes you
wonder, why did it take so long for this book to make its way to
readers? Why, even now, is there no discussion of including it in the
so-called complete works? Why, even as late as 1986, was it more
convenient to publish it in English than in the Russian translation?

What is more, in addition to this book about the history of our
country, there are a lot of other articles and speeches by Marx that
also remain generally inaccessible.

What's going on? Do Marx's views really seem so foreign and
terrible to our publishers?

A. KARP
Mathematics teacher, School No. 30
Leningrad
Received by *Ogonyok* Spring 1989
Unpublished

GLASNOST . . . BUT

In issue no. 9 of *Ogonyok* this year, a very good cartoon was published showing a bureaucrat shaking his finger in a threatening way, with a caption that read *"GlasNOst."*[1] The cartoon was very timely. Just as in the old days, we know much more about events in other countries than about problems in our own country. For instance, you can find out any time you want what is going on in the Middle East; all you have to do is turn on the TV or radio. But all we hear about the events in Azerbaijan and Armenia are the most general statements about the "need to pay greater attention to the issues of relations between the nationalities" and about the fact that "the situation there is being normalized" (after what?).

[1] In Russian, *"no"* means "but."

Ogonyok: M. Belomiinsy.

On the "Vremya"[2] program on March 9, the only information presented about the events in Sumgait[3] consisted of the words "What happened, happened" and "negative phenomena." What a wonderful lesson for diplomats: talk for ten minutes and provide literally no information! Incidentally, we have more of these "diplomats" on TV than we need. Our participants in "space bridges" are particularly skillful at getting around tight spots. Take any one of them and send them to the States or China. It doesn't matter; nothing will faze them! In the latest Moscow–London "space bridge" our beloved compatriots evidently got a little carried away and forgot that it wasn't only the English who were watching. I certainly would like to know where in the Soviet Union you can find these people who have everything, who are excellently dressed, who like to go shopping and don't mind standing in lines, and who always agree with everything.

I think that by showing models of this kind of *glasnost,* our television demonstrates an elementary lack of respect for the people, and ignores everyone's right to timely, full information about what is going on, not only in New Zealand, but in our country, too.

S. I. GORYACHEV
Geophysicist
Murmansk
Published April 1988

[2] "Vremya" is Soviet Central Television's nightly news program.

[3] Sumgait is a city in the Republic of Azerbaijan. On February 28, 1988, massive disorders occurred there, during which crowds of Shi'ite Muslim Azerbaijanis reportedly beat, raped and killed members of the city's Christian ethnic Armenian minority on sight. The official death toll from the incident was thirty-two, but Armenian nationalists insist that the number killed was at least ten times higher.

THE "SURPRISING" TRUTH ABOUT SAKHAROV

Probably all readers of *Moscow News* noticed the article in issue no. 20 about Academician Sakharov. For many, it seems, the article was a revelation. It turns out that Academician Sakharov is not swimming in luxury from the money supplied by foreign intelligence, and his wife, Yelena Bonner, is not simply an amoral adventurist who married the academician for money. But that is exactly what the Soviet population has been hearing about Sakharov and his family for so many years.

The article refers to the author of "a written account distributed in millions of copies." That account was slanderous, a falsification. But why, then, wasn't the name of that author mentioned?

Frankly, even in the old days, before we knew all the details, it was unpleasant to read the pages of that book about Sakharov and his family life. And now it turns out that it was all a lie? I would like a more detailed explanation from the people who created and disseminated that misinformation about Andrei Sakharov and his life.

A. Yu. SHCHERBAKOV
Moscow
Published July 1988

WHO'S GUILTY?

Please help me find the answers to three questions. First, why is it that people whose abuses have already been covered in the press still have not been publicly tried? Second question: if the accounts of their activities are false, then why haven't the journalists who wrote those accounts been prosecuted for libel? And third, what, in that light, does *glasnost* look like to the readers—an effective instrument of *perestroika* in a state ruled by law, where not a single publicized crime goes unpunished, or merely a means of arousing the reader's interest in any possible way?

> O. BUSHKO
> Veteran of the Great Patriotic War
> Member of the Union of Writers of the USSR
> Kaluga
> Published September 1988

THE GREAT PAPER SHORTAGE

During the summer of 1988, the media received a secret directive from the Central Committee, informing them that an acute paper shortage had abruptly developed in the Soviet Union. One of the emergency measures the Committee invoked to conserve paper was to institute a limit on the number of subscriptions available to certain newspapers and periodicals— including Ogonyok.

If the Committee had hoped that the new subscription curbs would be accepted as quietly as their directive had been circulated, they were in for a rude surprise. A rash of editorials and reader complaints immediately began appearing in several of the more progressive journals, including the following three letters to Ogonyok.

The ridiculous way our planned economy is developing boggles the mind. Here are two figures taken from the weekly *Argumenty i Fakty* (issue no. 27 of 1988): we produce almost 6.5 times more tractors than the USA, but more than 5 times less paper (19 percent of their level). It would seem there is no connection between those two figures. In fact, there is, and a very direct one at that. After all, what is an acute paper shortage? Ignorance. And what could have produced that monstrous armada of poor-quality tractors? Pure ignorance.

We were about to do away with limits on periodicals, but now we have gone back to them at perhaps the most critical moment of *perestroika*. What a disgrace—limiting the intellectual needs of the people.

Urgent measures are called for. We desperately need paper in order to eliminate as quickly as possible this ignorance that is so dangerous to our development and to the fate of socialism as a whole—in order just to stand on an equal footing with the civilized countries of the West. We won't even have enough bread until we understand that, along with implementing the land-lease system, we need to get rid of ignorance. Socialism, by Lenin's definition, is a system of *civilized* cooperatives. And the bread of civilization is . . . paper.

V. MAZURIN
Ivanovo
Published August 1988

It seems to me that the paper situation could have been created to limit subscriptions to progressive magazines and newspapers and artificially to increase subscriptions to some other publications. I do not understand why there were unlimited subscriptions in 1988, but not in 1989. Has paper production really slowed down that much? *Glasnost* means the availability of information. Even in the most "stagnant" years of stagnation this could not have happened. The situation with subscriptions is one of the most important subjects of discussion for all members of our society.

D. S. LIKHACHEV[1]
Academician
Published August 1988

For the first time in my life (and I'm seventy years old), I have given a bribe. Do you know what for? For a subscription to *Ogonyok*. How much? Fifty rubles more than the cost of the subscription. And my pension is only eighty rubles a month. I am forced to act dishonestly because I can't get along without the magazine.

---

[1] One of the Soviet Union's most distinguished medieval scholars; also well-known as a political activist. In 1989, he was elected to the Congress of People's Deputies, where he became allied with such reform-minded legislators as Boris Yeltsin, Gavriil Popov and Vitaly Korotich.

Whenever there's a shortage, there's speculation. The organizers of the limit on subscriptions should have foreseen that, too. I'm giving my name only to the editors—you can understand why.

> N. R——VA
> Moscow
> Published September 1988

Not long after these letters appeared, the Central Committee suddenly lifted the curbs on magazine circulation. Just how the paper shortage problem was solved remains a mystery—as does the identity of the specific person responsible for imposing the subscription limits in the first place.

"NOW WE'VE SEEN THE LIGHT"

In the recent past it would have been impossible to imagine that not only our friends, but even the "rotten" class—the capitalists—would react the way they did to our tragedy in Armenia. Now we know the reason: it's because of our positive initiatives—of Gorbachev's steps—toward peace.

But the recent past is fresh in our memory. It used to be that you would go into your kitchen, where the radio was, and you'd want to turn it off: all you'd hear about was missiles, explosions and confrontation. "Lord," said a man who suffered his fill in the war, "We can bear anything, just as long as there is no more damned war." Our conviction grew, at last, that we were going to be able to survive, thank God. The refrigerator wasn't empty; we weren't living in bunkers and wearing military jackets. And the man who had suffered so much thanked Leonid Brezhnev for his wise policy (can you imagine, forty years without war?), for his skillful deterrence of the capitalists.

But now we've seen the light. It turns out that missiles can be cut one and a half to two times, and that the danger of confrontation can be reduced by withdrawing ten thousand tanks. It makes you wonder: How did all this start, if we're not millionaires? To this day, our ears are ringing with that unpleasant word: *the Pentagon*. But it's time to ask *our* Ministry of Defense, too, where they got those insatiable appetites, and why there was no serious attempt to control them. What kind of closed agency is the Army, and will it be held accountable to the people, who support it? It's time to tell us what we have and what they have over there, across the ocean. Secrets unmasked will bring nations closer together and will stimulate activism in the Soviet people.

> N. KALININ
> Member of the Writers' Union of the USSR
> Mtsensk, Orlov *oblast*
> Published February 1989

"OLD THINKING" IN A NEW AGE

Our teachers love to repeat that the future belongs to us, the young people. The kind of future the leaders of our state talk about in negotiations is very attractive to me. It is one that people who participate in "space bridges" and international meetings truly believe in.

But in school we are not being prepared for that kind of future.

My literature teacher says that we would be better off not reading *Ogonyok, Novyi Mir* and *Znamya* magazines, or the sharp letters in your magazine. And like a true pedagogue, she sets an example: she doesn't read them herself. In her opinion, everything is caused by the "rotten intelligentsia" (naturally, she doesn't consider herself to be in the intelligentsia). In history class to this day they pound into our heads that our country is ahead, and decadent capitalism is in constant, deepening crisis.

Starting in fourth grade, the most important activity was "standing in formation" and singing songs. And from ninth grade on, retired colonels in our military preparedness classes have been scaring us with tales of crafty enemies. They teach us where to put our heads if there's a nuclear explosion next door. The textbooks are decorated with portraits of Brezhnev and Ustinov,[1] the very people, as I understand it, who made the decision about Afghanistan. And, finally, we are told what miracles (no kidding) the atom bomb can achieve!

We are taught blindly to repeat obsolete views of reality, as if we were living not in the time of "new thinking," but at the height of the Cuban Missile Crisis. They teach us to submit blindly to someone else's will.

I write and sing antiwar songs. At a recent concert at school, all the kids in the auditorium sang them with me. The teachers objected to them as "songs that were not agreed upon in advance."

For some reason, they think that military training will make real men out of us, but I think that its basic purpose is to inculcate a cult of force and the desire to obey without thinking.

A man should be brave, clever and strong, but he has to be capable of independent and proud thinking and use these qualities for the good of the people and society.

Andrei GUBIN
Moscow
Published March 1989

NO *GLASNOST* FOR EARLY BIRDS!

I am one of those many people in the country who goes to bed between 10 and 11 p.m., and if I don't, the next morning I just don't feel like myself.

For more than a year, Central Television has been waging a war with us early birds. They just can't seem to find any way to broadcast the most popular television show, "Glance," at the most popular time—between 7 and 9 p.m.—or to repeat it a week or two later at a time that is convenient for everybody.

The arguments by the producers at Central Television that the "Glance" program is for "night owls" and is a youth program

---

[1] Brezhnev's Minister of Defense.

(and when you're young going to bed at 1 or 2 a.m. is perfectly natural) aren't very convincing.

Why shouldn't people who aren't night owls—for age or health reasons, for example—have the chance to watch the most popular program on TV? Why do the Central Television producers find the time to repeat all kinds of broadcasts, but not the most popular ones?

Why should mothers of internationalist soldiers[1] who are dead or missing not sleep at night, hoping to hear even the smallest little tidbit of news about their loved one on "Glance"? Why do thousands of handicapped people and low-income retirees, people who are anxiously waiting for a real solution to the food and housing problems in our country, have to sit up past midnight every week because of the reactionaries at Central Television?

Personally, I watch "Glance" to the very end standing up so I won't fall asleep; and in the morning (at 7 a.m.), while I'm getting the kids ready for school and myself for the trek to the market and my head is pounding, I angrily sing out the words from the show's theme song: "Oh, that 'Glance.' "

A. OLEGOV
Gukovo, Rostov *oblast*
Published April 1989

AN INNOVATION TO "HELP" OUR PRESS

In the newspaper *Izvestia,* the commentary "Pass to an Extraordinary Event" talks about the fact that the Ministry of Defense of the USSR, the Ministry of Internal Affairs of the USSR and the Union of Journalists of the USSR have all now approved "Regulations for the Access of Representatives of the Mass Media to Locations Where Public Order Is Being Maintained and for Their Presence Therein."

According to these "Regulations," before being admitted to a meeting, gathering, demonstration, march or other "extraordinary

---

[1] i.e., the troops fighting in Afghanistan.

event" such as these, a journalist must now get a special pass granted
by the Ministry of Internal Affairs.

The head of the press office of the Ministry of Internal Affairs
of the USSR, Colonel B. Mikhailov, the holder of a candidate
degree in legal sciences, comments on this event with rather cheer-
ful words: "The decision to issue special passes to journalists should
not be viewed as detrimental to democracy (how else?). . . . The
working relationship between the agencies of internal affairs and
journalists remains the same: open and public . . . I am convinced

Ogonyok: Vladimir Soldatov.

Рисунок
Владимира
СОЛДАТОВА

that under today's circumstances of a democratizing society and
expanding *glasnost,* this innovation will help our press, radio and
television cover items related to 'extraordinary events' and will also
help them avoid conflicts (with whom?), which, unfortunately, we
have already had." (Isn't he referring to the events of October 30,
1988 in Minsk?[1])

[1] Minsk, the capital of the Byelorussian SSR, was the scene of a demonstration on
behalf of the victims of Stalinism which was violently dispersed by the police. A subsequent
article about this episode in *Ogonyok* sparked a major controversy about the proper role of the
press.

So, in other words, everything is allegedly for the better. But what if you take a closer look? I am a journalist, and before going to a fire, I first have to get a special pass from an official at the Ministry of Internal Affairs and only then go to the scene. . . .

Every employee in the mass media has an identification card indicating the organization he represents. If this document isn't enough, there is also the internal passport, membership card for the Union of Journalists of the USSR, birth certificate, public service certificate (for example, the one for getting sugar ration coupons), etc.

Why was it necessary to introduce yet another document? In my opinion (following the failure with the limits on subscriptions), this is just another attempt by anti-*perestroika* forces to put a muzzle on *glasnost* and get it under their control. (After all, they could now introduce limits on special passes, too.) What is more, the abovementioned document will go first and foremost to the more obedient types who are skilled at mimicry, and those who write the truth will have to run around, trying to get the necessary piece of paper so as to "avoid conflicts."

It is with good reason that the Minister of Internal Affairs of Byelorussia, V. Piskaryov, warns, "If they do not have a pass, journalists will be considered people who are violating the law and public order."

I. BOZHKO
Member of the Union of Journalists of the USSR
Odessa
Published April 1989

If one can speak of any guarantees of *perestroika* at all, the first such guarantee should be *glasnost*. In and of itself, *glasnost* will not feed people, give them drink or build homes for them, but if *glasnost* ends, then we will certainly have no food, homes or *perestroika*— we will not have anything at all, except the omnipotence of the authorities and the old, familiar stagnant swamp.

Glasnost, so far, is *perestroika*'s only REAL achievement. It is horrifying to think about it, but if the editorial boards of a dozen or so magazines and newspapers were now to be replaced, we would suddenly find ourselves thrown back a decade, as if there had been literally nothing: no new thaw, no hopes, no prospects on the horizon. *Glasnost* must be protected. For the time being, it is all we have. And it sticks in the throats of the secret and open proponents of stagnation, like a bone they can't spit out or swallow. And oh, how they would like to!

The January "Regulations for the Access of Representatives of the Mass Media to Locations Where Public Order Is Being Maintained and for Their Presence Therein" are yet another attack on *glasnost,* ever so barely covered up by the rosy mist of soothing commentary. From words about the "press unleashed," the authorities in question turn to action. It does not take much imagination to see how events are now going to proceed. The authorities will begin dividing journalists into good and bad (from their own bureaucratic point of view, of course). The "good" ones will receive passes; the "bad" ones will not. And if a "good" one lets himself publish something he shouldn't, he will lose his passes on the most legitimate, formal basis. . . .

Incidentally, these are all details. The crux of the matter is that the bureaucratic regulations DO NOT serve to expand *glasnost,* DO NOT help the efforts of the mass media; they serve the bureaucratic authorities as a convenience and help them give out information in "doses," placing yet another yoke on *glasnost.*

The position of the Union of Journalists is astonishing! It not only allowed itself to be constrained by the authorities but was eager to help them do it! Naturally, this is not the position of the entire Union; of course, hundreds and hundreds of real journalists, genuine fighters for *perestroika,* who understand their duty and see the danger, will raise their voices against this bureaucratic action. We join them and call on all those who cherish freedom of speech and the cause of the true restructuring of our society to rally around them.

Arkady STRUGATSKY
Boris STRUGATSKY[1]
Leningrad—Moscow
Published March 1989

*   *   *

---

[1] The Strugatsky brothers, Arkady and Boris, are a best-selling team of fantasy and science-fiction authors whose specialty is allegorical satire.

The "regulations" requiring special press passes were repealed by the Congress of People's Deputies during its June 1989 session.

A LEXICON FROM COLD WAR TIMES

I have in my hand the dictionary *The Modern Ideological Struggle,* edited by Politizdat Publishers in 1988, which went on sale in the beginning of 1989. When you start to read this book, you get strange feelings.

You will not find the concept of "Stalinism" or "Stalinist horror" in the dictionary, but you will read that the "Cult of Personality, of course, was not able to divert the Soviet people from the path of the October revolution and the construction of socialism" (see page 171). Do the authors of the dictionary really think Stalin's repressive regime is synonymous with socialism?

This publication does not contain the word "rehabilitation," but there are sections that condemn "Cosmopolitanism" and "Trotskyism."

There was no room in the book for the terms "Nazism" and "fascism," but there is a lengthy chapter on "Masonry."[1]

Nowadays, the Soviet people are creating a new, open society, free from the paranoid ideas of the steel curtain[2] and the atmosphere of a "besieged fortress." But on practically every page of the *Modern Ideological Struggle* dictionary we can read about the psychological war against the USSR, ideological diversions and bourgeois subversive propaganda. Who needs this lexicon from Cold War times now?

We are grateful to the international philanthropic funds that

---

[1] Since Stalinist times there has been a conviction in some circles that Soviet Communism is threatened by an international conspiracy of Freemasons.

[2] This is a play on Stalin's name, which means "steel."

gave humanitarian aid to the earthquake victims in Armenia, who suffered so much. But what feelings arise from phrases in the dictionary to the effect that " 'philanthropic' funds . . . are often used by the intelligence forces in NATO countries?" The compilers of the dictionary include the concept of "philanthropy" only in quotation marks, and the concept of "charity" is missing altogether.

I was amazed to learn from this book that there is no antisemitism in the USSR, that the socialist revolution solved the nationalities question, that stereotypes are prevalent only in the bourgeois press and that economic crises are possible only under capitalism.

When, oh when, will sociologists learn to speak the language of today and not use words that are forty years old?

Or maybe the half-baked specialists in the struggle against bourgeois propaganda are simply afraid that *perestroika* will put them out of a job?

D. LEVCHIK
Graduate student
Institute of General History of the
Academy of Sciences of the USSR
Published April 1989

20 PERCENT ACCURATE

Today at work, a lecturer from the Chelyabinsk Party *Oblast* Committee announced the following: "A competent group of historians has checked the articles published in *Ogonyok* magazine during 1988. The reliability of these materials is 20 percent."

Please tell me, is this true? I am very concerned about this! Was there really a verification committee, and, if so, where were its conclusions published?

N. P. VOLOSNIKOVA
Age 29, engineer
Chelyabinsk
Published July 1989

From the editors of Ogonyok: *We are directing your query to the lecturer from the Chelyabinsk Party Oblast Committee, who appears to be the only person in the possession of this unique information.*

GLASNOST À LA VYSHNY

Nowadays, a lot is being said and written about *glasnost,* democratization and *perestroika.* But more and more on the local level you hear: just where is it, this *perestroika?* Things have stayed exactly the way they were; they've even gotten worse. One of the reasons, I think, for people's distrust of changes is the lack of *glasnost.* Take the local press. Four years ago, when the central press and television began a direct, open discussion of our shortcomings, we at the local level hoped that this discussion would continue in the local press, too, because our national shortcomings pop up in just about every city, district or factory. But the district, city and even *oblast* newspapers pretended that there was no such thing on the local level then, or ever. People find out the truth from the central press. But just let someone try to mention that there is *blat,* corruption in the police and bureaucracy and contempt for people on the part of official agencies in the city and *oblast,* and he will quickly be shown how wrong he is and accused of demagoguery and a hundred other deadly sins. . . . True, there are people who get to and find the truth with incredible effort, but at what price and at the cost of how many nerves? How can we change all of this, and who is at fault? The newspapers? The journalists?

Take, for example, our *Vyshnevolotskaya Pravda,* the newspaper of the City Committee of the CPSU and of the City and District Councils. The residents of the city say unabashedly that the paper blatantly touches up reality and often trumpets phrases such as "Let us fulfill and overfulfill," "outstanding labor," etc. It sees only what is convenient and what it isn't afraid to see and shies away from the most controversial social conflicts. It would seem that it is clear: the journalists are at fault. But no. I personally know that the journalists have not been and are not happy with this situation. They write sharp, topical articles with civil courage. But these articles don't get to the readers; they are not let through. There are lots of examples of this: the workers of the electric utilities elected their own director, but the higher authorities did not confirm him—the newspaper could not write about it; one worker, as a sign of protest, announced a hunger strike—information about that was banned, too; environmental subjects are especially taboo, etc. And if something does get into print, it is so glossed over that it doesn't affect anybody. In *Kalininskaya Pravda* of April 2, 1989, you can read the opinion of the journalists themselves on this subject. They talk openly about the pressure put on the newspaper by the City Committee and its first secretary, and about the fact that a whole series of items have been vetoed.

There is also a ban on the publication of anything I write. I am a deputy in the City Council, but I can't address the residents of the city through the newspaper. So what can I tell my voters? That somewhere in Magadan things are getting better? Or how government by the people is gathering force in Moscow and Leningrad? People are waiting for changes on the local level, and until they see them, they won't believe in any *perestroika*.

A. ISAKOV
Milling machine operator in an experimental factory
City Council deputy
Vyshny Volochek
Published August 1989

"THAT KIND OF PUBLICATION ISN'T NECESSARY"

On June 27, 1989, in the Kharkov *oblast* near the "865-km Stop," car no. 17 of a twenty-eight-car express train from Kislovodsk to Moscow, in which the author of these lines was riding, after swaying from side to side repeatedly, left the tracks and came to an abrupt stop. The front end of the undercarriage of the car on the right side as you face forward was torn off, and only a prayer was holding up the left side. Car no. 18 came to a rest 600 to 1,000 feet from the remainder of the train. At first, panic set in among the people in our car, but a short time later, when the passengers got out and understood that they were not in danger, they started to discuss the accident with remarkable calm.

Fortunately, the people were all right. However, the railroad car itself ended up almost perpendicular to the rails, the concrete ties behind it were broken, the fasteners were cut and the rails themselves were left in terrible twisted shape.

Three hours later, the train took off for Moscow, leaving two cars (nos. 17 and 18) on the tracks. In Kharkov two more cars were attached, and the passengers went on to Moscow.

But the fact of the catastrophe itself is not the most important thing in this story.

I am amazed that the mass media didn't carry a single announcement of the accident. One could think of a lot of reasons (no one was hurt, only one car was damaged, etc.), but they all look rather laughable compared to the real reason for the silence: it is to someone's advantage for the people to know as little as possible about how many accidents there are in our country. That is the only way I can explain the fact that twice someone tried to prevent me from collecting information about what happened (I am a freelance correspondent for the newspaper *Za Kommunism* [*For Communism*] in the town of Shchelkovo in the Moscow *oblast*).

Several hundred miles away from the site of the accident, in the middle of the night, an athletically built man came by and asked me to step out onto the platform at the end of the car. I was expecting him for some reason to get rough with me, but that did not happen. Our discussion took place in a more or less civilized manner. First of all, the unknown individual presented me with identification which indicated that his name was Vladislav Viktorovich and that he worked in a respectable organization, whose name included so many words and was written in such small print that I could not read it. My nighttime "guest" started the conversation with some questions: he was interested in knowing why I had been collecting bolts, railroad spikes and pieces of the track at the site of the accident. When he found out that I had been doing it out of a professional interest, he grimaced involuntarily and said to me, "There is the opinion that that kind of publication isn't necessary!" I tried to find out whose opinion it was and why, but my efforts were unsuccessful.

Seeing the impossibility of finding a "common language,"

Vladislav Viktorovich changed the subject of the conversation and inquired, to put it mildly, for which publication the material was intended. I refused to answer, with the same stubbornness he had displayed. With the threat that I would "get mine," he was gone.

When I woke up the next day, I could not find some of my materials that were lying on the table the night before. But that is not the main thing. The main thing is that someone tried to pressure a journalist, and that has to be considered very alarming.

A. MUSORIN
Freelance correspondent for the newspaper *For Communism*
Shchelkovo, Moscow *oblast*
Published October 1989

WHY ONLY NOW? WHY SO LATE?

Now that I have turned the last page of the great book, I cannot get over the feeling of gratitude and joyful shock. Bitter, perplexing questions still haunt me: why only now, why so late? Half of my life is already over and so much water has gone under the bridge. Oh, if it had only been ten years earlier! . . .

At the age of thirty I have read the Gospels for the first time.

This miniature book reached me quite by accident, and I approached it purely out of literary curiosity. But the text gripped me: I was impressed by the austere power of the words, the elegance of the finely tuned aphorisms, the subtle poetic quality of the images. It became clear that the aesthetic importance of the volume was indisputable, and gradually I became very angry: what a treasure they have been hiding from me! Who decided, and on what basis, that this was bad for me—and why?!

No, I did not run off to church, and my forehead is not black and blue.[1] I simply understood that I never was and never will be an atheist.

A state that is separated from the church should also be separated from atheism. Isn't spiritual totalitarianism more terrible

---

[1] Prostrating oneself is a common ritual of the Russian Orthodox Church.

Pavel Krivtsov, *Ogonyok*

than the political kind? In returning social freedoms, a democratic state has no right to continue to lay claim to its citizens' freedom of spiritual quests.

In our dangerous and critical time, when crystal palaces are turning out to be houses of cards and kings who once spoke so majestically are now covering up their shame in dismay, when the clay foundations under the granite colossuses are crumbling, I know that there is a book I can always turn to, and it will help, console and support me in my darkest days.

Sergei ZUBATOV
Novosibirsk
Published October 1989

SECRETS AND MYSTERIES

From earliest childhood our life is surrounded (and fenced in!) by mysteries and secrets which, very often, insult our dignity.

Geologists, mountain climbers, hunters and tourists are dying because they're not permitted to use modern instruments of communication. You see, radio transmitters could be used to reveal some secret. Well . . . they *could*. You could also die from eating too much black caviar. You could have a car accident. You could jump from a fifteen-story window. Everything is intended for reasonable use, not for gluttony, crazy driving or suicide.

We continue to curse Trotsky at a time when no less than two generations of our people have never set eyes on a single line of his and have no clear sense of what Trotskyism is. Is Trotsky an enemy of Stalin and Stalinism or—which is not the same thing—an enemy of Soviet power? And if he is an enemy of Soviet power, then which version, the Stalinist or the Leninist? And if it's the Leninist version, then why did Vladimir Ilyich value Trotsky so highly? Why don't you give us a few of his works to read, for heaven's sake? Let us think for ourselves; after all, we are adults, citizens and workers in our own country—we're either Communists or non-Party members, fans of Glinka or jazz, pensioners or just starting our careers. There shouldn't be someone constantly thinking, feeling and making decisions for us, because each individual has only one life of his own, and it is precious only because of its unique experiences and its achievements.

Defending and building up the homeland is everybody's duty, but not everyone is allowed to know the factors that could lead to armed conflict or to a significant expenditure of resources. We trust our elected bodies, but they don't trust us. Why is that? Don't we have any brains? Are we unreliable? Don't we deserve trust?

Why is it that laws that prohibit something, or that prevent access to accurate and complete information, are adopted much more quickly and easily than ones that allow something? Are the governments of, say, Honduras or Switzerland afraid of their own citizens to the same degree? And if not, why not? Excessive secrecy breeds ignorance and failures in people's memory, and the impossibility of free development and of a critical evaluation of reality, as well as a lack of resistance to potential dangers that threaten society. An unnamed, undivulged evil becomes even greater and grows like a tumor that isn't treated.

And to this day:

- archives historians need have not been opened;
- a scholar can't get clearances in time to travel to a foreign congress;
- it is very hard for an economic planner to contact the company he needs to reach.

It's time to understand that every wasted day is turning into a year's lag, and a ban on photographing the banks of the Moscow–Volga canal in the days of satellite reconnaissance is, at the very least, a joke. Indeed, we have too many secrets per square mile here. . . .

Yet another dramatic example: we almost never have concrete evildoers—they are nameless and "absent." That's why the construction of utterly pointless canals and industrial behemoths (that obsolesce during the design stage), the transformation of swamps into deserts and deserts into swamps, the dying out of rivers and of cultural life, and the long undeclared wars and unconcluded peace treaties, all of them go unpunished. Our misfortune is that, because concrete individuals are not linked with this or that fact, the responsibility is carried by the *whole system,* the *whole structure* and the *whole apparat.*

These secrets, big and small, new and ancient, keep us from living and working at full speed, from developing and being civilized. . . . Is there another people that has endured so much—day and night—both from secrets and from their keepers and defenders, in uniform and out?

I am not calling for all national borders to be opened, for the numbers of diplomats and General Staff to be made public, for tourists to be allowed on the sites of the remaining missiles or for divulgence of the newest technology to go unpunished. But it is time to make life freer, more open, more favorable. It is time to start living as befits the great people of a great nation. We, today's generation, want to see a "bright today," in other words, something that was promised over seventy years ago and for which tens of millions of people gave their lives.

M. SHUR
Member of the CPSU
Gomel
Received by *Ogonyok* Summer 1989
Unpublished

DEMOCRATIZATION

TIME TO MOVE ON

There seems to be no end to our intoxication with *glasnost*. Oh, how marvelous it is that you can say what you think! Of course, it's hard to get used to it. For so many years our mouths were kept shut, and all we could do was stand by and watch as boorishness and brazenness crawled their way up the ladder. But isn't it time to move on? Haven't we sat long enough on this platform of euphoria? We must climb higher. *Glasnost* should become a genuine institution of democracy and a guarantor of *perestroika*.

It has often been said that, because our thinking has been formulated along dogmatic lines, we do not have the experience to deal with a clash of ideas under democratic conditions. Well then, we'll have to do some learning. Dialogue, a polyphony of ideas, a culture of thinking—this is what we need.

N. K. KOZYREV
Krasny Luch
Voroshilovgrad *oblast*
Published March 1988

BALLOTS AND MERINGUES

Last year I was a member of the electoral commission for the elections to the local soviets.[1] I sat at one of the tables, handed out ballots, watched and reflected on things. Of course, not all voters are the same, but most of them look like this: they rush in, give their name, take a ballot and drop it in the ballot box without even looking at it or turning it over. No questions, no conversation. Pick it up, toss it; pick it up, toss it. One woman brought in three passports—one for each member of the family—and she was given three sets of ballots. Behind her was a man with four passports— same procedure. Outwardly, everybody was more or less ceremonial, solemn. One flight down, at the snack stand, the situation was completely different, because they had some boiled tongue down there, and all that was left was fifteen portions which had been reserved for the members of the commission. There was a restless line waiting for meringues. They were arguing about how much to give each person. It was really embarrassing. Then I remembered that for the forty years of my life I "voted," too; I just didn't know for whom and for what. But the vote was "99.9 percent in favor" every time.

Elections, soviets. . . . They were once the very basis of our people's state, our Soviet system. I remember books and movies about those not-so-distant days. I recall heated discussions, differences of opinion. It's no joke, after all—whom do you trust with power over people; who should run the country? We didn't vote on the basis of hearsay; we elected people we knew, people we trusted.

It's important for us, now, to realize the fundamental need for giving elections back their meaning. It would be good for everybody—from the worker to the minister, from the nurse to the Central Committee member—to ask himself: can a society develop normally, can democratization successfully take place, in conditions where the very essence, the fundamental basis, of elected Soviet power is, in many cases, something very close to a travesty? To a great extent, the dynamics and depth of the improvement of our

[1] Councils with specific local administrative powers. In the early days after the Bolshevik Revolution, members of the local soviets were chosen in elections in which workers, peasants and soldiers were eligible to vote.

entire life will depend on the honesty of the answer to that question, and on our determination to correct the situation.

L. D. BORISOV
Ulyanovsk
Published May 1988

"ALL POWER TO THE SOVIETS"

If one believes books and articles, our country is governed by the people—by the power of the soviets. The local soviets, the regional Executive Committees, the Supreme Soviet, the Soviet Workers— all of these terms have become a fixed part of our lives, through and through. And we repeat what we've learned by heart: the power in our country belongs to the people. But what is really the case?

The years of the Stalin era and the so-called stagnation period showed clearly who is at the helm of the country. On the level of the republics, *oblasts* and districts, the Party Secretary was always considered number one. The economy, agriculture, the law, culture, medicine, education and people's fates—everything depended on his will, and revolved around him. . . .

As before, all issues, from disarmament to the battle with alcoholism, are being decided in the Central Committee of the CPSU. And where is *soviet* power? It is dolefully dragging along behind . . .

One hopes that the Party Conference that will convene shortly in Moscow will solve the issue of power in favor of the soviets. Without that, *perestroika* and democracy are merely empty words. If we are going to follow Lenin's behests, then we have to start by implementing the principal motto of the Revolution: "All power to the soviets!"

E. N. SMIRNOV
Terney, Primorsky *krai*
Published May 1988

A week after this letter was published, Mikhail Gorbachev addressed the Communist Party Conference and proposed a sweeping liberalization of the Soviet electoral system, calling for the creation of a new "Congress of People's Deputies," two thirds of whose members would be elected directly at the local and regional levels. The Supreme Soviet approved these reforms the following December, and the first round of elections was scheduled for March 26, 1989.

HOW WE "MET" THE CANDIDATES

On March 18 of this year, at the Moscow Council movie theater, there was a meeting with the candidates for People's Deputy of the Supreme Soviet of the USSR for voters in the Kuibyshev Voting District in Moscow. We, the residents of the district, came to the meeting to get acquainted with the candidates, discuss their platforms and make our selection. But the impression we were left with was very disheartening. We witnessed an outrageous incident. During the discussion, in response to a command spoken into a microphone by the First Secretary of the District Committee of the CPSU, Comrade Panteleyev (he presided over the evening), two of the speakers were forcibly dragged away from the microphone in full view of the entire hall and taken backstage. All of our attempts to find out what happened to them got nowhere. The people that did this disgusting thing said they were *Druzhinniki,*[1] although they had no armbands and could not show any identification. At our insistent request, Comrade Panteleyev ordered the instructor of the District Committee, Comrade Sokolov, to find out what happened, but Comrade Sokolov "found out" in such a way that the so-called *Druzhinniki* disappeared from the scene and remained unidentified. The only thing we managed to get during that hour was the spoken assurance of a lieutenant colonel in the 101st Precinct of the Moscow Police that no one had been taken to the precinct from the meeting.

---

[1] *Druzhinniki* are volunteer auxiliary police, identifiable by their red armbands.

We see this whole story as the rudest trampling on the principles of democracy, and we want concrete information about who was responsible. Please inform us of the answer in the press.

> Residents of the Kuibyshev District:
> V. B. SEDNIN
> V. A. KHAUSTOVA
> A. A. KHMARA
> L. I. DYAKOVA
> G. P. PODGORNOVA
> V. V. GULYAEV
> 19 March 1989
> Unpublished

THE NOS HAVE IT

I want to share some thoughts with you about the elections for People's Deputy of the USSR that were just held. Frankly, I voted against every single one of the three candidates on the ballot in our district. I wasn't happy with their election platform or the principle of nominating people at district preelection meetings.

I don't think I was the only one who did so since, based on data recently published by the district electoral commissions, the number of votes against each of those candidates was significantly higher than the number of votes *for* them.

And so we are now facing a runoff election, this time with only the two candidates who got the "most" votes. But based on the Law on Elections for People's Deputy of the USSR, one way or the other one of them is guaranteed to get elected: all he has to do is get more votes than the other candidate. Even if one of them gets only 5 percent, and the other, 4 percent of the overall number of votes!

What kind of logic is that? And what kind of incentive is there for me—or, I'm sure, a lot of other voters who share my position— to vote again if one of the remaining candidates will definitely become a Deputy anyway, even if he doesn't get the support of even half of the voters?

> A. VERSHININ
> Graduate of the Moscow State University
> School of Journalism
> Published April 1989

KHARKOV DEMOCRACY

After March 26 the city authorities took measures clearly aimed at blocking at any cost the democratic nature of the upcoming second round of congressional elections. They prohibited any preelection meetings and gatherings and the collection of signatures in areas not specifically designated for such purposes. For some reason, those areas—there were two per *raion*[1]—were located far from the center of town and from major subway stations, squares and streets. The decision (supposedly at the "request of the workers of Kharkov") was motivated by the fact that holding meetings in "sacred places" would lead to "unsanitary conditions." Official parades and people's outings are always held in Gorky Park or in Shevchenko Park, but suddenly it seems the immoral preelection gatherings are going to defile them.

It wouldn't be bad for Mr. Timoshin, who has worked for a long time in the City Executive Committee and is so concerned about the city's sanitary conditions, to turn his official attention to the city cemeteries, or to housing conditions in that same center of town he is now so eager to protect, or to the utter filth in the streets. They were cleaned up—as I recall—for the first time when Leonid Brezhnev came to Kharkov. The *second* time, when Yegor Ligachev[2] arrived in February 1989, there was also a memorable

---

[1] An administrative unit or district within a city.

[2] A hard-line conservative member of the Politburo; appointed Secretary of Agriculture in 1988.

food surplus—there were ducks baked with apples at the markets, fish fillets in cooperative stores turned into ordinary stores, turkeys at the *state price*—and speeches by responsible workers on the subject of how we managed to achieve these results. . . .

I don't want to give my name because of the specifics of Kharkov "democracy."

> Irina SH.
> Kharkov
> Received by *Ogonyok* April 1989
> Unpublished

"I'M VOTING FOR THE BOTTLE"

On May 21, 1989, the second round of elections for the Congress of People's Deputies of the USSR took place in our town of Vershino-Darasunsky, in the Chitinskoy *oblast*.

The high point of the campaign to "get out the vote" was as follows: An announcement was made that anyone who came in to vote would be given ration coupons for alcoholic products. And that's exactly what happened. The procedure was simple: You'd come up to the electoral commission's table, say your name and address and they'd give you a ballot with the names of the candidates for Deputy and a coupon allowing the purchase of one bottle of vodka. And, so that there would be no confusion with the *monthly* ration coupons, the "election" coupons were printed on colored paper. [Note: The ration coupon for April is on white paper with the number 4 on it, and the "election" coupon is on colored paper with no month indicated.] Only the "election" coupons were being honored. In the town of Svetly, they made it even easier for someone showing up at the town soviet to vote: they gave out election ballots and you could buy vodka and *zakuski*[1] right there at the snack stand.

---

[1] Russian-style hors d'oeuvres.

The reactions of the town's residents varied:

1. Some said: "I'm not going to vote. They want to buy me with a bottle of vodka?!"
2. Some came in, took a coupon and a ballot, and, without crossing out a single name (there were two candidates for a single Deputy seat), dropped the ballot in the ballot box.
3. Some voted and used the coupon as intended.
4. Some voted, but did not take the coupon.
5. Some voted and took the coupon, but did not use it as intended (or just destroyed it).
6. Some voters wrote on the ballot: "I'm voting for the bottle."

In conclusion, I would like to ask a question: Can you imagine a better way to discredit the elections to the Congress of People's Deputies?

> Residents of the town:
> L. M. KARTUZOVA
> and dozens of other signatures

P.S. All of the above signed work for the Darasunsky Geology Research Expedition.

> Received by *Ogonyok* June 1989
> Unpublished

THE FIRST CONGRESS OF PEOPLE'S DEPUTIES

On May 25, 1989, the First Congress of People's Deputies convened in Moscow. The sessions were televised live over Soviet Central Television— the first time ordinary citizens had ever had the opportunity to watch their government in action. Within hours, a torrent of telegrams, messages and letters began to arrive at the offices of Ogonyok.

*   *   *

Finally, they have let real democracy into the Kremlin Hall of Congresses! The Deputies are open, principled and aggressive. Sometimes they are too quick-tempered and combative, but I think you can attribute that to the newness of *perestroika* and the new political system. I believe that the Congress will be able to find a common language, that it will discuss all the painful issues, think through all the urgent questions and set a government in place that is capable of giving the country and the people what they have been waiting for since 1985.[1]

Valentin STYDEL
Chairman, Voikov Collective Farm
Minsk *oblast*
Published June 1989

Eight thousand kilometers and seven time zones lie between Moscow and Khabarovsk. But we, the residents of Khabarovsk, don't feel the distance. Live television broadcasts give us Far Easterners the chance to participate in the events in the Hall of Congresses. In my opinion, this is a wonderful lesson in people's political education. How can you help but be upset about the letter M. S. Gorbachev read from a group of delegates who proposed stopping the live coverage of the Congress? It seems that there are people in the Hall who yearn for the formulas of the stagnation period, when everything ran along tracks laid down in advance by the *apparat*. No doubt, Gavriil Popov was correct when he said in his speech to the Deputies that "Congress—which itself was elected on a new basis, in a competitive system and by secret ballot—has in essence now set out to offer the same number of candidates for the Supreme Soviet as there are positions to be filled.[2] It is becoming obvious

---

[1] 1985 was the year Gorbachev became General Secretary.

[2] One of the duties of the People's Congress is to elect, from among its own ranks, the 542 members of the USSR's permanent legislature, the Supreme Soviet. Popov's speech complained that since the conservative majority of the Congress permitted only 542 names to be placed in nomination, there were no alternate candidates for the Deputies to vote for. Hence, mere nomination to the Supreme Soviet was tantamount to election.

that the *apparat* is blatantly trying to take revenge, blatantly trying to have a direct influence on the course of events at the Congress."

A. LYUBYAKIN
Khabarovsk
Published June 1989

The election of the Chairman of the Supreme Soviet[1] without a preliminary report from him and a subsequent discussion of his remarks is a caricature of *perestroika*. Don't forget whose Deputies you are; become politically literate.

A. SHILO
Saratov
Published June 1989

On June 2, Andrei Sakharov shocked the Deputies—and the national television audience—by delivering an angry denunciation of the Soviet intervention in Afghanistan, calling it "criminal adventurism . . . , a war of destruction waged against an entire people."

Despite his protest that he meant no disrespect for "the soldier who shed his blood there and heroically followed orders," Sakharov was jeered and heckled by members of the Congress and was forced to relinquish the podium before he could finish his speech.

A disabled veteran, Sergei Chervonopisky, then addressed the Congress, and received wild applause for his assertion that Sakharov's remarks had been "irresponsible and provocative."

I would like to express my amazement at the reaction of some people in the Hall to the speech by Andrei Sakharov. Academician Sakharov is a person of rare spiritual courage and does not need me to defend him. But I would like to know who got up the "courage" to interrupt him? I would like to look those people in the eye. Apparently, some Deputies have a perverse understanding of equality, and think that their heckling can be equated with Sakharov's statements.

[1] The writer is referring to Gorbachev, who, during the first day of the Congress, was elected President of the Soviet Union—a revamped office carrying broad new powers.

Ogonyok.

Andrei Sakharov and Mikhail Gorbachev at the Congress of Deputies.

I wish the impatient members of the audience, in addition to recognizing their false equality with the academician, would also understand their mission as elected representatives of the people.

O. FROLOVA
Moscow
Published June 1989

The tormenting of Andrei Sakharov organized by some of the Deputies, and the fact that he was not given the right to defend himself, are infuriating, but perfectly easy to explain. These Deputies, who have now cloaked themselves in the mantle of ardent *perestroika* supporters, at one time contributed—by their obedient silence—to many ugly episodes in the life of our society, including the tragedy in Afghanistan. Sakharov, though, did *not* keep silent. And that is exactly what they cannot forgive him for, and never will.

Outbursts like the one provoked at the Congress are nothing more than attempts on their part to deflect responsibility from the people who were basically guilty for the tragic page of Afghanistan in our history, and to relieve themselves of any responsibility. But the most frightening and painful thing is that the group hurling the abuses is also being joined by Deputies who still have a very vague notion of what Sakharov means to this country. The herd instinct, it seems, is still alive and well. Under these circumstances, I find the neutral position taken by the Presidium unacceptable. After all, it knows the truth about Sakharov all too well.

Forgive all of us if you can, Andrei Dmitrievich.

> A. CHEPIGA
> Yar-Sale, Tyumen *oblast*
> Published June 1989

Sakharov, Sakharov . . . He only became a Deputy on the foam of a street-meeting, anti-Communist wave.

Don Quixote fought against windmills, and you, *Ogonyok,* are fighting against dead people.

I believe that the working class, which you and all kinds of informal groups[1] have deceived, in the next elections will throw those intellectual motormouths like Sakharov out of the workers' and peasants' parliament. The way, for example, the miners did during the strike, when they chased out all the informal groups who had tried to infiltrate their ranks.

For fifty years I subscribed to *Ogonyok* when it really was a "small fire"; you have turned it into ashes. And while you are all

---

[1] Since the state has traditionally permitted the existence of only one *formal* party, other political organizations—operating outside the official state and Communist Party machinery—have become known as "informal groups."

sitting there in your editors' chairs—because of some misunderstanding perhaps?—I refuse to subscribe. I am going to do everything in my power to keep other people from subscribing to your
magazine, too.

> P. BLINOV
> Veteran of the Party, war and labor
> Nikolaev
> Published October 1989

On June 3 I sent the editors a letter about Academician Sakharov's
speech at the Congress of People's Deputies. Please don't publish
my letter or print my name. I've lost my nerve.

> N.N.
> Chernovtsy
> Published June 1989

One of the most unusual events in the Congress of People's Deputies was the vote to eliminate special VIP waiting rooms for deputies in airports and train stations. This idea was unexpectedly
proposed to the Congress by Yevgeny Yevtushenko[1]—so unexpectedly that not even the most "obedient" Deputies or the opponents
of *perestroika* figured out what was going on before they had already voted for the change. I emphasize this: they *voted* for it! In
other words, those very rooms and halls were eliminated throughout the USSR by the highest power in the country.

But . . . the rooms and halls continue to exist as if nothing
happened! How are we to understand this?! That a vote by the
entire Congress is nothing more than a cute little joke and should
not be taken seriously?! Or that the authorities (or the *apparatchiks*
who prepared the decisions of the Congress) didn't give a damn
about what the Congress said? Or that some invisible person is
taking it upon himself to correct the decisions by the highest body
in the country?

And another thing . . . I cannot understand the psychology of

---

[1] A world-renowned Soviet poet, noted for his anti-Stalinist activism. In 1989, he was
elected to the Congress of People's Deputies.

the Deputies who first voted to eliminate this inequality and then, as if not a thing had happened, sat in those despicable "Stalin-Brezhnev" waiting rooms on their way out of Moscow and were not bothered by any troubling questions or by their conscience! And this is just a month after all their talk, during the election campaign, about their dedication to social justice!

What's going on here?

M. TUKALEVSKY
Veteran of labor, member of the Communist Party
Vuktyl, Komi ASSR
Published July 1989

Think about this. Only 431 of the 2,250 Deputies voted in favor of roll-call voting. The rest preferred to vote anonymously. What does that say about the deployment of forces at the Congress? During the entire time the Congress was in session there was not one roll-call vote, even in those cases when what was at stake was the determination of a political post for one of the Deputies. Most of the members were by no means eager to state their position on such matters publicly. To say yes or no as a part of the general chorus is far more convenient. Who's going to hear you singing off-key if the entire chorus is off-key? It looks as if you're not the one to blame, and you won't offend those who are truly concerned about the issues.

The people in charge of counting the votes walked up and down the aisles, revealing to the entire world the level of our "electronic technology." They counted and recounted the votes as if someone were deliberately trying to kill precious time. But recall, by contrast, how well the electronic voting machines worked at the beauty contest[1] or at the musical show. Just remember how those numbers bounced around!

Could those who prepared the Congress really not have anticipated that there would be voting at it? Or did they merely assume, given the experience of past decades, that it would be obediently unanimous? No. I think that there was a specific goal of making the People's Deputies safe from popular control.

---

[1] The first "Miss Moscow" Beauty Pageant had been broadcast by Soviet Central Television just a few weeks prior to the Congress.

Of course, even with the current voting system, there is still a certain risk. What happens if, at the critical moment, you wind up in a closeup on the TV screen, and the voters find out that at the preelection meetings you promised one thing and then, in fact, you voted for something else—the exact opposite? In this context, why should we have been surprised when Gorbachev reported that among the participants in Congress there were those opposed to live broadcasts? Unfortunately, these Deputies remained anonymous; we never found out their names. But we can say with certainty that they were from the majority which still, on numerous occasions, is going to say its triumphant no when they are voting on radical changes needed by the people. And behind that no, there will continue to be the protection of personal interests, which, alas, by no means in all cases coincide with the interests of society.

A. PUTKO
Member of the Writers' Union of the USSR
Published June 1989

After the final session of the Congress, an electronic voting system was installed in the Palace of Congresses, and immediately put to use in the Supreme Soviet. Indeed, as Lev Gushchin and Valentin Yumashev note in their essay "A Word About 'A Word From the Reader' " (page 17), Ogonyok published the account of a television viewer who had noticed a deputy pushing two buttons during a single vote—one at his own desk, and one at his neighbor's—thus touching off a furious debate on the floor of the Supreme Soviet.

STANDING ON TIPTOE

We were so glad about the live broadcasts of the Congress of People's Deputies! Even with all its problems, it was a forum for genuine democracy.

That's why it seemed to go without saying that the work of the Supreme Soviet of the USSR would be open as well. Alas, no! On June 26, the Chairman, A. I. Lukyanov, announced that, by decision of the Presidium, live broadcasts would be discontinued. A summary would be provided in tapes, played in the evening, of the most important moments. Everything else would be behind closed doors. Apparently the people had no need to know.

Well, the "democratization" in our lives is just one more illustration of the famous Chinese proverb: "He who stands on tiptoe cannot stand for very long." Without consulting the people, the Presidium once again clamped the lid down on information to us. And none of their arguments—such as their complaint that too many people were sitting in front of their TV sets instead of working—was very convincing. As it is, with luck you can count on the fingers of one hand the people who were satisfied with the last Congress. The number of people with the opposite opinion is far greater. So why create even more? Rumors, assumptions and theories will abound. In the end, this kind of selectivity in covering the sessions will not work in favor of the authorities.

After all, selecting information (who, one wonders, will decide which sessions are important to us, and which ones are not?) is a fundamental part of the old way of thinking. It is our leaders' desire to cut themselves off from the people at any cost that has led us to where things stand today. . . .

L. ZHAVORONOK
Tallinn, Estonia
Published July 1989

SIMPLE QUESTIONS FROM A SEVENTEEN-YEAR-OLD

I don't intend to get into politics, not now or later. Everybody should mind his own business. But I want to ask several questions about the Congress of People's Deputies and the Chairman of the Presidium of the Supreme Soviet (the President). First, can even one person explain to me this difference between the elections for President here in the USSR and in other countries: in most countries the President is supposed to be elected by *direct* vote of *all* citizens with the right to vote, but here, it's only an extremely insignificant part of the population. Is that really democracy? And is it democratic that we have one single candidate, M. S. Gorbachev, all the time and everywhere? He *already has* a post; we

Reuters, UPI/Bettman Newsphotos.

A lone Moscow picketer demands electoral reform as the Congress of People's Deputies prepares to choose a President. The placard, decorated with a photograph of Boris Yeltsin, reads: "Deputies, elect the President by secret ballot and majority vote."

don't need to hang all the basic duties in the country on him. And then, as long as Mikhail Sergeyevich is for *glasnost* and democracy, I don't get this: why at all the congresses and sessions of the Supreme Soviet does everybody have to stick to the time limit on speeches, everybody except him? And why in the USA can you see lots of people criticizing George Bush, you can see cartoons of him and other politicians who are in office *now,* but here you can criticize Yeltsin, but not Gorbachev; you can draw Stalin and Brezhnev in all sorts of uncomplimentary poses, but not Gorbachev?

Second, why elect directors and chairmen, etc., as Deputies since, if they're going to "work" as politicians now, who is going to work as directors? And where are our politicians, anyway, if we have such a thing, which I doubt?

And don't think that just because I'm only seventeen years old, I don't understand anything. I've seen plenty of "stagnation" and *"perestroika."* Only under "stagnation" there was something to eat and drink, and sometimes you could get made up like a French girl, and you could buy cassettes for your tape player at the state price, and lots of other things. But under *"perestroika,"* not only can you not get by on just your salary (much less on a pension or stipend), but on any kind of legal earnings at all, because you're forced to buy everything at double or triple the state price.

You might not publish my letter. That's your right. You hold the cards. But there's no way *everybody* can possibly be satisfied with things as they are.

> Olga BELOVA, age 17
> Student
> Received by *Ogonyok* Summer 1989
> Unpublished

ONE MAN, TEN VOTES

Why is our President here elected not by the people, but by a bunch of cronies? We've had four General Secretaries (I mean those who were in for a long time), and four different stages of socialism. How much harm have these four General Secretaries brought us? Why do they have a mandate for such unlimited power? I lived in the times of Stalin, Khrushchev, Brezhnev and now under Gorbachev. Well, it was never worse than it is today.

Nobody—not at the top, not at the bottom—believes in this *perestroika,* which Gorbachev is so pigheadedly trying to shove down everybody's throat. But nobody can object, because in this country everything is headed up by one man. Everybody is afraid for his own cushy position. We all live by the principle: "The new one kicks out the old one, we 'wipe' our tears and everything goes on just the way it was." One man runs everything; he has the final say.

We now have half-capitalism. A worker gets 150 rubles a month; the cooperative people get 800 rubles (Of course they're going to be looked at as "enemies of the people"!). All the crooks and speculators can do anything they please. They even have their own saying: "Strike while the iron is Gorbachev!"[1]

General Secretaries Khrushchev and Brezhnev were the laughingstock of the whole world. One banged his shoe in the UN; the other couldn't even read his notes. We have so many talented people in our country, but our presidential elections are a mess! Why are our Deputies here elected by the people, but the General Secretary by ten people?[2] I think, if they put Gorbachev to a vote, it's hardly likely he'd get enough votes for the post of General Secretary.

Please publish my letter no matter what. After all, we *do* have democracy here.

> S. N. LANIN
> Village of Kushchevo
> Krasnodar *krai*
> Received by *Ogonyok* Summer 1989
> Unpublished

---

[1] In Russian, this is a pun: the words for "hot" and "Gorbachev" sound somewhat similar.

[2] The writer is referring to the Politburo, the highest decision-making body of the Soviet Communist Party.

THE MONOPOLIZATION OF POLITICAL POWER

During the period of Stalin's Cult of Personality, a stereotype was created, and became entrenched, that a socialist state, in particular our country, had to be a one-party state. Even if there were non-Communist parties in that state, all of them were obliged to recognize the leading role of the Communist Party, which de facto also meant accepting a one-party system. At the start it must be noted that, in these remarks, I am not questioning the conscientiousness of the Party or its ability to run the country. What I am questioning is a one-party system which intrinsically, by virtue of its structure, inevitably forces the Party to make serious mistakes.

"In preserving the Soviet organization of society and the one-party system, are we in any condition to guarantee the democratic organization of public life?" Academician L. I. Abalkin asked at the Nineteenth Party Conference. Indeed, is it possible, under the conditions of a one-party system, successfully to create a functioning democratic state ruled by law? Unfortunately, not a single one-party state in the history of mankind has been fully democratic. All of the one-party bourgeois states in recent decades, for example, were to some degree authoritarian or outright fascist.

All socialist countries have entrenched one-party regimes, either in form or in content. And the socialist states, just like the bourgeois ones, have failed to prove that they can be consistently democratic. All socialist countries have to a greater or lesser extent carried out unfounded repressions, where millions of innocent people have died. Despite all their radical political measures, these countries have not been able to achieve any real leap forward in their socioeconomic development, or to reach the level of the developed capitalist countries. The main obstacle here has been the one-party system.

A one-party state, by virtue of the very logic of its political structure, cannot be completely democratic. It is governed not by the people, but by the party, a fact often directly confirmed in the constitution. Thus, Article 6 of the Brezhnev Constitution of the USSR now in force reads: "The leading and guiding force of Soviet society, the nucleus of its political system and of all state and public organizations, shall be the Communist Party. . . . The Communist Party shall determine the general prospects for society's development and the direction of the domestic and foreign policies of the USSR; it shall lead the great constructive work of the Soviet people, and shall provide for the planning and the theoretical basis of their struggle for the victory of Communism. . . ." Here is the complete, 100 percent monopolization of political, and consequently state, power. No matter how the Party behaves, it will still be in power, even if its current policy, as was the case in the time of Stalin and subsequent years, is not always correct.

The Party de facto, and for that matter de jure, runs the country, although strictly speaking, it has no right to do so, since it is not an elected or representative body. The Party represents first and foremost not the people, but itself. It itself selects for its ranks those citizens who appear to be suitable based on its standards.

We are now governed by a Party most of whose members joined it during the Stalin and Brezhnev years in accordance with the demands of those times. The most important of these demands was, in practical terms, loyalty to the Party leader. And experience has shown that those who became Party members were by no means always the best people in the country. In Lenin's words, "sometimes even people with the most self-serving notions wangle their way into the ruling party." In a one-party state very often not only do the lives of non-party members mean little, but so do those of the members, because the monopolization of political power unavoidably leads to a concentration of extraordinary power in the party leadership—especially in the party leader—and to a split between the leaders and the party masses.

A one-party state unavoidably engenders a cult of the party leader, even if only for a limited time, and this always has negative consequences. This kind of state offers the most fertile soil for the appearance of a regime of personal power, or authoritarianism. And such regimes have existed in all one-party countries and have caused great harm to the people.

A one-party state necessarily creates a party and state bureaucracy, which constantly renews itself. The party and state bureaucracy are, in fact, uncontrolled. The people do not control them; on the contrary, since they wield complete power, they control the people. In order to control the Party there must be other organizations that have equal political and legal status, i.e., other political parties. Democracy exists only where there is full political, practical and legal equality of citizens and their associations with each other. If one citizen or one organization possesses more rights, there is no democracy. Try as you might to build a state ruled by law in a one-party system, it will always be first and foremost a party state, i.e., one-sided and partial, and will represent the interests above all of one portion of society—the party and its leadership.

In our country the period of democratic development was very short. It began in October of 1905, during the first Russian revolution, following the announcement of the Tsar's manifesto of political freedoms. Party activities were then legalized, and the first Russian parliament—the state Duma—came into being. This period ended in 1918, when the Bolshevik Party, which had banned factions in its ranks, became the sole party.

During the years of Stalinism and in subsequent years, the idea was hammered into the minds of the Soviet people that the Soviet one-party state was a good thing, and that a multiparty system, where the issue of the popularity of this or that party, its programs and its leadership were decided at the polls, was a bad thing—an institution of a bourgeois exploitative state. This Stalinist stereotype of the benefits of a one-party system weighs down on us to this very day.

The one-party system is the *main culprit in our tragic history.* I am certain that we would not have had the massive repressions of the 1930s and 1940s, stagnation, the introduction of troops into Afghanistan or many other similar episodes if we had had a multiparty system. In a situation where several parties are forced to struggle for power on an equal basis, leaders like Stalin and Brezhnev could probably not come to power, or if they did, could not remain there long. The opposition parties would sound the alarm and start a campaign against incorrect policies and specific dubious actions.

The illusions of a one-party system go back to Russian absolutism, to the ignorant peasant's faith in the kind and wise "Tsarfather" in a country with a low level of political culture. This faith was adeptly exploited in the struggle for power by Party functionaries who acted dishonestly. The one-party system was created by people, and it can be destroyed by them.

A multiparty system, like elections, parliaments, freedom of speech and assembly, etc., is an achievement of all mankind, not an invention of the bourgeois to addle the simpleminded. Parties express the interests of various classes and layers of society, various

Ogonyok: Aleksei Merinov.

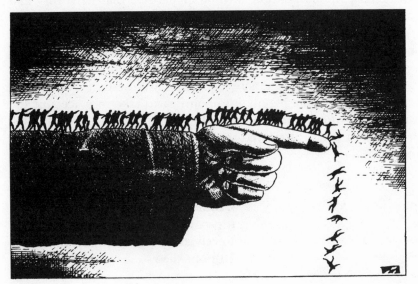

ideological and political trends, various approaches to solving concrete problems. Progressive forces have always used political associations to struggle against tyranny and exploitation and to fight for
socioeconomic reforms and personal and political freedom.

In our country, for more than seventy years now, politics has
weighed heavily on economics. All our economic failures were due,
above everything else, to the one-party system. No kind of *perestroika* will be successful, nor will the state become one "ruled by
law," as long as the monopoly on political power remains in the
hands of a certain segment of society. The reforms will either be
throttled back by the bureaucracy, which has a centuries-long history in Russia, or they will be carried out very slowly (delay is also
a serious mistake), and we will always lag behind the capitalist
world.

The political structure that created Stalinism and stagnation,
which has to this day remained basically unchanged, must be re-
formed at its very roots; the monopoly on power must be liquidated
and the political system decentralized. Only equality for the participants in the political process and the play between political forces
will allow us to deal with the bureaucracy and to set up a regime of

true democracy. The Party should rule not because the Constitution and other laws proclaim it the leading force, but by proving with deeds, in competition with other parties, that its theory and policies are the only correct ones.

We must reject the Stalinist stereotype of the benefit of a one-party system and move toward creating a multiparty state. How many parties we need and which ones will be decided by the people themselves. The introduction of a multiparty system will make it possible to bring the people into politics; to take into account the broad spectrum of their interests and opinions; and to guarantee that the best procedures are used for selecting programs, measures and leaders.

G. I. NIKEROV
Candidate in juridical sciences
Moscow
Received by *Ogonyok* Summer 1989
Unpublished

On February 7, 1990, the Communist Party's governing Central Committee, after three days of stormy debate, voted to accept a proposal from Mikhail Gorbachev repudiating Article 6 of the Soviet Constitution. The vote effectively relinquished the Communists' "monopolization of power," and set the stage for the development of multiple parties.

GLASNOST AND DEMOCRATIZATION
An Afterword by Andrei D. Sakharov

The growing stream of letters from ordinary readers to the mass media, especially to popular publications like *Ogonyok,* demonstrates how the range of activity of our country's people—so long bound by bureaucratic fetters, administrative pressure and a system of prohibitions, and by the existence of areas beyond criticism—is now, finally, expanding. The first Congress of People's Deputies played a critical role in this process; it greatly politicized our society. People awoke to the possibility of an active political life; they stopped feeling they were "cogs" without rights of their own, and showed that they wanted to do something for their country. This politicization process became very strong as a result of the twelve days of live broadcasts of the sessions, during which the majority was exposed for what it was, and it became clear that there were those in the hall who could propose real alternatives that left an imprint on people's minds. What is more, the Congress revealed the full tragedy of the situation in the provinces with a clarity greater than any our press has been able to achieve over the entire period of *glasnost.*

Now the huge sea of popular grief and unsolved problems has exploded into a cascade of complaints and requests directed at newspapers and magazines. Instead of appealing to City Executive Committees, courts or procurators' offices, people are turning, as a last resort, to periodicals. *Ogonyok*'s mail shows that the press has become the final hope of a people in despair. Now it is time for the People's Deputies to come to the journalists' aid. Some letters, though, reflect a surprising sense of helplessness on the part of the

People's Deputies in the provinces—helplessness arising from the
fact that they do not yet possess real power. People need to be
defended against the lawlessness, and arbitrary will, of local authorities.

It is gratifying that more than half of the voters in the elections
of March 1989, in contrast to what happened in years gone by,
made an independent, conscious choice in favor of one or another
candidate. Moral and ethical qualities like integrity, justness and
responsiveness took a front seat. It appears that this concern with
the moral aspects of the people's representatives is one of the characteristics of the new times, a far cry from the conformism and
indifference that characterized past elections, when the director of
an enterprise or yet another *apparatchik* were the nominees. I think
that the Law on Elections to Local Soviets should be changed to
take into account the experience we gained from the elections for
People's Deputies of the USSR.

It seems to me that alternative choices should be mandatorily
offered in all elections. All the candidates should have equal access
to the mass media, and there should be no mechanism for the sifting
out of "undesirable" ones. As a consequence of this mechanism in
the People's Deputy elections, a great many wonderful candidates
were lost. And this was no accident; it served the interests of the
apparat.

In other words, the laws should be changed so that the *apparat*'s chances of dictating the results of elections are minimized.

And, of course, a law on the use of power must be adopted.
Judging by the letters from the provinces, far from all economic
managers have yet seen the link between political and economic
reforms. Power is the key; without power all the problems facing
the nation cannot be solved: not the economic ones, not the social
ones, not any of them. Unless the soviets have real power, the
diktats of the authorities cannot be overcome; truly self-managed,
free enterprises cannot be created; and land reform cannot be implemented. Nor can a general agricultural policy be instituted sub-
stantially different from the current, absurd attempt to resuscitate
the unprofitable *kolkhozes*—which are in the process of falling
apart.

Our nation's economic problems must be solved by the soviets
at all levels, and for that, the soviets need to be independent.

Perestroika must reach the stage where it can be considered
irreversible. It seems to me that this is not yet the case, a fact

which—unfortunately—is confirmed for me by reading *Ogonyok*'s mail. Readers' letters have helped me to delineate the circle of most urgent problems in society that need solving: we need political and economic reforms, and a higher standard of living for the people. We must go down the path of reforms more firmly. We can no longer put off adopting fundamental economic laws about property ownership; the most important law on Earth, the law on freedom of speech and the press; and other acts necessary to create a state governed by law. The Congress cannot feed the country, solve the nationality problems and eliminate the budget deficit all at once. It cannot immediately give us back clean air, water and forests. But creating the political guarantees that will enable us to solve these problems—that is what it is obliged to do. And that is precisely what the country expects of us.

Andrei D. Sakharov

Editor's note: Andrei Sakharov completed this afterword in December 1989, just as the Congress of People's Deputies was beginning its second session. Less than a week later, after returning home from an arduous day in the Congress, he suffered a fatal heart attack. Sakharov had lived to see a commission, appointed by the same body of legislators that had shouted him down in June, officially condemn the USSR's intervention in Afghanistan as a "criminal" act. President Gorbachev eulogized him as "a man of conviction and sincerity."

DAILY LIFE

"GONE WITH THE WIND"

People who have been to Paris are ecstatic over the women there. They all look so young and so elegant. In our opinion, the point is not the women themselves. How are you supposed to be young-looking when you're prematurely gray and there's no hair dye available to give your hair the right color? Very recently you could find "Coleston" and "Topaz" and "Gamma" on the shelves. And now they're gone with the wind! There were so many crèmes—"Spring," "Youth" . . .

We're no worse than Parisian women, but the perfume industry and its enterprises aren't concerned about us. Or is it the same old story—no raw materials? We can just imagine the statistics that will be thrown at us when those whose job it is to be concerned about our beauty and youth answer our letter, and how they're going to brag about all their accomplishments!

E. FROLOVA
A. GOVORUKHINA
N. BORISOVA
Morshansk, Tambovsk *oblast*
Published December 1987

LET US EAT CAKE

For the first time in my life, my family and I have celebrated a holiday without any cakes or pies. Yes, that's right, no pies. Why? There's no yeast. My birthday is coming up soon—my sixty-ninth. But what am I going to serve my guests? I can't bake a pie; you can't buy a cake anywhere in this city; there are no cookies or candy, either. What am I going to do?

There's no yeast because of the war against alcoholism.[1] I'm against alcoholism, too, but the war has to be fought some other way, so that people who have nothing to do with that vice don't have to suffer.

A. D. CHERNYSHOVA
Borovsk, Kaluga *oblast*
Published December 1987

DIAL "B" FOR "BLAT"

Writing you this letter makes me feel like I am committing treason, but my conscience forces me to speak out. Let me begin at the beginning. I had to make an urgent telephone call to my sister in Central Asia. The operator said that the connection was very hard to get; it would take a week. I told my neighbor how upset I was. That evening I gave her my sister's address. She dialed some number, joked a little and kidded around with somebody. And exactly twenty-two minutes later, a voice at the other end of the line said, "Your call is reserved for tomorrow at 9 a.m.; because of the time difference, everybody has left work already today." In the morning I talked with my sister for seven minutes, and, to show my grati-

---

[1] Since Gorbachev's anti-alcoholism campaign began, products, such as yeast and sugar, that might be useful to moonshiners have intentionally been kept in very short supply.

tude, I gave my neighbor a five-ruble contribution toward the phone bill she was going to get. Imagine my surprise when she would not take the money! "You know, where I work I don't get billed for phone calls," she said. I was in an awkward position; I bought her some flowers anyway, but I still felt badly. And then suddenly I understood: my own money isn't good enough to order a phone call, but a few lucky people can call anytime, anywhere in the country. A telephone engineer friend of mine opened my eyes. It turns out that the telephone system, like everything else, works according to the principle "You scratch my back, I'll scratch yours." Every telephone operator has her own circle of friends, and the money streams and streams out of the State pocket. It's all very simple: an order from a friend doesn't get entered on a form; the operator just connects you, and you can talk as long as you want. According to regulations, any communication through the switchboard is supposed to be checked by the controller at the office and by the technical engineers who service the switchboard rooms at least two or three times a month. So this service through *blat* could be exposed. But then the chain of mutual favors would be broken. . . .

If you could count up all the kopecks the state loses on conversations such as these, if you could make the figures public, this loophole would close very quickly for those who enjoy living at other people's expense.

I. V. PETROV
Automobile plant mechanic
Svetlogorsk, Gomel *oblast*
Published March 1988

SLOW BOAT TO KAMCHATKA

Our son studied at the naval institute in Petropavlovsk-Kamchat-sky, graduated in 1970, got married and stayed in that area to work. The climate there, as you know, is harsh, and they don't grow very many vegetables, but we have our own garden and we used to send the kids tomatoes. We would take them green right off the vine; the packages would arrive in twenty to twenty-five days—not a single tomato would spoil—and they would get them red. We did that for about five years. But then the packages started to take longer, at first thirty-five to forty days, and then this year over sixty days. For three years we haven't sent tomatoes because as soon as he gets them, my son has to throw them out. We tried sending them air mail—the package gets there in ten days—but it's expensive: we paid more than twenty rubles to send eight kilograms. We are retired and just can't afford it.

Why on earth has the Ministry of Communications started charging us over one and a half times more for packages and tele-grams, while their delivery time gets longer every year? Maybe our trains and ships have started going slower or the storms in Kam-chatka are more frequent than in previous years?

Perestroika is under way, but our communications system is being restructured too slowly, at speeds that remind one of the times when couriers used to make deliveries.

K. R. POPOVA
Novosibirsk
Published April 1988

A SOLUTION
FOR SINGLE MOTHERS

In issue no. 12, research worker A. Solovyov proposes prosecuting single mothers who leave their children in orphanages for the state to raise. But here is another question: how is a young, single woman supposed to raise and educate a child with a monthly state allowance of twenty rubles? And you have to run around all over the place with your baby to get that money. The bureaucrats who allocate the funds to care for abandoned children moan that this costs the state a lot of money—a whole 300 rubles per month! But a single mother for some reason gets twenty rubles a month, and they think that's enough.

Do people like Solovyov know how hard it is for a young, single woman to decide to have a baby? And once she has decided, she is left with her child in unbearable financial conditions. Twenty rubles is no solution to the problem. And at the same time the state spends 300 rubles a month on an orphanage child. What kind of logic is that? If you want fewer children to be abandoned, then give 100 rubles a month to the single mother and let her raise her son or daughter to her heart's content. And the state will get a normal, healthy citizen and save 200 rubles. I would like to see Comrade Solovyov with a baby in his arms and a twenty-ruble stipend from the state.

And as for putting those mothers who abandon their children in jail: well, why not have little girls in school, along with their Pushkin readings, go through a compulsory labor camp regime during their home economics lessons. Then I'm sure they would not have any babies. And the Solovyovs of the world could sleep in peace.

V. D. ZHULYOV
Village of Yurevo, Sumskaya *oblast*
Published April 1988

SHOW TIME IN KRYLATSKOYE

We were lucky. Several years ago we celebrated our housewarming in the new Krylatskoye "microregion" in Moscow. We moved into the apartment almost with a parade and drumrolls. That's how festive the mood was. The former Moscow leadership had told us that a unique experiment was under way: a residential district was being built all at once, that is, cultural and consumer facilities were going up right along with the apartment houses. Alas, the promises were just promises. Three years went by, and to this day Krylatskoye has no movie theater, not a single library, no public baths and no household supplies or furniture store.

But that's not the worst problem! From time to time, most of the major stores here close down. And these closings coincide, in the most remarkable manner, with visits to this country by foreign VIPs. About two weeks before the visits, the stores start remodeling. Our huge microregion, for all practical purposes, goes without bread, and to buy groceries, you have to travel to downtown Moscow. Right now, in fact, in the middle of May, two department stores, a shoe store, a vegetable store and the major supermarket are closed for repairs, all at the same time. The residents of the region say, "Well, Reagan must be coming soon. . . ."

Judge for yourself: just how lucky is it to be living in a region built for show during times of *perestroika?*

O. KARMAZA
L. KOVALENKO
A. CHURKIN
Residents of the Krylatskoye microregion
Moscow
Published May 1988

Reuters/Bettman Newsphotos: Denis Paquin.

A Soviet woman spreads asphalt in front of Spaso House, a U.S. Embassy residence, as Moscow prepares to host the May 1988 summit meeting between Ronald Reagan and Mikhail Gorbachev.

ADVICE REQUESTED

I would like to ask for advice from the readers of *Ogonyok*. Maybe somebody has some experience and can help me solve my problem.

I live in the town of Rtishchevo, in the Saratov *oblast*. Since the beginning of the second quarter of 1989, soap and detergent have been rationed by coupons. The ration per person for a three-month period is:

2 packages of detergent powder
1 bar of household soap
1 bar of bath soap.

Okay, we figure, we'll wash our clothes less often and walk around a little dirtier. But what about the bath soap? After all, even doctors recommend washing your hands and face when you come in from outdoors.

And what about the children?! They have to be washed every night, to clean off the dust and dirt they bring in from playing outside that day.

And so I am writing to you editors. Help me. Do you know who introduced these ration amounts, and if they are the same everywhere?

One hundred grams of bath soap for three months. How do you divide it? Please publish my letter in your magazine so I can get an answer and some advice about how to stretch out 100 grams of soap for three months. . . .

L. U. YEGOROVA
Rtishchevo
Received by *Ogonyok* Summer 1989
Unpublished

CHILD'S PLAY

My daughter is nine years old. Today I took a look into a small corner of her imaginary play world, which we adults ordinarily don't take very seriously. But in that small corner, I saw us adults, with all today's cares and problems.

I am sending you a coupon drawn by a child's hand—yes, that's right, it's a ration coupon for sugar. This is the kind of game my little girl plays when she's at her grandmother's.

Well, kids are kids . . . let them play. But sometimes their games make us adults very uncomfortable.

Anatoly SMIRNOV
Journalist
Kostroma
Published September 1988

VETERAN'S BENEFIT

Since I am old and it is harder for me to move around now, I decided to purchase my own car.

Remembering that, since I was a war veteran, I could buy one "out of turn," I went to the Social Security Department of the Signakih region of Georgia to find out when I could get my car. The head of the department, a woman named Kurdashvili, explained, "The line for buying a car is already 250 people long—all of them war veterans. If you consider that we receive only three to four cars a year to satisfy the demand of veterans, you can easily calculate when your turn will come."

I immediately did the simple arithmetic, and it turned out that I should come back for the car in . . . sixty-two years, in other words, in A.D. 2051.

I thought, ecstatically, God let me live to that day. I would probably be the oldest person not only in our small village, but in all of Georgia, and I would be able to drive around and visit all my heirs, who would also be happy to drink to the health of their 130-year-old great-great-grandfather.

That's what it means to buy a car out of turn these days.

> Shalva Solomonovich ZEDELASHVILI
> Veteran of war and labor
> Personal pensioner
> Village of Dzhugani
> Signakih *raion*
> April 15, 1989
> Unpublished

HOW I GOT A "BONUS"

I want to tell you about how I got a "bonus." I am on a pension, and, since I am a librarian and bibliographer, for my whole life my pay has been minimal. Correspondingly, so is my pension. I work, so my pension-plus-salary is set at 150 rubles per month. Not a single ruble more, period. That's the ceiling! But the museum (that is, the library in it) was awarded a bonus. It was earned by everybody, including me. My allocated portion of the bonus was ninety rubles, but since the bonus put me over the ceiling, they immediately deducted ninety rubles from my pension. In addition, they deducted income tax from the bonus. Eighty-three rubles of it were left. Plus sixty rubles pay. All-in-all, 143 rubles. Without the bonus I would have gotten more. Is that absurd? No, that's our law on pensions.

From this I have concluded that working hard doesn't pay.

> E. I. DOROGINA
> Leningrad
> Published May 1989

SOS!

To the Editors of *Ogonyok*
cc: The Minister of Health, Comrade E. Chazov

SOS! We don't want to die! We are people who suffer from bronchial asthma, heart disease and other ailments.

There is no medicine! None at all! You might as well close the pharmacies. Who is going to save us?

I am a disabled person, unable to work. Over a number of years my doctors took great pains to work out a system of treatment for me that kept me more or less in balance. Now the medicines involved in that treatment have completely disappeared, and there aren't any other ones, either.

It's so terrifying to wait for the unbelievable agony to come. Better to end life while I still have the strength.

Over the last seven years I have gone through intensive care six times, experienced "clinical death" from suffocation, and broken four ribs.

Are our health services (or rather death services) really trying to get rid of all the weak and sick people? Nobody needs us. Comrade E. I. Chazov, when he became the Minister of Health, promised the people great improvements. Well, where are they?

It's gotten a lot worse. We're being condemned to such unimaginable pain!

All we can do is wait for death to deliver us.

> Lidiya Nikolaevna YAKOVLEVA
> Dnepropetrovsk
> Received by *Ogonyok* May 1989
> Unpublished

HOW THE RAILROAD "TOOK CARE OF US"

On August 1 at midnight on the dot we boarded train no. 1, the *Rossiya,* in Vladivostok. We got as far as Spassk, where we found out that the tracks had been washed away by a flood and we couldn't continue our trip from Vladivostok to Moscow. After the train had stood in Spassk for several hours, we were told that some of the passengers would be sent back to Vladivostok, and from there by plane to Khabarovsk; others would be offered a comfortable hotel. Passengers with children and older people could not go to the airport. We were taken off the *Rossiya* and, after lengthy wrangling, were given the cars of train no. 5, which had been temporarily turned into a hotel.

For three days, we and the children (some people had as many as three) suffocated in the intense heat of the boiling cars. No help whatsoever came from the railroad authorities; on the contrary, there was only a war of nerves. And finally, on August 4, we accidentally "found out" from the TV program "Diapazon" ["Range"] that we, the passengers who were stuck at the station because of a natural disaster, were being housed in a comfortable hotel and provided with three meals a day, and that a substantial sum had been allocated for us.

Understanding that the state was already suffering enormous losses from the natural disaster, we made no claims to any benefits; we just waited patiently, that's all. But when we found out about the benefits allegedly provided to us by the railroad, we were completely incensed. Whose hands did that money fall into? We don't want to believe that someone was actually trying to get rich off a natural disaster. More likely, this was just the usual case of irresponsibility.

And another thing. A warning about the typhoon that caused the flooding had been issued in advance. But for the umpteenth time, the machinery of apathy and complacency set in: "Maybe it'll just pass us by."

O. TOKAREVA
R. YARULLIN
E. NAZAROV
V. GOLUBEVA
G. MEDVEDEV, etc.
[eleven signatures in all]
Published September 1989

DOESN'T ANYBODY NEED OUR FAMILY?

My name is Valentina Pokhodnya. My husband and I have been together a little over two years, but we already have three children. My son, Misha, the oldest, is seventeen months old, and the twins, Varya and Nastasya, are six months old. Our five-member family is living in one room (approximately 100 square feet) of my in-laws' small, three-room apartment. Four more people live there besides us: my husband's mother and father (who at present is in the hospital with a second heart attack); my husband's very ill, eighty-two-year-old grandmother; and my husband's younger brother, a drunkard who, since the age of eighteen, has been on the clinic's list of patients with drug problems. The apartment is impossibly crowded; the twins don't have their own bed and sleep either in the little bathtub or on a chair—and they're already sitting up and crawling! There have been times when they fell out of their little "beds." The air in the apartment is stifling; when the weather is cold, you can't open the windows because of the sick grandmother, and the babies' diapers and playsuits have to be dried all over the apartment because all three of them still wet their pants and diapers. But that is probably not the most important thing . . .

There has not been a single month yet when our children haven't been sick. The little girls were born very weak, with rickets, and Varya also has a hernia. They often get colds, and then our home turns into a living hell because all that has to happen is for one to get sick, and then they all do. It's impossible to isolate the sick child. One will start crying, and then they all cry. And it's the same thing every night. If one of the kids wakes up to go to the potty and starts to cry, so do the rest of them; and then the chorus becomes so loud that nobody's nerves could take it. My in-laws are very upset about it; they constantly pressure us by complaining that we can't solve our housing problem and are torturing the kids and them, too. Several times, when the father or grandmother had heart problems, or because of the drunken uncle, we simply had to leave in the middle of the night and just go outside with the children. My mother-in-law, who has gone completely mad (and it's no wonder that someone would go mad or insane in that kind of situation) is constantly threatening to throw our "runts," as she says, out on the street.

When the twins were born, people in the know advised me not to leave the maternity hospital until the authorities gave us an apartment; if I didn't do that it would take a long time to get housing. Now I understand how right they were.

We have been on the list for an apartment for about two years, and that provides people with just the excuse they need to pass the buck to somebody else. We have gone to so many places and stood in so many lines waiting to see somebody. Just let me tell you all the places: Chairman Geraskov of the Lenin District Committee, Chairman Generalov of the Soviet District Committee (because we are on two lists, one based on the workplace and one based on where we live), Secretary Mindolin of the Party District Committee of the Soviet District, Secretary Bochkaryov of the Komsomol District Committee of the Lenin District, Chairman Indenok of the City Executive Committee, Skasyrsky of the *oblast* cultural department, Secretaries Morozov and Fadeyev of the *Oblast* Committee of the Komsomol, Deputy Chairman Kasaurov of the *Oblast* Executive Committee, and People's Deputies of the USSR Demakov and Kozlov.

Unfortunately, none of them has ever been to our house, and the only one who agreed to help us was the *Oblast* Committee of the Komsomol: they agreed to donate money without compensation so we could pay for a cooperative apartment. In almost nine years of working for the Komsomol, I never once heard of such generosity on the part of the *Oblast* Committee; obviously this was a result of *perestroika*. But it was no cause for rejoicing, because none of the other authorities was willing to cooperate.

I think I'm going to go out of my mind soon from the constant humiliations and indifference of bureaucrats. After all, at work they need us so badly. I am an honored Komsomol worker, a teacher. At one time the magazines *Sobesednik* [*Interlocutor*] and *Komsomol-skaya Zhizn* [*Komsomol Life*] wrote about my Komsomol achievements in the north in Tyumen. My husband is a talented theatrical director whose career is very promising. He graduated from the Leningrad Cultural Institute and conducts many district and city events himself; he writes scripts for the city and teaches students in the Institute of Culture and the Arts.

Can it really be that the state or society or *perestroika* doesn't need our family? Maybe this sounds pathetic, but the family is the heart of the state. And the state can't be well-off if our family is doing so badly. Yes, I know there are problems in the country with housing, that we aren't the only ones like this, but how am I going to explain that to my children, who are growing up fast, who need a place to sleep, someplace to crawl and develop, who need fresh air?

I feel guilty in front of my children. If I had known ahead of time what fate had in store for a Soviet mother with several children and few financial resources, I would never have started having children in the first place. If we end up on the street tomorrow, with no means to live, I don't think any of the local authorities would be overly concerned.

Dear comrades, I am asking you, I am begging you: help us! Save our family! I am appealing to your human feelings. I am

Ogonyok.

at the point of despair. Did I really not have the right to have these children?

Valentina POKHODNYA
September 16, 1989
Unpublished

SO YOU SAY YOU WANT A TELEPHONE?

New apartments are being built in Alushta, and telephones are being installed in apartments for people who are coming to live in the city. Our district was built in the 1950s, but underground telephone cables were not planned for, so we were left with no telephone. I have lived in the city for thirty-two years, worked hard all my life, and grew old here. You can imagine how angry I became when I asked a telephone worker when our street was finally going to get telephones, and he said, "Buy a telephone pole, put it up, buy a telephone cable, string it up, buy a telephone set—and then we'll hook you up."

Excuse me, but where can I get a telephone pole?

T. ZAKHAROVA
Retired
Alushta
Published November 1989

WHAT IS A STATE OF LAW?

What is a state of law? As I understand it, it is a state where letters like THIS ONE should disappear from the pages of the newspapers and magazines once and for all!

It is impossible to imagine a state of law where the media publish letters about broken toilets, leaky roofs, rude salespeople, late trains, broken promises and ruined plans! In the civilized world they have courts to get rid of all of this! Courts! Every individual should go about his own business, but if he does it poorly, he is liable under the law!

We, on the other hand, are used to issuing threats: "I'm going to write a letter to the newspaper!" Now the standard answer to that is, "Go ahead and write one, if you're such a big author! You scribblers are popping up all over the place!" So, the recent Central Radio morning broadcast with the old recommendations to turn to the Party, to go to the *Raion* Committee with your troubles, is nothing but an appeal to old stereotypes! We will never become a state of law if we keep putting our faith over and over again in some menacing person, instead of in the law!

A. GROSSMAN
Engineer
Leningrad
Published September 1989

PEOPLE AND
POWER

Ogonyok: Vladimir Uborevich-Borovsky.

"KEEPING ORDER" ON THE SEVENTH OF NOVEMBER

I am working in Yamburg on a special assignment. For the November holidays[1] I went to Moscow, where I live permanently. Being in a holiday mood, I went to the parade and took my granddaughter with me, because my friends, who work in a factory in the Moskvoretsky district, had agreed to take us in their group. The right-flank man vouched for us. But as soon as we ran into a police unit along the street, my granddaughter and I were taken aside. They found out that, although I really was a Muscovite, I worked in Yamburg. No matter how much I tried to convince them that there were no columns of workers from Yamburg with whom we could more properly march through Red Square, they refused to listen; they grabbed me by the arm and out! And even the tears of a child who had gotten up so early had no effect on the people with red armbands or the ones in police uniforms. They used force and tore the sleeve off my coat, but the irate column gathered around us and would not let the "keepers of order" remove us. Thanks to them, we went on to Red Square, but the anger and bitterness are with us still. How long are people in power, with Party cards in their pockets, going to use their sticks however they please?

T. AKHMATUKAEVA
Yamburg, Tyumen *oblast*
Published December 1987

---

[1] November 7 is the anniversary of the Bolshevik Revolution.

SENSELESS BANS

We are used to senseless bans and to the fact that they sometimes turn into a farce. Last summer I witnessed a ridiculous scene. At the Zima railroad station a line of policemen approvingly watched some Japanese tourists taking group photos on the platform. But when Soviet citizens did the same thing, their film was triumphantly taken away and exposed. The policemen announced, "Taking pictures in the station is prohibited.[1] If you argue, we'll take you to the KGB."

Friends of mine got into a similar situation when they decided to have their picture taken on an embankment of the Neva river in Leningrad. The picture had a railroad bridge in it, a bridge that just happens to be in the middle of a city with millions of inhabitants.

And now new regulations have been posted in subway cars with a paragraph that prohibits taking photographs in subway stations without the "written permission of the Subway Administration"! Here is yet another example of bureaucratic state activity. We see foreigners happily photographing the inside of Mayakovskaya station, or the stained glass in Novoslobodskaya station, or the bronze sculptures in Revolution Square station. How will the subway police react to this now? And where will they take Soviet citizens who violate this ban?

B. CHIMIT-DORZHIEV
32 years old, member of the CPSU
Moscow
Published December 1987

---

[1] Presumably for the purpose of safeguarding national security, Soviet law has long prohibited the photographing of railroad stations, airports or bridges.

"BY THE WAY, WHO'S YOUR HUSBAND?"

I was surprised to read in *Literaturnaya Gazeta* no. 49 a letter from a minister's wife who tried to justify the special privileges of the staff workers in the *nomenklatura*[1] by referring to the difficulty of their daily lives, the responsibility of their office and the length of their workday. I would like to respond to her in the pages of *Ogonyok:*

You complain that ministers (including your husband) work twelve to sixteen hours a day. I can certainly believe that. But I don't see any particular tragedy in that because I work just as long—eight hours at my regular job as a junior researcher in a museum, and then I work on the side as best I can. There is no other way. I have been renting a room in an apartment for six years. Your husband isn't by any chance the Minister of Housing Construction?

You didn't say what his salary is. Mine is 110 rubles a month. Your husband isn't by any chance the Minister of Finance?

I was surprised that you carry heavy bags home from the market[2] yourself because the special stores[3] "don't always have what I need." I suppose I'm in a better position there. Although I don't always find what I need in the city stores, I don't carry any heavy bags—I can't afford to go to the market. Your husband isn't by any chance the Minister of Agriculture?

You complain that every morning you leave for work at 7:30. I can certainly relate to that. I leave the house at 7:15. But I don't have a black car waiting for me; it takes me almost an hour and a half each way. Your husband isn't by any chance the Minister of Transportation?

I also very much sympathize with you that your family only

[1] The vast hierarchy of officials appointed by the Communist Party and the government.

[2] After meeting governmental quotas, growers are allowed to sell surplus produce in special markets. Prices here are usually much higher than in the state stores.

[3] Stores in which only specified categories of VIPs are allowed to shop. Such stores invariably carry a wider selection of better-quality merchandise than do the ordinary state stores.

gets to use its state *dacha* one month out of the year, but you have to pay for the telephone for the *whole* year. And I am prepared to sympathize quite deeply with many of the other things you write in your letter. But as long as not everybody in our country has his own apartment and dacha, a black car and money to shop "at the market," my sympathy will hardly be sincere.

V. PRIBYLOVSKY
Istra, Moscow *oblast*
Published December 1987

RECIPE FOR CHANGE

Thousands of people are clinging to the special privileges you described ("No Problems," issue no. 36) with both hands. These privileges affect one's psychology; they raise their holders' opinions of themselves and often make them callous, indifferent and blind.

If a "Big Boss" stood in line to see a local doctor at a regular clinic for two or three hours, and the doctor then treated him in five minutes; if he had to wait for two or three years for dentures; if he lay in a hospital hallway for a while, and they didn't have the medication he needed; if he went on a tourist trip around the country on our trade-union passes, ate foul-smelling meat with the same old rice, stood in line all the time for the toilet, and didn't get even half of what he was promised for his money; if he tried to repair his car without using connections or bribes; if he got back torn sheets from the laundry and had his brand-new sheets stolen; if his wife started wearing the kinds of boots they sell in the ordinary stores . . . *then* we could really expect some changes!

N. NIKOLAEVA
Leningrad
Published November 1987

"FOR THINGS LIKE THAT, YOU DON'T GET VISAS?"

I am a sailor. I'm fifty years old, and I have spent thirty of those years dealing with the sea. By profession I am a radio operator on fishing boats in the Kaliningrad area. Since 1972, when I returned from a scheduled trip on the whaling ship *Yuri Dolgoruky,* I've had "suspended status," or to be more exact, I've been a person who is no longer trusted to go on vessels that sail abroad.

The reason for my suspension was my interest in English, which I tried to improve by talking with two Japanese representatives who were on board the *Yuri Dolgoruky* to observe our whaling procedures. To my chagrin, neither of them spoke English. I discontinued my efforts, but my "contact" with them was noted, although such contact was not prohibited. I was then categorically forbidden to meet with them. Later accidental meetings (a ship is not land—you can't go very far) did, of course, take place. I didn't run off and hide whenever there were foreigners on my ship. More than once I'd had occasion to deal with them, during previous calls at foreign ports.

Someone got the idea that since I was a radio man, I could reveal the secrets of codes used in radio communications. And we were off and running. These suspicions showed up in my trip report, in the form of such phrases as "apolitical," "sloppy attitude toward his work," "does not attend Marxism-Leninism classes. . . ." I found this out only after many unsuccessful attempts—which were indescribably nerve-racking—to learn the truth from the *Oblast* Committee of the CPSU. Finally, they agreed to read me excerpts from information kept in the archives of the Kaliningrad fishing industry producers' association. I listened in shock and then asked, "So, for things like that you don't get visas?" Their response was to shrug their shoulders and ask me to come back later.

I never really managed to break through that deaf, secret wall of silence and indifference. My friends sympathized, but they didn't know what to do. They advised me to drop it and switch to shore duty. Luckily, there were *real* Communists around who delved into the details of my case. They were able to arrange for me to continue working on ships, with the condition that I no longer had the right to call on foreign ports. I didn't need to visit other countries, anyway; I was at sea, on a ship, doing my favorite work and proud of it.

But nevertheless I never lost the hope that justice would triumph and that some day I would again become a full-fledged sailor-citizen and would remember everything that happened to me only as a horrible dream. In the meantime I am still interested in the English language and I sail around the Baltic Sea, but no further. And I am still hoping for my non-posthumous rehabilitation.

V. S. DMITRACHENKOV
Radio operator
Kaliningrad
Published April 1988

Lev Gushchin, Ogonyok's *deputy editor-in-chief, provides the following commentary: "To date, the instructions requiring people in certain official positions to inform their superiors about all contacts with foreigners have not been rescinded. For example, it is still officially forbidden to visit citizens of another country, or to receive them in your home, without your superiors' permission. These are concrete manifestations of the 'iron curtain' which was used to separate the USSR from other countries."*

BORDER INCIDENT

On February 10 I was scheduled to travel from Odessa to Moscow on train no. 24, car 2, seat 7. When I went into the car there was a border guard, a sergeant, blocking the entrance to my compartment. "Where's your ticket? Seat 7 is taken," he said, and reported into the walkie-talkie hanging on his chest, "This is Buran-4. There's a passenger here for seat 7."

From the loudspeaker on his chest came the loud question, "Military or civilian?"

"Buran-4," the sergeant replied. "Civilian."

The loudspeaker barked again, loudly enough for the whole

car to hear, "Buran-4, detain the citizen; do not let him into the compartment. We're going to figure this out."

People were starting to gather around us and discuss the situation, not maliciously—they were Odessans, after all!—but with a sense of humor. "Uh-oh, none of us have visas!" "Tell me, which way does the border run here: along the length of the train or across it?" Easy for them to make jokes. . . .

The military commander's adjutant came by, took my ticket, wrote down the number and said, "You'll have to get off the train." What was I supposed to do? I use up my entire reserve of personal-conflict energy at work; in situations like this I am practically helpless. I left. "Does this happen a lot?" I asked the conductor.

"Yes, every time there's a general on board. One or two soldiers come by and guard the seat."

So that's it. Well, in my case, everything worked out all right thanks to the efforts of that conductor, who found me another seat in the car. But one question still remained, and I think it's a pretty fundamental one.

I have two grown-up sons. One graduated from the university with an officer's rank; the other served in the Kantemirov Division. The latter has strong, pleasant memories of his military service—he served in training and education. And what about our boys who came back from Afghanistan? They are justifiably proud of their difficult stints.

But what is that sergeant, who spent part of his service standing in a sleeping car, going to say when he gets home? What "border" did "Buran-4" patrol? And there's also the question of our national budget. Of course, you can't put the Army on an independent, self-financing system. But, somehow, like other organizations, it should feel the changes going on in society.

The general came in wearing civilian clothes: a calm, intelligent (and, I think, not only in looks) person. Maybe he, too, is sick of this kind of "service." But if, in principle, it *is* necessary, then surely it needn't be performed in such a blatant, high-tech, loud and—excuse me—tactless way.

O. MELNIKOV
Agronomist
Odessa
Published May 1988

WHY DO POLICEMEN GUARD MOSCOW UNIVERSITY? WHAT ARE THEY GUARDING IT AGAINST?

In *Ogonyok* no. 9, the article "On Wheels" has kind words for the guards at Moscow State University. One can only rejoice that a handicapped person with practically no friends can always get assistance from the "kind policemen." But, one wonders, how did the police end up in the main building of Moscow University in the Lenin Hills in the first place? Why has the "temple of science," which was always famous for its democratic nature and love of freedom, been literally cordoned off by the police? What are they guarding here? Against whom? Why can't I, who studied at Moscow University for eight years, come here to see friends and professors and walk in freely, instead of being humiliated by having to explain to the sergeant the purpose of my visit? (Incidentally, I don't always get in—not by a long shot!) But never mind me! What about the eminent academicians, the recipients of various awards, professors at Moscow University, who have given decades of their lives to their university? Why do they have to shuffle through their pockets looking for a pass?

Recently, I was at Moscow University again. With me were two of my students. They were genuinely surprised at how seriously our nation's main institution of higher learning is guarded. And I was embarrassed, just as I was embarrassed on other occasions in front of undergraduate and graduate student friends from Bulgaria, the GDR, Lebanon, Greece and Colombia, who had traveled and seen a lot, but were coming up against this phenomenon for the first time.

Why am I writing about this now? Because I am convinced that, in these days of *glasnost* and *perestroika,* the time has come to review the nonsensical prohibitions of the past, and to trust the students of Moscow State University to be their own masters in the "temple of science."

Ivan Georgyevich DZHUKHA
Assistant professor, Vologdu Pedagogical Institute
Published May 1988

KGB, OPEN YOUR DOORS!

Every time I walk past the solemn facades of the buildings housing the KGB, I have a feeling of vague alarm, puzzlement and, I admit, fear. It would seem I am no threat at all to our country's security, but so many people were no threat at all. . . . I am also stunned by the grandeur of the new building on Lubyanka. The effect created by the architect is extremely imposing.

Like it or not, I get the impression (maybe a wrong one) that the agency is living some kind of independent life—that there is no social institution controlling its activities, that it has no accountability to society. I am also puzzled by the complete silence of the people who work for the KGB: there hasn't been a single major article or statement from them in the press or on the radio. Incidentally, a happy exception to this was the recent interview in *Pravda* with the Chairman of the KGB, V. M. Chebrikov.[1] Perhaps from now on the agency's silence will not be so mysterious, and so deliberate. Indeed, why don't KGB officials openly express their attitude toward a subject that right now is at the very nerve-center of social awareness—the Stalinist repressions? In addition to its human considerations, this subject has another important aspect for KGB workers—a professional one. The tragedy that afflicted our country from the 1930s through the 1950s is probably just as painful for today's *Chekists*[2] as it is for the rest of us. I believe that they are a different breed of people from those that worked there in past years. And, if my observations are correct, the majority of our population believes this. But why not give us visible confirmation of our belief?

In this connection, I have a concrete proposal: invite a correspondent from *Ogonyok* to Lubyanka. Let him walk around the hallways and offices, let him go down into the cellars—whose existence we know about from the memoirs of those who resided there during the Yezhov-Beria period and survived to relate their experiences. Let him talk with the people who are guarding the security

---

[1] In 1989, Chebrikov was succeeded as KGB Chairman by Vladimir A. Kryuchkov.

[2] The *Cheka* was the original name of the KGB.

of our fatherland, let him interview the KGB leaders. And then let him write about everything he has seen, for the public at large.

O. FISHER
Moscow
Published September 1988

Lev Gushchin comments: "This was the first letter published in the Soviet press that spoke so openly about the KGB, and it sent shock waves through the KGB apparat. As funny as it sounds, the censors attempted to force Ogonyok to have the letter checked out by the KGB!"

In the meantime, hundreds of the magazine's readers wrote letters in support of O. Fisher. Within the next twelve months, Ogonyok had taken Fisher's advice and published two articles by Yaroslov Karpovich, a former KGB colonel, in which he spoke candidly about the agency's activities during the Stalin and Brezhnev years.

GLASNOST IS ALL VERY NICE, BUT . . .

I read the material by Ya. Karpovich, a former officer of the KGB, entitled "I'm Too Ashamed to Remain Silent," in issue no. 29. First of all, these questions came to mind: What was the goal of the magazine's editors in publishing it? Why did we need to consume, with relish, various facts about the agency's activities in the years of the Cult or stagnation? Does that contribute to strengthening the moral and political fiber of Soviet citizens in these times—which are not particularly calm as it is?

In my opinion, the article was aimed at undermining the authority of the KGB.

Of course, the Party and the Army and the KGB had and still have shortcomings, and they can and should be criticized. That's what *glasnost* is for. But, obviously, there has to be moderation in every criticism, and whenever critical material is published you have to ask yourself these questions: Who will benefit from this? Does this serve the cause?

Is Karpovich's statement, that the KGB from the mid-1950s to the 1980s (or right up to today) was doing things it was not supposed to do, really true? Who gave him the right to make slanderous statements like that? Even if he did see occasional shortcomings in the work of the agency, can its employees really just blab about anything, anywhere they want? *Glasnost* is all very nice, but you have to know where to stop.

One can agree with some of the critical remarks the author makes. But why such an outpouring of facts about the demonstrations at the U.S. and West German Embassies by Jewish "refuseniks," or about the inappropriate activities of the KGB and its staff, etc., etc.

The article is clearly aimed at undermining the authority of the agency, and it cannot be ignored. The not-so-noble role of the editor-in-chief of *Ogonyok* magazine is very much in evidence here.

In my opinion, what should be done—and right away before we're awash in more articles like Karpovich's, before slandering the KGB becomes a regular habit of the mass media—is for the Party to issue a sharp censure, on principle, of the article, its author and the editor-in-chief of the magazine.

And, I think, this should be done publicly, in the press, so that all Soviet citizens can read it and draw the proper conclusions.

V. ZHUKOVSKY
Member of the CPSU since 1947
Veteran of war and labor
Borisov, Minsk *oblast*
Published October 1989

SILENCE IS GOLDEN?

In July and September 1989, I wrote two articles in *Ogonyok* magazine (issues nos. 29 and 37). In these articles, I referred to well-known examples and names in making the case that on many occasions during the so-called stagnation years, the state security agencies carried out the function of persecuting dissidents, an activity that cannot be permitted in a state ruled by law. And I did not hide my own participation in all of this.

At first, the reaction was very democratic: there were numerous responses and telephone calls, of every stripe. Former colleagues responded in different ways to my first article in *Ogonyok;* the Chairman of the KGB, in an interview with *Izvestia,* confirmed that the agencies had indeed engaged in certain improper actions in the past.

However, in November of 1989 everything changed. Within the KGB, three highly placed officials twice accused me of slander and distorting facts, and, on November 28, a decree was issued by the Chairman of the KGB depriving me of my award as an "Honored State Security Officer."

In light of the processes of democratization and *glasnost* under way in our country, the goal of creating a state ruled by law, and the unqualified condemnation of the fundamental precepts of the "stagnation period"—in particular the active persecution of dissidents—it is difficult to agree with the arguments brought forward in the Chairman's decree.

For one thing, I cannot understand where, in the material I wrote, I ever disclosed a classified secret. In discussing the unjustified harassment of Sinyavsky and Daniel,[1] Sakharov, Solzhenitsyn or Grigorenko?[2] All this had already been widely reported, with pain and bitterness, in the mass media. In presenting examples of the unlawful persecution of Jewish "refuseniks" or Crimean

---

[1] In the first of a continuing series of showcase trials, writers Yuli Daniel and Andrei Sinyavsky were convicted in 1966 of having published "anti-Soviet" works abroad. They spent eight years in a labor camp.

[2] P. G. Grigorenko, an honored general from the faculty of the Soviet War Academy, was denounced as insane, fired from his job and stripped of his citizenship after he went to Tashkent in 1969 in an attempt to aid eleven Crimean Tatars who were on trial there.

Tatars?[3] Everyone already knew about that! Or perhaps in my statement that the upper levels of the state security agencies were overflowing with incompetent and incapable Party and Komsomol functionaries, and that, quite naturally, the KGB's level of efficiency was reduced as a result?

The decree asserts that, in the article "I'm Too Ashamed to Remain Silent!" I painted a tendentious picture of the work of the state security agencies and, for opportunistic reasons, resorted to slanderous fabrications that distorted the essence of KGB activities. But, in fact, weren't the KGB's activities in a number of cases during the "stagnation" years, by their very essence, themselves a distortion? (The Chairman of the KGB went so far as to point this out in his *Izvestia* interview.) Just consider the incidents I cited. And there are so many more. Therein lies our tragedy. . . .

As a circumstance aggravating my guilt, the decree of November 28 pointed out that I myself was directly and actively involved in the work of the state security agencies but expressed no disagreement with it at the time.

Although it may not sound logical, here I fully agree with the decree of the Chairman of the KGB. And if this were the only reason I was being deprived of my award as an "Honored State Security Officer," I would be ready to go to the head of the ranks of those who were deceived by the times, who were misled, who were afraid, and who, during the "stagnation period," did something they were not supposed to do. So fine, I'd say, punish me! But somehow I haven't heard anything about punishing the people who actually persecuted the dissidents (for example Sakharov, Solzhenitsyn and many others).

Sometimes, in fact, just the opposite occurred: the Chief of the Fifth Administration of the KGB, General Abramov, succeeded in becoming Deputy General Prosecutor of the USSR. Perhaps because, in the career game, silence is golden?

A great Russian said, a long time ago, that "in the human soul's recognition of its past errors, in the act of cleansing itself of those errors, in atoning for them—that is where the highest meaning of man's existence on Earth is to be found."

---

[3] An ethnic group accused by Stalin of collaborating with the Nazis, and deported by him to live—under terrible conditions—in Kazakhstan. After four decades of struggle, Crimean Tatars were granted legal permission to return to their homeland. However, housing shortages and registration requirements continue to make such moves virtually impossible.

A process of renewal—of washing away the old, the harmful and the criminal—is under way in our society. The leaders of the KGB are among those who have repeatedly made statements to that effect. But all one man had to do was cite specific facts and call for deeper restructuring, and—in the great tradition of the stagnation period—his persecution began. Everything is just as it was then: pressure and humiliate anyone who ventures his own opinion.

By pointing out concrete facts and names in my articles, I wanted to demonstrate what the security agencies should avoid in these complex times we live in.

I cannot help but feel a part of the past, present and future activities of the state security agencies.

We live in a society in which profound changes are needed. And we are the ones who will determine what is to come: darkness, chaos, catastrophe—or a new, happy and just society.

Ya. KARPOVICH
Published January 1990

BUREAUCRACY AND DISASTER

We are members of an independent rescue group certified by the Control Rescue Service with experience in saving people's lives in extreme conditions. When we heard about the earthquake in Armenia, we immediately let it be known that we wanted to go to Leninakan and participate in the rescue operations in the ruins of the city.

As early as the ninth of December we were ready to leave for the site with all our necessary equipment. We went to the City Executive Committee with our request. There we were advised to register on a list at the office of the District Executive Committee and wait for an answer. At the District Committee, they referred to instructions from higher up and told us they couldn't send us down there. We called the headquarters of the Komsomol Central Committee in Moscow on December 10 and repeated our request to the

Ogonyok: Igor Gavrilov.

official on duty. His response was, "Listen, guys. There are already so many people down there; you'll just be in the way. Leave me your phone number. If you're needed, we'll call." Only by going to the Kharkov Komsomol *Oblast* Committee did we manage to get through to the headquarters of the Central Committee of the Armenian Komsomol, where we heard that rescuers were needed more than anything.

We arrived in Leninakan on December 12. We worked there until the twenty-fourth, and during that whole time there was a catastrophic shortage of qualified rescuers. If we had gotten there even by December 10, we would have saved more people—on the twelfth they were pulling out the dead bodies of people who had been alive two or three days before. . . .

Our group worked side by side with American and French rescuers, and they often asked us, "Why did you get here so late? After all, this happened in your own country." They really could not understand it, and we couldn't give any kind of informed answer. And even though it was not our fault, we could not stop feeling ashamed and angry.

When our work was finished, we left Leninakan for Kharkov with free tickets we had been given. In Moscow, when we were changing planes, there was a very ugly incident: at Vnukovo Airport we had to pay extra for overweight baggage. We really did have a lot, because we were carrying all our rescue equipment with us. The point is not the money we had to pay, but that the airport officials knew very well who we were, where we were coming from and what kind of baggage we were taking back home.

This natural disaster showed how unprepared we Soviets were to react quickly. There was no coordinated, centralized information service to supervise the rescue workers on hand. We are sure that there were other groups of rescuers who either could not get to Armenia or came late.

We are not writing this letter to have someone punished; that will hardly make any difference now. But as the concepts of mercy and compassion come back to us with their full meaning, we must learn to feel shame for the many "trivial details" in our day-to-day life that cost us so dearly, and deprive us of the most important thing there is—the feeling of our own self-worth.

O. RYZHENKO
A. KHYANNIKYAINEN
V. KOBZEV
[Eleven signatures in all]
Members of an independent rescue unit
Kharkov
Published January 1989

FREEDOM OF RELIGION, BUT . . .

In our city of Ivanovo, which has half a million residents, there is one functioning Russian Orthodox Church, the Preobrazhensky Cathedral. On holidays and on Sundays so many people crowd inside that the congregation stands there in a solid wall with the doors open, in the draft. The church has a capacity of more than two thousand people. On holidays, though, there are twice, sometimes even three times, as many, and people are crushed in the crowd. Perhaps statistics are not appropriate here, but over a six-month period (and this includes only the holiday services) there were sixty-four accidents, including some fractures and concussions. And how many times have they had to call an ambulance to the church . . . ?

On November 23 last year in Moscow, the Council on Religious Affairs, overruling the local city authorities, registered a second religious community of Russian Orthodox Christians and recommended that it be given a place of worship, with the Vvedensky church in mind. It was built in 1907, sanctified in 1912 and closed in 1935. It is 580 square meters in size and conveniently located. Since 1938, the church has housed archives. A nine-story building has now been built for the archives. But last August—that is, the moment the members of the faith put in their application for registration—the final work on the new archives building came to an abrupt halt. Since November our new community has been in limbo, because the local authorities will not supply even a temporary facility on the grounds of the Vvedensky cathedral. We understand that both another building and time are needed to accomplish the removal of the archival documents from the cathedral. But all

Ogonyok.

that one would need to vacate several rooms from the buildings *adjoining* the church is the desire to do so, which our local leadership does not have. We contacted the Chairman of the City Executive Committee and were told that the new nine-story building was not big enough to hold the archival documents.

So the result is that nobody is openly harassing us, but at the same time our problems are not being solved. Are half-baked measures really democracy?

> Members of the religious community
> L. KHOLINA
> V. TUVIN
> L. ZOLOTUKHINA
> M. PILENKOVA
> T. ALEKSEYEVA
> and others
> [3,000 signatures in all]
> Ivanovo
> Published February 1989

Lev Gushchin comments: "After the publication of this letter, events continued to unfold. The authorities made no concessions, and fifteen activists in the church association announced a hunger strike [see the accompanying photograph]. Ogonyok came out with an article in which it defended the religious believers against the Party bureaucracy. Then— and only then—was the church returned to the believers."

A PROPER BURIAL

Moscow, 30 May 1989

To Her Royal Highness, The Queen of England, Elizabeth II
To His Majesty, The King of Spain, Juan Carlos I
To Her Majesty, the Queen of Denmark, Margrethe II
To His Imperial Highness, Grand Prince Vladimir Kirillovich
To His Holiness, The Most Right Reverend Vitaly, The Patriarch of the Russian Church Abroad

LETTER OF APPEAL

At the present time here in Russia, an independent Russian Ortho-dox Initiative Group has been founded, to establish an independent public commission to identify and decide on the ultimate fate of the remains of the Imperial Family, which was brutally murdered in 1918.

The Initiative Group issued an Appeal to the population of the country, the text of which follows. Right now signatures are being collected under this Appeal throughout the country.

At the same time, the Initiative Group has begun the estab-lishment of the Commission, which is to include independent rep-resentatives of the public, as well as specialists: criminologists, historians, physicians, photographers, cinematographers and so on. It is proposed that a bank account be opened to collect funds for the Commission's work.

We ask that you, for your part, participate in the solution of this question. We think it would be desirable to set up a similar Commission made up of people and specialists involved abroad, and to establish working contacts with us.

After publication of the material on the discovery of the re-mains, the situation for those who made the discovery and for the burial site itself could become extremely difficult at any moment.

In view of the general situation in the country, the issue of the fate of the remains of the Tsarist Martyrs, in our opinion, should be resolved immediately.

In the hope of your assistance, we humbly ask you to respond to this Appeal.

Archdeacon Dionisii MAKAROV   Lev VOLOKHONSKY
Geliy RYABOV   Pavel LITOMIN
Natalya GOLOVANOVA   Andrey ILLARIONOV
Olga KORZININA   Vladimir ANISHCHENKO
Mikhail TALALAY   Vladimir YEROKHIN

APPEAL

Recently, publications in *Moscow News*, the magazine *Rodina* [*Homeland*] and *Samizdat* revealed that G. T. Ryabov has discovered the remains of the Imperial Family, brutally murdered in the city of Yekaterinburg (now Sverdlovsk) in 1918.

It is essential to establish an expert commission composed of professionals and representatives of the Russian and foreign public who wish to participate in its work, in order to identify the discovered remains. The work of the commission should be broadly publicized by all the media.

If the commission confirms that G. T. Ryabov has actually found the remains of the Tsar's family, it is the moral duty of the people and the government to give them a Christian burial. The fate of the Tsar's family is a model for the fates of millions of families in Russia. A people that spits on its past is unworthy of a future. The place of burial should be the historic burial vault in the Petropavlovsky Cathedral.

Since the majority of Russian Orthodox believers consider these murder victims to be new martyrs, it should be proposed to the Moscow Patriarchate that they be canonized at the next Synod, following the example of other Russian Orthodox Churches.

In the event that a Christian burial in Russia is impossible, the question of the burial of the revered remains of these new martyrs should be remanded to the Russian Church Abroad.

The Editors of the journal *Rossiskie Vedomosti* [*Russian News*]
c/o Archdeacon Dionisii, Moscow
Received by *Ogonyok* June 1989
Unpublished

TRAGEDY TAX

I had a tragedy in my family. At the age of eleven, my son drowned. My wife and I have no other children. There is no point in going into the reasons why my wife could not get pregnant again. For five years now we have both been paying the notorious childlessness tax, and this will continue until I am fifty and my wife forty-five. I'm already forty-seven, and my wife forty-three. Tell me, please, how are we guilty before the state for the fact that we couldn't have any more children?

We have been traumatized and wounded by fate enough as it is: we're facing old age without children. What could be more painful when you think about the future? And every month you're reminded about it when you get your pay because you see that special column on the payroll voucher. Please understand, I'm not upset about the money; it's just that I feel humiliated by this tax, especially at my age. Let alone the psychological effect on my wife: after our son's death, she went gray overnight.

So I would like to ask the Ministry of Finance of the USSR this question: does such a tax really help fill up the treasury? And haven't the bureaucrats thought about the fact that this tax insults human dignity?

O. AKIMOV
Pathologist-anatomist
Salekhard, Tyumen *oblast*
Published February 1989

MARRIAGE OF CONVENIENCE

As you know, our laws and decrees are supposed to serve people and defend their interests. Only that is far too often not the case. Many of our decrees became obsolete long ago and are now contrary to people's interests. However, they continue to exist to this day and make life immensely complicated. For example, consider our housing law.

I have been living in a cooperative two-room apartment for fourteen years now. Last year my husband died and I was left completely alone. I am already eighty-two and have very bad arthritis in my legs. I have to take care of myself, and what is more, I am very lonely now that I have lost my husband. My adopted son lives in Kiev. He has agreed to come live with me and help me. This is a very nice wish. However, according to the regulations I cannot have my son registered to live with me but can only leave him a share in the apartment and property, which he will receive only after I die. But then I won't need his help anymore; I need it now, in my ninth decade of life. In order to will him the apartment now, I either have to leave it myself or marry my adopted son.

Only our housing laws could create a situation as ridiculous as this!

L. GARBUNOVA
Leningrad
Published February 1989

TELEPHONE TURNOFF

I recently received a notice with the following text: "Dear comrade residents! Come get your monthly payment book[1] within three days. Have with you your old book for apartment payments, your telephone payment book and your electricity payment book. Otherwise your telephone will be turned off."

Why this high-handed tone? Why make threats of punitive action? Why turn off a telephone that is fully paid up?

I did not accept the challenge: let them put the payment book in the mailbox, the way they always did. But when I come home from work one evening, I discover that the phone has been turned off.

Three days later I go to Maintenance Center 2 of the Volgograd district and find a commotion. The young, radiant women who work there are in a happy mood. They are pleased with their work. They explain that they have just turned in the next list of residents to have their phones turned off. "Now they'll come running in to exchange their books. As soon as we find out the phone numbers, we make up the list for the turnoffs." In a word, business is booming.

I hand in my paid-up books for exchange, and they hand me a form to pay a fine.

"What's this for?"

"Two rubles for turning on the phone."

And I thought they would apologize for the moral insult and compensate *me* for turning off a fully paid-up telephone.

---

[1] A book containing coupons which accompany bill payments.

I ask on the basis of what order they are cutting off phones for not turning in payment books.

It turns out that they are doing it without any orders or decrees; they're taking the punitive measures on the basis of a directive given over the phone by one V. P. Peskova, an employee of the Lyublin telephone exchange.

I ask for the complaint book.[2] They answer very politely that they don't have one.

Today we don't have an agency that deals with violations of civil rights and that defends such rights. That's why all the levels of the bureaucracy consistently violate them with impunity.

Only complete irresponsibility explains the statement made by the head of the accounting department of Maintenance Center 2: "Write whomever you want and whatever you want!"

I am following that recommendation and writing to *Ogonyok* magazine in the hopes that it will raise the question: who will defend us against violations of our civil rights?

E. V. RAZUVAEVA
Moscow
Published May 1989

HARD ROAD TO MURAVLENKO

My daughter works in the oil industry and lives in the village of Muravlenko in the Tyumen *oblast*. I can't go see her when I need to. Not a single ticket office will sell me a ticket without a special pass.[1] But to get a pass, I have to receive an invitation, which my daughter has to pound the pavement to get from her local authorities. After I get the invitation, I have to go to my police office for

[2] A book supposedly available on request at all public service establishments, in which customers can write complaints and suggestions.

[1] Certain areas of the Soviet Union are considered "off limits." They are so designated because, in theory, they are near sensitive foreign borders, or are the site of classified industries.

the pass, which I can get two weeks later. The pass is issued only for the specified time of my stay, and if I need to go a second time, I have to go through the same procedure all over again.

By the way, the village of Muravlenko is in the taiga more than 1,000 kilometers from the Arctic Ocean; there isn't even a hint of a foreign border there. There's freedom of movement for you. It's time to open the northern areas of the Tyumen *oblast* the way they did in the Far East.

And registration for a residence permit[2] is the same story. If your health prevents you from living in a certain place, or you have some other reason for moving, just try to go live somewhere else. You can't get work unless you're already registered, but they won't register you if you don't have a job.

I agree with those who say that residence permits shouldn't be necessary.

V. V. BURDAKOVA
Pensioner
Izhevsk
Published May 1989

PLEASE SAVE MY DAUGHTER!

Please save my daughter, who is only twenty-four years old and the mother of small children. At Trauma Hospital No. 50 in Kharkov she had a stomach operation and was released too soon, and that was a crime. On May 21, in Hospital No. 26 in Kharkov, they operated on her again along stitches which hadn't healed yet. And now she is dying. I sent a telegram to Minister of Health Chazov in Moscow. The Chief Surgeon of the USSR, Knyazkov, forwarded it on to the Ukraine, which to this day hasn't answered it. The doctors here insist on big bribes, even though they know ahead of time that the patient is going to die.

[2] All Soviet citizens must be registered in the place where they reside. One cannot move until one has obtained a new residence permit.

Twelve of my relatives and I are announcing a hunger strike as a sign of protest outside Hospital No. 26 in Kharkov. The ground is burning under our feet! Help!

M. A. KTITAREVA
Kharkov
30 May 1989
Unpublished

LET'S SPEND OUR MONEY ON THE LIVING!

After the Soviet troops were withdrawn from Afghanistan, the Central Committee of the Komsomol and the local Komsomol committees started work on creating monuments to the internationalist soldiers[1] in every city. Special funds are being set up and money has been collected for some time now.

I would like to express my opinion on this subject.

As we heard at the Congress, our country is in a very difficult financial position. Therefore, we can't allow ourselves to throw millions around casually for the erection of monuments which, as a rule, don't have the slightest artistic value.

For a long time our country was under mass hypnosis. It followed the uniform policy of building gigantic monuments to deify its leaders. Are we ashamed of that now? Somehow we don't seem to notice that times have changed. The country is infected with the virus of self-adulation.

The boys who were wounded or died in Afghanistan and even those who came back in one piece, are victims. Of course, you can hardly blame them: every one of them claimed he was doing his

---

[1] A term frequently used to describe the soldiers who fought in Afghanistan.

A decorated Afghan veteran as he enters Gorky Park for a "Victory Day" celebration, May 9, 1989. To his left is a veteran of World War II, also heavily bedecked with medals.

military duty, that he was only a soldier. As Bulat Okudzhava[2] says in one of his songs, "How simple it is to be a soldier. . . ."

On the other hand, those who came back include a lot of disabled people, with ruined health and shattered nerves. Very often these men need improved housing and financial help. Why does the money from the fund have to go into dead, lifeless stone, instead of being used to build homes for Afghan vets, and to assist parents who were left without any support and the wives of those killed in action? Why not invest this money in the construction of homes for the disabled, and establish treatment centers for them and buy medical equipment? Why do we invest money over and over again in stone and think least of all about the living?

Perhaps the most reasonable way to use the money that's been collected so far would be to help the families of those killed to put monuments on their graves. After all, not every family has the wherewithal or the strength to do that. And then let all the remaining funds be used to help the living Afghan vets.

N. SARSAKOVA
Murmansk
Published June 1989

WHO'S BEEN READING MY MAIL?

For a long time I have been maintaining creative contacts with the organizers of international photography contests and exhibitions. In this connection, I receive mail from abroad. On every occasion it arrives opened, patched up with Scotch tape or adhesive tape. In other words, every time, some stranger is carefully acquainting himself with the contents of these packages, without leaving any official inspection stamps behind.

I have never been investigated, convicted, indicted or informed that I was not allowed to go abroad. My exact address is

---

[2] A famous Russian balladeer and poet.

always correctly indicated on the outside of each envelope. So how does one explain this remarkable interest in my correspondence? If it is so important for envelopes to be opened, isn't it time to introduce regulations concerning the inspection of mail? Then, at the very least, we will be able to know at what stage, and by what official, our mail is being opened.

N. NIZOV
Photojournalist
Kaluga
Received by *Ogonyok* Summer 1989
Unpublished

POLICE TERROR IN LENINGRAD

To: *People's Deputies of the USSR*
     Deputies of the Supreme Soviet of the RSFSR
     Deputies of the local soviets
     Public organizations and the mass media
     All people of good will

APPEAL

Fellow citizens! August 23, 1989 is yet another black mark on the recent history of our city. On that day, the Palace Square—the most beautiful square in Leningrad—was witness to harsh reprisals by the police against people who had gathered to express their views on the Molotov-Ribbentrop Pact,[1] which for fifty years now has been a disgrace to our country.

But a free exchange of views turned out to be too terrifying for

[1] The Molotov-Ribbentrop Pact, which surprised the world when it was concluded on August 23, 1939, was ostensibly a straightforward treaty of nonaggression between the Soviets and the Nazis. But it also contained a secret protocol partitioning much of Eastern Europe. Under the terms of this agreement, Finland, Estonia, Latvia and Bessarabia were allotted to the USSR.

the city authorities, and they did not stop short of lawlessness to avoid it. First, they denied the Democratic Union's request to hold the meeting, basing their refusal on the "pointlessness" of the announced subject matter. This was a direct violation of the law, which states that the only reason for a refusal is a contradiction between the announced subject of the meeting and the Constitution of the USSR. And when the Democratic Union decided to hold the unsanctioned meeting anyway, the police "preventively" dispersed the people who had gathered (twenty minutes before the announced start of the meeting). Not a single banner had yet been unfurled; not a single word had yet been spoken, but people were already being grabbed, beaten up and taken to buses, where the sadistic beatings continued. They beat people horribly until they had concussions; they beat women and grabbed not only those who had come to the meeting, but also passersby who happened to be near the Palace Square at the time.

Fully aware of the illegality of their actions, the police preferred at the "hottest" points to act through people in civilian clothes (with *Druzhinniki* armbands and without). All the detainees were then taken to the police station, where they were held for several hours and then sent off to the district courts. There, under the cover of night, a shameful legal farce was played out: people were tried without lawyers and without witnesses for the defense. . . .

What happened on August 23 should be given the widest possible publicity. Silence in this situation would mean betraying the ideals of morality, freedom and democracy. Tbilisi, April 9,[2] should never again be repeated!

We call on the People's Deputies of the USSR, the Deputies of the Supreme Soviet of the Russian Republic and of the local soviets, public organizations and the mass media, and all people of good will to raise their voices and demand that everyone guilty of arbitrary will and cruelty—all those, without exception, who gave the orders and carried them out—be punished. We call upon all democratic forces to unite in the struggle for democracy.

To freedom, yours and ours!

Commission for Social Assistance and Legal Defense
Leningrad Popular Front

---

[2] In Tbilisi, Georgia, on April 9, 1989, Soviet Army troops killed eighteen unarmed civilians during a nationalist demonstration.

P.S. The Commission has numerous items of evidence demonstrating the arbitrariness and cruelty of the police (eyewitness reports, photographs, medical certificates) and is prepared, immediately upon request, to present them to all interested organizations.

> Received by *Ogonyok* August 1989
> Unpublished

THIEVES AND LEADERS

Now that the existence of privileges can be admitted, all the objections against revoking them go something like this: "Can our rich nation really not guarantee our leaders a life worthy of their efforts, like any civilized country?"

But are we able to guarantee an acceptable standard of living for a normal working engineer or a skilled laborer or a talented scientist? Unfortunately, ours is a poor country, and its political leadership is obliged to live with this indisputable fact.

The only thing that can now prevent the Party and the people from openly opposing each other is voluntary and conscious asceticism on the part of the Party *apparat,* right up to the very top, because the rank-and-file members of the Party are ascetic enough as it is.

If *perestroika,* which was begun by the Party, succeeds, living conditions worthy of human beings will cease to be the prerogative of only thieves and highly placed leaders.

> N. SERGEYEVA
> Kharkov
> Published June 1989

CURRENT ISSUES

CRIME, PUNISHMENT AND DRUGS

NO PITY

In early 1988, Ogonyok *published an article, "The Barbed Sky," which described inhuman conditions in Soviet prison camps for juvenile offenders. The exposé prompted the following response from a reader.*

There's no point pussyfooting around with criminals; they poison the life of society. Your correspondent decides to write an article about juvenile offenders, and he immediately starts feeling sorry for them. Out come the tears. And what if these creeps had held a knife to his throat or raped his daughter, I wonder what tune he would sing then? And where did he get those ideas about "lice" and "hun-

Ogonyok: Igor Gavrilov.

gry eyes"? I worked for twenty years in these labor colonies as a deputy warden, and I know what they're like. The young men say openly, "This is no labor colony; it's a Pioneer camp!"[1] They have it better than soldiers in the army. When they're released, they don't want to be useful to society. They simply take up their criminal ways again, and start corrupting others.

Prison life should be made harsher, so that when they get out, criminals will say "I can't go back in there." And drug addicts and alcoholics should be sent off to the taiga to cut wood for six months. Let them work it out with their hands and if they don't come around—send 'em back. Then we'll have medicine in the drugstores and cologne will be back on the shelves.[2]

---

[1] Pioneer camps are Communist Youth camps which millions of Soviet children attend every summer.

[2] Medicine and cologne have been in chronic short supply in the Soviet Union because, since Gorbachev limited liquor supplies as part of his anti-drunkenness campaign, alcoholics have bought up everything with even the slightest alcohol content.

And that goes for moonshiners, too. Don't feel sorry for that scum, because that isn't going to help create order.

I. G. YENBAYEV
Pensioner
Chelyabinsk
Published July 1988

THE TAIGA IS NO ANSWER

I would like to respond publicly to pensioner I. G. Yenbayev's letter from Chelyabinsk, printed in *Ogonyok* no. 27.

I have also been working in a correctional labor facility, not for twenty years, but only for six, as the head of a prisoner's brigade. Oh, what a wonderful solution Comrade Yenbayev is proposing for society and the state! It seems that every societal disease should be combatted with repressive measures. Alcoholics? To the camps! Drug addicts? To the camps! Prostitutes? To the camps! Everybody to the camps!! What wonderful order there will be in the country then!

Well, what kind of order would it be? A forceful, strict, "special"[1] Stalinist one? From the style of Comrade Yenbayev's letter it is obvious that he, as a deputy warden, maintained strict order in his area and did not spare the prisoners. But after all, the way we treat them, that's how they'll treat us; we are all people. There are, of course, exceptions. I know because I work in a "special" prison—they lie and hurt and do nasty things. But no one has the right to destroy someone's soul and humanity. I don't know whether any of the prisoners Comrade Yenbayev has released ever said "thank you" to him for the lessons about life, for his humanity. But I am glad when even one out of ten especially dangerous repeaters thanks me when he is released, because it offers the hope

[1] The labor camps of the Stalin era were commonly referred to as "special" camps.

that he will not be back here again. What kind of Communists are we, what kind of "engineers of human souls," if we want to heal human souls with a hammer behind barbed wire?! Who is guilty for the fact that ex-convicts when they are freed don't want to "be useful to society"?

We are! After all, they were entrusted to us. We don't need tears here, or painful measures—we just need to do our work with heart.

And drug addicts and alcoholics should be treated—treated in somewhat different conditions than are found in today's forced-treatment centers. These are mainly sick people. And in the battle against private stills and prostitution and so on, we need to eliminate the reasons—both social and economic, not the consequences. No matter how many weeds you pull out, until you pull them out by the root, you won't get rid of them. And the taiga is no answer. Hard physical forced labor that gives no satisfaction makes a person cruel. Order, in Comrade Yenbayev's opinion, is fear. We have already lived in a society of fear. Enough already!

V. POPOV
Vologodskaya *oblast*
Published November 1988

THE DRUG CRISIS: ONE ADDICT'S SOLUTION

I think nobody would argue with this obvious fact: the drug problem is now as far from a solution as it was ten years ago. And so many have tackled this problem! The agencies of the Ministries of Internal Affairs and Justice, the Ministries of Health and Agricultural Industry, psychologists, sociologists, pedagogues, people with candidate and doctor's degrees, professors and academicians. . . . But the problem hasn't budged an inch. The number of drug addicts is growing every year, and all the efforts in the battle with drugs have had practically no positive results. In fact, the results have been plainly negative.

Take, for example, the universal ban on cultivating poppies, whose oil is used to make most of the drugs Soviet addicts use. What has it accomplished? Well, it has made prices for those drugs immediately jump ten times higher. If four years ago a jar of poppy extract on the Leningrad black market cost fifteen rubles, now it goes for 150 rubles. It's just as easy now as before to get, as long as you have the money. The drug market goes on flourishing, only now it gives the dealers ten times more income, and the addicts— whether they want to or not—are forced to steal, rob, cheat, etc., ten times more "productively."

And there is one more unforeseen consequence of operation "Black Poppy." Along with naturally grown drugs, synthetic drugs, produced from inorganic substances in unknown laboratories, are also helping to satisfy the demand. These have similar effects—and completely unpredictable fatal consequences for those addicts who switch to them. The harder it is for traditional addicts to get to the black market, the more actively the underground chemists will "provide" addicts with newer and newer poisons, in comparison to which morphine will soon look like vitamin C.

Of course, it would be unfair not to mention that the need to "earn" two to three hundred rubles *a day* just for drugs has forced many addicts to switch to using drugs occasionally. But has that brought them back into society?

They turn to drug addiction specialists for help; they go through detoxification treatment, and for a period of time truly believe that they have left drugs behind forever. But as a rule there is, unfortunately, no way back for them anymore. The psychological enslavement turns out to be much stronger and more debilitating than the physical so-called state of abstention. And besides, unlike the latter, it is lifelong.

Society should have understood a long time ago that drug addiction in the overwhelming majority of cases is just as incurable a disease as cancer or AIDS. There isn't a single drug addict who wouldn't like to get rid of his narcotic bondage, just as there isn't a single person with cancer who wouldn't like to get well. But only very few, including the author of this letter, have found the strength within themselves to renounce drugs completely. However, even those few are not ensured against a relapse. Giving up drugs—even for as much as fifty years—is nothing more than a "state of remission," which can end at any time. . . .

All in all I took drugs for about fifteen years. Of those, I spent ten trying desperately to crawl out of the quagmire of this disease. Over and over again, I tried all the existing methods of voluntary and forced treatment. Twice I was convicted on criminal charges of acquiring, producing and storing narcotics for the purpose of use, and was sent to prison, where I spent about four years. I was treated both by doctors who were professionally and morally at the highest level of their profession, and by sadists in white coats, with whom the infamous Dr. Mengele might not even have been willing to shake hands. I was treated by officers of the Ministry of Internal Affairs and ensigns in the Internal Forces. I was treated with medication, hypnosis, hard labor, hunger, cold, beatings, and simply by humiliation at the hands of bastards who were given unlimited power. But throughout those ten years the disease turned out to be stronger.

I am now in my eighth or ninth (I've lost track) remission. I very much want to believe that this time there will be no relapse. Very much! But the issue here isn't my life, which is basically almost over, or the individuals who have gotten off drugs forever. The issue is all the rest. Much more than I hope for my own final cure, I hope that someone in power will listen to my opinion. It is the opinion of an old drug addict who doesn't want millions of children—both those who haven't been born yet and those who are still playing dolly and hide-and-seek—to go down his road.

One thing seems to me beyond dispute: DRUG ADDICTS ABSOLUTELY MUST BE ISOLATED FROM SOCIETY. The social danger from people who are suffering from drug addiction is extremely high. It is much higher than the danger from all those suffering from the most infectious diseases combined. There isn't a single drug addict who has not infected someone else with his disease, that is, gotten at least one other person hooked on drugs. As a rule, though, every one of them has many more victims on his conscience, and the spread of drug addiction throughout the world is a real chain reaction, with all the attendant consequences.

BUT IT WILL BE PRACTICALLY IMPOSSIBLE TO ISOLATE ALL OR ALMOST ALL DRUG ADDICTS FROM SOCIETY *UNTIL THEY THEMSELVES WANT TO BE ISOLATED.* AND THEY WILL WANT THIS UNDER ONLY ONE CONDITION: *IF IN THEIR LIFELONG ISOLATION THEY ARE GUARANTEED THE RIGHT TO TAKE ANY DRUGS THEY WANT.*

Over the last ten years I have managed to poll more than a

thousand drug addicts. I asked every one of them the same question: Suppose they built "narcosoriums"—zones or reservations for drug addicts, surrounded by "fences" with watchtowers and machine guns. Entry would be free but there would be no exit. Drug addicts could take any amount of any kinds of drugs free—or at the state price of a few kopecks—for the rest of their lives. Those who wanted to be released would have to go through treatment and a five-year quarantine in another zone, sort of like today's forced-treatment camps. If you didn't make it through the quarantine, you'd have to go back to the narcosorium. Would you go there voluntarily?

About 90 percent of those asked (I guarantee their sincerity) answered yes without hesitation.

"You need to ask? Of course, I'd go!"

"I'd run right in there before all the places were taken!"

"What do I need their freedom for without drugs? Let 'em shove it up their . . ." These are the three most common answers.

And I guarantee that they would "run right in there," if they believed that the narcosorium wasn't going to be a "garbage heap," and that they really were going to be able to get enough drugs there. And they'd even sew some mittens or something for a couple of hours a day to earn a piece of bread and a two-hundred-ruble dose of heroin, which in reality isn't even worth two kopecks. And they'd be deeply grateful to you, and would die within a year or two in front of the television cameras with happy smiles on their dried-out faces and needles in their veins. And those smiles alone—which look more like grimaces of disgust—would be an infinitely more effective deterrent for children and teenagers than any number of warnings and quotes about "trips to hell."

It goes without saying that, in connection with the opening of even a first, experimental narcosorium, the punishments for any illegal drug activities *outside* the walls of the narcosorium would have to be made even harsher, and a more active war would have to be waged against unprotected poppy and hemp fields, so that the number of drug addicts who didn't want to live on the "outside" would be as close to 100 percent as possible. In the end, those who didn't want to go into the narcosorium would—and should—be sent there by force. And no one, including themselves, could accuse society of being inhumane.

This is the only way, in my view, of getting started on a solution to this problem, and of turning two upward curves—the number of drug addicts and the crime rate—into downward curves, and very sharp ones at that. (Note: I mean crimes like burglary and pickpocketing, theft, muggings, swindling, speculation and, of course, all types of crimes related to the drug business.)

And one more request: Don't be too quick to say, "Oh, what a bunch of nonsense from a guy who's flipped his lid because of drugs." Moving along by inertia is always much easier than overcoming that inertia. If you doubt what I say, just poll the drug addicts. Only don't ask the ones who are now in prisons or forced-treatment camps—they might in good conscience be mistaken because they overestimate the importance of freedom. And don't forget to ask which they think is more humane: what I propose, or their present situation—death in a year from a drug overdose, or in fifty years in the "freedom" society offers them?

Vitaly SHAKHOV
Leningrad
February 9, 1989
Unpublished

THE "RULE OF THE GRANDFATHERS"

Lev Gushchin writes: "The Constitution of the USSR stipulates universal military service for all young men who have reached the age of eighteen. The term of duty, as a rule, is two years.

"It has become commonplace in the Soviet Army for soldiers who are in their second year of service to humiliate and, for all practical purposes, make slaves out of the newly arrived recruits. This practice is commonly called the 'rule of the grandfathers.'

"A similar phenomenon has also appeared in juvenile technical schools, and it has become typical in prisons.

"The first to call attention to this problem were the young people's publications; then the campaign to expose the 'rule of the grandfathers' was joined by the 'heavy artillery' of the Soviet mass media.

"Until recently, the Army leadership has insisted that the 'rule of the grandfathers' was an invention of the press."

"AN ISOLATED PHENOMENON?"

I have read the materials of the Twentieth Congress of the Komsomol, and I won't deny that I was hurt by the words of Hero of the Soviet Union I. Chmurov, who said that the " 'rule of the grandfathers' is an isolated, atypical, dying phenomenon." What good fortune that he apparently managed to serve in a good unit.

I am the mother of two sons. The older one came back from the Army in 1982, and we expect the younger one home this spring. I went to see my sons in the service and saw a lot for myself. My boys are not whiners—they can stand up for themselves—but the weaker soldiers are broken there. My younger son wrote after his "training," "Mama, don't worry. The worst part is behind me now." After he was transferred to a new division, he was able to tell us that he himself had experienced this "rule of the grandfathers." How much he had to put up with to keep from being crushed!

My sons are physically strong, and their friends and school-mates, who were called up at the same time they were, write to one another, urging each other to have "square iron fists." A friend of my son's wrote home from Kazakhstan about how, on his very first day, the "grandfathers" pulled off his watch; he strictly ordered everyone at home not to send him money or packages because of the massive stealing going on. A colleague of mine from work just got back from Chita. We all think of her as a woman with an iron character. But you should have seen her, all swollen with tears and grief. Her son had been beaten up so badly that there wasn't an untouched spot left on him: he had refused to wash the "grandfa-thers' " socks. Newcomers were beaten with belt buckles so hard that the stars were imprinted on their behinds.

Where are the commanders? Where are the political officers? It seems impossible that they don't know anything. No one is saying that soldiers need to live in hothouse conditions. They need to be hardened—but by means of work, army training and marches, not by being humiliated or by being beaten up. It is urgent that something be changed in the Army, and this won't be accom-plished by arguing about whether the "rule of the grandfathers" is typical or not.

KUZNETSOVA
Chelyabinsk
Published December 1987

A "BARRIER AGAINST FAIRNESS"

I am a student, and I have just gone into the reserves. Right now a timid attempt is being made to tell the truth about life in the Army. Of course, the hardest thing is the beginning of Army ser-vice. But I would like to tell you about my final months on active duty, because it would be cowardly to be silent simply on the pretext that "I myself went through all of this already, so now let somebody else make it through—it's none of my business."

Yes, of course I knew about the "rule of the grandfathers," but I'm not ashamed to admit that I still had respect for the officers' rank. But thinking back on my days in the service, I remember, unfortunately, an entire chain of violations on the part of my commanders: their use of military technology and soldiers' labor for their own purposes and the unfortunate "personal example" they set for the soldiers.

The commander of the unit, in order to have a wine cellar built for himself, arbitrarily kept soldiers "in the service" until June 19, despite the fact that an official discharge date of May 31 had already been stamped on their military cards. Of course, he didn't simply detain them; the excuse was that they had to prepare some technical equipment. They worked with the equipment—a tow truck—exactly one day, and the rest of the time they dug the pit for the cellar. Put yourself in their shoes: since they had been officially discharged, they were counting every hour.

Another captain, the head of the motor pool, who had been put in charge of a truck that was supposed to transport weapons, spent his time drinking in a neighboring village. And he got away with it, despite the fact that the weapons were never delivered. I have also met soldiers who were forced to be servants for their commanders.

Last spring, the first men to be discharged were the ones who were on "good terms" with the bosses. A sergeant who had many times been caught drunk or ripping off technical equipment or beating his subordinates was the first to be discharged. My comrades coming back from the Army confirm that there is a kind of mutual protection everywhere (only the locations and the players change), which serves as a barrier against any attempt to reestablish real fairness.

So where are those ideals that were hammered into us in political education classes in school? The "grandfathers" could not have appeared out of nowhere. The responsibility has to be carried first and foremost by the officers.

V. CHAPLINSKY
Third-year student
Leningrad University
Published September 1988

"THIS TRAGEDY
IS NOT UNIQUE"

I cannot understand how this ugly tradition of hazing new recruits became a fixture in the Army. And it is not being done by some Tsarist drill sergeants, but by their own brothers—soldiers and seamen, recent graduates of schools where they were taught the same subjects and instilled with the same ideals. All right, never mind about the schools. But people have always thought that if a boy was wild before going into the Army, then after his tour he would come back a different person, a serious person who had learned the meaning of genuine comradeship.

I'm holding in my hands a copy of a sentencing by the military tribunal of the Vladivostok garrison. It describes in detail how a certain S. A. Bizov, born on 8 February 1966, a Russian by nationality, a member of the Komsomol with a high-school education, was in charge (because of his rank) of Seamen Shakirov, Balakay and Lezov, whom he beat up day in, day out. What for? For not bringing his cigarettes in time or for not making tea. One day before going into the reserves, this Bizov hit my son, Seaman Lezov, one more time. That was on November 30 of last year. On December 1, Bizov left, and on the fourth my son went to the hospital with a ruptured spleen. An operation did not help him, and he died the next day.

During the six months my son served on a ship, he was given responsibility by the unit commanders and was preparing to become (at my urging) a candidate member of the Party. He received a certificate of honor from the Navy and passed all of his exams to become a Seaman Second Class. During those months, his letters did not even hint at how hard it was for him to serve in that unit. Only later, at the trial, did I find out what life had been like on that military vessel. There was no friendship or discipline. The former captain of the ship admitted that he had no authority; he had reported on this situation to all the higher-ups but had received no help.

One can understand why my son, who was a former school Komsomol leader, took those beatings by his "elder" in silence and shared what was going on only with a seaman from another ship when he got the chance. It was because he did not see his commanders as intelligent leaders, comrades and protectors.

The military tribunal sentenced Bizov to nine years in a maximum-security labor colony. But does that really make it any easier for my family or for Bizov's own family? I am not looking for sympathy for my grief. I want to ask this question: why is something like this possible in our Army and Navy? Why aren't the officers, Communists and Komsomol members watching? Since when is the danger of an Army tour of duty determined not by the kind of military situation one finds oneself in, but by the relationships between various age groups within the military units?! My second son is growing up; in six years it will be time for him to go into the Army. Will he believe the lofty words about military comradeship, where brother helps brother, knowing what happened to his older brother? This tragedy with my son is not unique. What steps is the political administration of our Army taking to reestablish a healthy moral atmosphere among the soldiers?

V. V. LEZOV
Workshop foreman, "Krasnaya Etna" Factory
Gorky
Published June 1988

THE AIDS CRISIS:
"REFLECTIONS ON ELISTA"

I just heard the horrible news on the radio: In Elista, twenty-seven infants, barely two years old, were infected with the AIDS virus. And it didn't happen just any place, but in one of our Soviet hospitals, and doctors and nurses, those whose duty it is to heal, were to blame. I remember very well the words of V. I. Pokrovsky, the president of the Academy of Medical Sciences, which were published in your magazine: "Can one get infected in a hospital or clinic? In general, no. There are instructions for sterilizing syringes and other medical instruments. . . ." And then he goes on in detail about how the syringes should be boiled, and how this is laborious work, and how if a nurse is careless, she may deviate from the instructions. The problem of carelessness could be solved in part by investing in disposable syringes, but, as Pokrovsky says, "we follow the proverb, 'Until the thunder claps, the peasant won't cross himself.' The millions of rubles we're saving now will come back to us, in five years, as billions of deaths."

So, isn't it time for us to stop trying to save money when human lives are at stake? Why should little kids have to pay for the criminal actions of our Ministry of Health? The thunder has clapped. . . .

And by the way, I would like to say this: Recently there was a television broadcast about AIDS. It was a thoughtful and serious program, hosted by the author and commentator, A. Gurnov. But the program ended at 12:30 a.m. This show—which everybody should see, especially young people—was broadcast late at night, just as, in the past, lively variety programs used to be shown during the Easter holidays.[1] Once again, hypocrisy on television? Yes, it's hypocrisy—because it's impossible to discuss AIDS without bringing up prostitution and homosexuality, and we are trying with all our might to show that these phenomena are not part of our society.

> V. KUZNETSOVA
> Mother of two
> Fryazino, Moscow *oblast*
> Published February 1989

When I found out about the tragedy in Elista, I thought it was my duty to propose the creation of a fund to purchase disposable syringes for children, since our state, quite possibly, does not have enough hard currency to use for this purpose. And if our Soviet money "won't go" abroad, then perhaps we could contribute gold and silver to this fund. I myself, as a first contribution, offer my gold wedding band (I have no other gold).

I think many parents would do this. Only all of us together can stop our people from dying.

> V. SHEVCHENKO
> Father of two
> Kiev
> Published March 1989

The tragedy in the children's hospital in Elista happened as a result of the indecisiveness and "cautiousness" of the Ministry of Health of the USSR in the battle against AIDS. Until very recently our country looked like an oasis of tranquility in a world gripped with alarm.

One gets the impression that the Ministry was afraid not so much of the disease, but of truthful and timely information about it! How costly the bureaucratic fear of "spreading panic among the population" is for us! If we followed the lead of television reporters and conducted a random poll of passersby on the street, only a few would be familiar with the issues in the battle with AIDS.

---

[1] Soviet Central Television traditionally made it a practice to broadcast particularly interesting programs on religious holidays, presumably to keep people home from church.

In conditions of reassuring pronouncements and carefully dosed information, not only the population, but even part of the medical community, apparently believed that the threat of an epidemic was not real and let down their guard. And one step beyond that was criminal negligence. . . .

I think that the bureaucratic machine will now end its period of "pulling itself together" and will start functioning effectively. But that is not enough. Since there is no time left, hard currency must be allocated to buy everything we need from abroad in sufficient quantity to satisfy our needs until Soviet industry can handle the job.

As far as the hard-currency shortage is concerned, if there is no other way, our list of foreign purchases has to be reviewed. After all, we are not talking here about satisfying people's desires, but about their very existence.

> V. NESTEROVICH
> Veteran of World War II
> Labor veteran
> Mariupol
> Published March 1989

Lev Gushchin writes: "Following the incident in Elista, outbreaks of AIDS were confirmed in other children's and maternity hospitals as well. The main reason for them was the almost complete lack of disposable medical supplies. After the appearance of these letters in Ogonyok, we published, under the title 'Better Not Think About It?,' a major article detailing the helplessness of the Ministry of Health in the face of the AIDS epidemic in the Soviet Union.

"Ogonyok has also established a charitable hard-currency fund, thanks to which hundreds of hospitals have been guaranteed the necessary supplies. Should any of our readers wish to contribute, they may submit funds to the Ogonyok Anti-AIDS Fund, c/o the Vneshekombank, USSR. The account number is 70000015."

Alla Alova's article "Better Not Think About It?," published in *Ogonyok* no. 26, is not only about AIDS, but also about the fact that, for many agencies, concrete people—patients, living men, women and children—are a much larger abstraction than this year's accounting statement or certificates of work performed. As we can see, even public organizations like the Red Cross demonstrate a bureaucratic, official indifference to human beings. I am convinced that one of the most important tasks for our Supreme Soviet is to change the state's attitude toward the people for whom it exists, to turn the faces of the agencies and governmental bodies toward their real "bosses"—all the country's citizens.

But that is a matter for the future. AIDS, on the other hand, does not want to march to our tempo. The enormity of our plans somehow has no effect on the ominous timetable of its spread. That is why I am in complete agreement with the decision of your magazine to take into its own hands at least part of the responsibility for saving people from this epidemic. By establishing its Anti-AIDS charitable hard-currency account, *Ogonyok* is demonstrating that deeds have indeed replaced words. It's good that the account has been set up at a popular magazine with millions of supporters. That will help in the collection of funds.

As a person who is alarmed about the AIDS situation in our country, I intend to become a contributor to the new fund, and as a Deputy to the Supreme Soviet of the USSR, I am petitioning the Ministry of Finance of the USSR to open it as soon as possible.

Boris N. YELTSIN
Moscow
Published July 1989

THE ENVIRONMENT

ONLY PEOPLE CAN
MAKE A BUILDING . . .

Nowadays, you read from time to time: They're cutting down trees in the cities. How can one explain this barbarism? It's hard to understand. But then, from somewhere, the memory comes back to you: they say it's being done to make the architectural structures more visible. Honestly, that's a laugh. The architecture in our time is no longer art but an appendage of the construction industry; it's embarrassing to exhibit today's "beauties." They should be hidden far from view. Of course, trees, bushes, climbing plants (roses, ivy, wild grape, etc.) actually serve a decorative purpose, hiding the cement monsters behind their green leaves. Not to mention the fact that the *principal* role of greenery in the cities and populated areas is to act as their "lungs"; that is, to clean the air of harmful pollutants, of which we have more than enough today. (Dyushambe is among the leading cities in the country in terms of level of air pollution.) But they are cutting down the trees anyway—not by the dozens, not by the hundreds, but by the thousands.

During my youth, twenty-five years ago, Dyushambe was called—and with good reason—a garden city. It was, of course, smaller, more compact, but attractive and comfortable. Old people, children, young people liked to walk along its streets, parks and squares. But now everybody is afraid to walk along the streets—because walking along in a leisurely manner is very dangerous: You could get sunstroke or a severe burn.

Last year, they chopped down all the trees in two squares along the main street in the city—Lenin Prospekt—and put up a couple of administration buildings. Next to one of them there still is a small island of greenery, but they put a concrete fountain in the middle of it and covered the area around it with cement. They forgot to leave even a few trees for those people who used to like coming here to relax (they're not likely to do that now).

You can imagine the temperature under our feet when the mercury climbs up beyond fifty degrees Celsius[1] in the sun. We have bitterly started calling our city "The Big Frying Pan." If you also take into account that you can count on two hands the number of fountains in the capital of sunny Tadzhikistan, with a population of over 600,000, then your sympathy for Dyushambe's citizens will grow into tremendous pity.

R. MAKHMUDOVA
Dyushambe
Published November 1988

A CLEAN BILL OF HEALTH

I have been working in Chernobyl in the nuclear plant for ten months as an electrician, and I am a member of the Communist Party. I very much want to tell the whole truth, but alas, I don't *know* the whole truth. Not long ago, in the newspaper *Evening Kiev,* a map was published showing the areas contaminated by cesium: in the Ukraine, 100 square kilometers; in the Russian Federation, 2,000 square kilometers; and in Byelorussia, 7,000 square kilometers. Well, better late than never, but that "late" has not even come yet for strontium, radium, polonium and other contaminants. Isn't that curious?

I take it upon myself to swear to you that this touches *every one of us*. Another curious fact: everyone knows that lead is not particularly healthy for the human body. Yet no one in a professional capacity has published an article or map that even begins to tell us that the lead—thousands of tons of it—which was used to put

---

[1] 120 degrees Fahrenheit.

out the burning reactor has now found its way into the Chernobyl water supply. Now we—and *you*—are eating it. And it seems we haven't gotten sick from it yet, because no one is saying anything. That must mean it's tasty.

We, you and everyone who is close to us shudder to think that we may have an untimely death—especially a painful one. But even in the best hospitals now, people are dying. More than 100,000 people have spent time in the contaminated zone. Our families will bury us. We'll be diagnosed with heart disease, with intestinal disorders, and with lung diseases.

It's all very well to complain about the excesses of Stalinism; and yet Stalinist methods—threats and punishment—are being used to chase workers into the contaminated zone. What else is there to do? Volunteers would have to be *paid*. And—merely because a life is at stake—no one wants to pay. Yet people are dying of heart attacks, the children grow up undernourished, undereducated—but all the same they grow up. Perhaps they're living on borrowed time, but they grow up, and that means there will be even more free labor. King Stalin is dead. Long live King Stalin!

Every day 10,000 people go into the contaminated zone, thereby taking upon themselves hundreds of different kinds of ailments. Even new viruses are being mutated. Some of these are rejected by our immune systems, but the viable ones remain and mutate further. And this has already been going on for four years. Of course, there's some small chance that we might contract some kind of virus of immortality. At least that would give us more time to think about all of this. Whether it's all been worth it or not . . .

Our immunologists will prove whatever you like. After all, the atomic engineers proved that a nuclear plant would melt down only once in a million years. Of course, it's too bad that our thirty-five years of atomic energy included that one dangerous year out of the otherwise harmless million. But there's a bright side to this: in the remaining 999,965 years, there should be no meltdowns at all.

The faint of heart and the downtrodden will probably complain about my letter. They'll say, "Why did he write such a letter? Even if that's his opinion. Why did he sign his name to it? It would have been better to *do* something about all this first; then the regime would be even more thankful to him."

What are you afraid of, people? I'm thirty-eight years old and up until this moment I have worked ten months inside the atomic energy plant at Chernobyl. In 1986 I buried my mother. She had breast cancer. The last month of her life I slept very lightly at night, listening to her breathing in the next room—just as a mother listens to the breathing of a child. When her breathing stopped, I'd get up and I'd run to her. . . .

I do not wish such nights upon any of you. But I must tell you that for some time now I've been in the care of a very competent specialist in the lymph glands. Now, at the medical commission which checks me out once a year, they told me that the key to lymphatic disorders is to be found in the teeth! I figure I've heard just about all I need to know about teeth—although they've yet to make it clear to me why it is that my *teeth* don't hurt, but my left *arm* does. (Perhaps if I were thoroughly checked out, they'd discover that my teeth have very long roots—roots that stretch all the way down into my armpit.) Simply put, the final result of my medical examination was that I am healthy, and that there's no reason for me to quit my work.

People, please listen to me. This touches everyone.

E. V. KORTOV
Kiev
Received January 1990
Unpublished

RADIOACTIVE SAUSAGES

Under the heading "Items of Interest," the Syktyvkar newspaper *Krasnoe Znamya* [*Red Banner*] published a collection of letters, entitled "For Purchasers . . . A Secret," which discussed the covert sale of products containing radioactive substances. These letters have given rise to a mass of rumors. Indeed, according to this correspondence, sides of beef having an unusually high content of radioactive substances *did* show up at a Syktyvkar meat plant. They were all dumped in a pile and distinguished from the regular meat by means of a cut in the shape of a cross. This meat, it turns out, was shipped in by order of the State Agricultural Industrial Association of the Russian Republic. Apparently, such meat has been shipped in before, beginning in 1986. And since then, guidelines have been drawn up by the All-Union Scientific Research and Design Institute for the Meat Industry to the effect that meat containing more than the permissible amount of radioactive substances is suitable for the preparation of sausages. But the guidelines do reveal a touching concern for our children. "This sausage is not recommended for use in kindergartens and schools."

The problem raised in *Krasnoe Znamya* is far from just a local one. Ales Adamovich,[1] writing in *Novyi Mir* [*New World*], offers the following explanation from Academician N. A. Korneyev: "There are thousands of tons of contaminated meat in the refrigerators of Byelorussia. Needless to say, the thought of simply destroying this horrible meat (and I think that every citizen of Byelorussia would pay to have that done) seems blasphemous to the officials of the State Agricultural Industrial Association. But it isn't the meat they're concerned about—it's the State plan!"

And so here in Syktyvkar contaminated meat is not being buried in the ground; it's going into sausage. And this has been going on for several years. Why hasn't anyone stopped this crime? Quite the contrary: men of science are quietly, in a businesslike way, continuing to draw up new and better methods for turning it into sausage.

This problem can hardly be solved at our local level. And we are not reassured by the promises of the chief physician of the republic's health services, E. Kanev, and the director of the radiology division of that organization, Zh. Kuznetsova, that after the meat is processed into sausage it becomes completely harmless to one's health. (Apparently it's all very uncomplicated: just wash the meat in saline solution and the high radioactive content simply disappears.) Their responsibility, in fact, should be not to allow this meat to reach consumers—as it never did in Pechora, where all of the workers refused to cut up the carcasses.

V. SELIVANOV
Syktyvkar
Published April 1989

[1] A noted Byelorussian writer and antinuclear activist.

LOST IN SPACE

The announced attempt to make a Soviet journalist the "first" to fly into space is particularly immoral since the Minister of the Chemical Industry of the USSR, wholly in the spirit of the old days, is prepared to provide the money for this venture. From where, his own pocket? Of course not! From ours, all of ours!

The plant in the port of Odessa produces 900 million rubles in income every year, 600 million of it in hard currency. At the same time, for two years now there's been no money to set up an ozonizer for the city's water pipes, and for several years already we've been drinking poisoned water.

The very existence of this plant constantly threatens the life of our entire city: according to expert predictions, an accident at our facility would be more expensive than Chernobyl and in one hour would kill 300,000 to 400,000 people.

This monster was built in a resort city on the seacoast with millions of inhabitants. At first, it was just a "transfer base" for very dangerous chemical products. But someone thought that wasn't enough: now they're reloading phosphates from Syria, which contain dangerous amounts of cadmium, thallium and beryllium. That's the reason other countries refused to buy them from Syria. Syria *itself* refused to build the necessary chemical industrial complex for them in its own country.

This all creates the impression that someone wants to get rid of the Odessans as quickly as possible. We are already in first place nationally in terms of oncological diseases. Specialists claim that if these phosphates are reloaded here, two years from now the Black Sea will finally die completely. Do we have a single other warm sea besides the Black Sea?

Well, how much can you take? Does our country's prestige really depend on a Soviet journalist's being the first to go into space? We're proud of the fact that the first MAN in space was our Yuri Gagarin. But so far, we have nothing else to be proud of because we are behind in so many other things. It would have been better for us to be first in health care; as it is, we are behind even the developing countries in that.

We're against throwing away our money—not into the wind, but into empty space—so that one of our journalists can take a little walk in the cosmos.

D. O. TSITKOV and family
Employees of Goskominturist of the USSR
[total of eight other signatures]
Odessa
6 April 1989
Unpublished

NATIONALITIES

UZBEKS NEED NOT APPLY!

Until very recently we were sure that our country's population had the proper "internationalist" education. And so, the news about nationalist demonstrations in Alma-Ata, Sumgait and so on hit us like a bolt out of the blue.

Aren't you surprised by this announcement in the Personals section of the Classifieds [a special supplement to the newspaper *Vecherny Kishinev* (*Evening Kishinev*)]: "A woman of varied tastes, 164 cm tall, wishes to make the acquaintance of a man who can become her faithful partner for life. He absolutely must be either a Slav, a Moldavian or a Jew." Notice, not just a good man, but a man who has to be a certain nationality. If you're not a "Slav," but merely a good man, don't bother applying to be her husband! It seems to me not only the would-be bride, but also the newspaper, showed the narrowness of their minds here.

I also can't understand why one needs to indicate one's "nationality" on the cards one fills out at the reading room of the library. Maybe so they can determine whether citizens of this or that nationality read more fiction; or, perhaps, to prevent Turks from being served in Moldavian libraries?

M. L. ZLOTNIKOV
Chief physician of a medical clinic
Dubossary, Moldavian SSR
Published June 1988

A FOREIGNER IN HIS NATIVE LAND

My husband is a German by nationality. During the national census, when the question came up, "What languages of the peoples of the USSR do you speak?," he answered, "Russian and German." It turns out that German is not one of the languages of the peoples of the USSR. I found that to be, at the very least, paradoxical.

There are about two million Germans living in this country. Now, if their native language is not a language of the peoples of the USSR, does that mean that it's a *foreign* one? Are Soviet Germans foreigners in their own country?

And here's something else I thought of. Why, after all, is "nationality" included as an item in one's passport? Is it perhaps so that, given a certain specific course of events, people will know who should be discriminated against first and foremost?

O. POPOVA
Sverdlovsk
Published July 1989

UNWRITTEN INSTRUCTIONS

My name is Tatevosyan. During the December earthquake I was in Leninakan, where I was living with my wife and two children. My wife died in the earthquake; my home was completely destroyed, and I have documentation to confirm it. I was left alone, with no home or relatives, with two children on my hands—a five-year-old boy and a three-year-old daughter. I had to move to Stavropol, where my late wife's brother lives; he is helping me raise the children. With the approval of the agencies of the City Executive Committee, I have been registered to live in Stavropol since January of 1989.

Nine months after I received my residence permit, I decided to buy a private house in the city, on Krasnodarsky Prospekt, No. 9. To fill out the deed of sale, you need a document from the Technical Inventory Office certifying the condition of the house. But citizens are not allowed to receive such certificates without the specific permission of the regional committee leaders. With great effort, and after a lot of humiliating scenes, I was able to make an appointment to see the deputy chairman of the Lenin Executive Committee of the City of Stavropol.

At the meeting, Deputy Chairman Strochkov informed me, in the presence of the owner of the house I was planning to buy, that according to an unwritten instruction of the City Executive Committee, the sale of houses to people of Armenian (specifically Armenian) nationality is prohibited. He would not give me a refusal in writing, thus depriving me of the opportunity to file a complaint with the courts. He also informed me of a second requirement of the Committee: a compulsory three-year residence in the city before the right to purchase a home could be granted.

I consulted attorneys and legal specialists, who unanimously confirmed that these actions of the City Committee were in violation of the law, that they were not supported by official directives, and that they contradicted the Constitution of the USSR.

On what basis can the Stavropol City Committee carry out a policy of discrimination for reasons of nationality, thereby prohibiting citizens from purchasing private homes in the city, even though they are officially registered?

What provisions in the Soviet Constitution of the USSR support the directive requiring a three-year residence period in a city before one can purchase a private home?

And on what legal basis can the City Committee prohibit the Technical Inventory Office from issuing a document certifying the condition of a private home?

I feel nothing but deep anger about the arbitrary will of the authorities, especially when I try to reconcile such practices with the latest statements of the Party and the government about the nationalities policy in our country at this time.

I am a simple man, and because I feel helpless in the face of the mute wall of the all-powerful authorities, I am asking for your help in resolving my problem according to my constitutional rights and the law, before which, in all civilized countries, both Presidents and beggars are equal.

S. A. TATEVOSYAN
Stavropol
Received by *Ogonyok* November 1989
Unpublished

LANGUAGE GAP

For fifteen years I lived in the Zaporozhe *oblast* in the Ukraine, and for the past fifteen years I have been living in the Russian Republic. When I was in school, I could speak both Russian and Ukrainian fluently. But years have gone by and I am starting to forget some words here and there from my one-time native language (although I do periodically read literature in Ukrainian). For this reason, whenever I am in Ukrainian cities, I stubbornly look for Ukrainian-Russian and Russian-Ukrainian dictionaries in the bookstores—but always without success.

As you know, the Ukrainian, Russian and Byelorussian languages are similar to each other. Since I know the first two, I could easily read and speak Byelorussian with the help of a dictionary. But no matter how persistently I've searched in the bookstores in Gomel, and last year in the bookstores in Brest,[1] I've been unable to find a single Byelorussian textbook or dictionary.

I've cited, by way of example, two particular national republics; but I would also be glad to learn to read and speak Uzbek or Kazakh, Georgian or Armenian. But where can I get textbooks or dictionaries for those languages?

This raises the question: why, in school, is one required to study a *foreign* language—German, French, English or Spanish—but not one single *national* language, except one's native one? Most of today's fourth-graders will probably never get a chance to go to the German Democratic Republic or the Federal Republic of Germany, but they will definitely travel in the Soviet republics; some of them, perhaps, will even have to live there. And when they're in some hotel room in Tashkent or Brest, listening to the local radio station, they'll feel extremely uneasy, because what they're hearing will sound like Greek to them. Of course, before one can offer the study of national languages in our schools, one needs dictionaries and textbooks, and there aren't any.

After the events in Alma-Ata, the Baltic republics, the Crimea and Nagorno-Karabakh, many articles have begun to appear in the press about national education and the strengthening of friendship. But without making possible the study of the languages of the Soviet republics, you can't completely bring all the nationalities and peoples together in spirit. In a word, *perestroika* of the study of Soviet republic languages is just as necessary as the general *perestroika* of society as a whole.

Pyotr Alekseyevich PANASEIKO
Engineer, Volga Automobile Plant
Togliatti

---

[1] Gomel and Brest are cities in Byelorussia.

TONGUE-TIED

For more than twenty years here the post of Minister of Education of the Mordovian Autonomous SSR[1] has been occupied by a respected comrade who, throughout his career, has never once spoken in his native Mordovian language either on the radio or at meetings. Is it any wonder that the Comrade Minister hasn't noticed how the teaching of national programs is being cut back?

Some of our Party and council officials are afraid that their authority will be reduced if they suddenly start speaking in their native language. And so, for years on end, such leaders don't reveal themselves to people, leave some things unsaid or sometimes even hide things. In time people manage to find out that their leader is a member of the indigenous nationality—one of "them." But no matter what they do, they still can't talk to "their" man in their native language because he shows no interest in doing so.

It seems to me such a leader is forgetting the principal reason he was promoted to a leadership position. Has it really not occurred to him that in advancing him for a leadership post, people were hoping that he would be an activist, not only for the general development of the economy, but also for national culture, the basis of which is language?

A. TYAPAEV
Member of the Union of Writers of the USSR
Honored writer of Mordovia
Saransk

[1] The Mordovian Autonomous SSR—also known as Mordvinia—is an administrative division of the Russian Republic. It is located in the mid–Volga River region.

"I THINK AND DREAM IN RUSSIAN"

In issue no. 11 of *Ogonyok,* a reader, S. Shelkova, writes, "For some reason only the Jews are trying to become Russian, and not even all of them. Intelligent and honest people write 'Jewish,' and no one respects them any less for it."

According to Shelkova's classification, I, apparently, am neither intelligent nor honest since, despite the word "Jewish" in item 5 of my passport, I firmly consider myself a Russian. For this simple reason: I was born in Moscow, in a Russian-speaking family, and was raised and educated in a Russian Soviet kindergarten, school and institute. I not only speak, write and read Russian, but I also think and dream in Russian. My major spiritual "sources" are Chekhov, Tolstoy, Pushkin, Yesenin, Bunin and Kuprin. . . . I never studied Yiddish or Hebrew.

And according to the 1979 census (the results of the latest census of 1989 are not complete yet), people like me, for whom Russian is the only native language, account for 83 percent, or approximately one and a half million people, of the 1.8 million Jews living in the USSR. It is not surprising that among Soviet Jews there is a strong tendency toward mixed marriages with Russians. The children of those marriages more often than not are registered as Russians.

Incidentally, it is by no means only the Jews who are "trying to become Russian." Many Ukrainians, Byelorussians, Moldavians, Chuvash, Marits and Tatars, especially those who live outside their own national territories and have gone to Russian schools, speak and think only in Russian and are, for all practical purposes, Russian. No one has yet become ill or lost from natural, unforced Russification. No such case has been recorded. The anti-assimilationist tendencies encouraged by nationalists today, when people who have "become Russians" are being urged backward (no one knows why) to the language and customs of their ancestors, seem to me to be detrimental to the unity of the country, and tactless toward those who've become assimilated. (Of course, the opposite—the forcible Russification of those who don't want it—is also unacceptable.)

If I have not convinced you, my esteemed Comrade Shelkova, allow me to call for help on Vladimir Ivanovich Dahl, the author of the *Interpretive Dictionary of the Spoken Great Russian Language,* the man in whose arms Aleksandr Sergeyevich Pushkin expired. Dahl wrote: "Neither name, nor professed religion, nor even the blood of his ancestors make a man belong to one or another nationality. The spirit, the soul of the man—this is where his membership in one or another people is to be found. How can the affinity of the soul be determined? Naturally, the manifestation of the soul is thought. Whatever language a person thinks in, that is the people to whom he belongs. I think in Russian."

Why did Dahl feel the need to confirm to himself and to other people that he was Russian? Because Dahl's father was a Dane who had come to Russia from Denmark. And his grandmother on his mother's side, Maria Freimag, was descended from the French Huguenots. But at home they spoke only Russian, and his father, recalls Vladimir Ivanovich, "reminded us at every turn that we were Russian."

If even Dahl is no authority in your eyes, esteemed Comrade Shelkova, let me risk turning, for my last argument, to the Gospels. In Saint Paul's Epistle to the Romans (2:28–29), we read, ". . . he is not a Jew, which is one outwardly; neither is that circumcision, which is outward in the flesh. But he *is* a Jew, which is one inwardly; and circumcision is that of the heart, in the spirit, and not in the letter; whose praise is not of men, but of God."

Understanding that I am depriving myself of the hope of earning the praise of the Almighty, I must still admit that I am a Jew only outwardly and by my passport, but at heart I am a Russian urban intellectual, which pleases me greatly. And neither I nor S. Shelkova are in a position to change this, as they say, objective reality.

Mark VILENSKY
Journalist
Moscow
Published April 1989

"AN ACCOMPLICE IN A CRIME"

It was with bitterness that I read the letter by Moscow journalist Mark Vilensky in *Ogonyok* no. 15 of 1989. In the first lines he says that he firmly considers himself a Russian, although according to his passport he is Jewish. Alas, history itself has dealt cruelly with the great Jewish people, scattering them around the whole world. Worse, when Vilensky listed the writers who became his "main spiritual inspiration," he did not mention a single Jewish one, not even the remarkable Sholom Aleichem. In other words, he doesn't want to know anything about his long-suffering people. He writes, "No one has yet become ill or lost from natural, unforced Russification. No such case has been recorded." He is wrong. The smaller peoples of our country have lost a great deal as a result of natural assimilation.

The absence of national self-awareness is vile pragmatism— "why should I beat myself and my children over the head to learn two languages when nowadays you can get by in any republic with only Russian?" Just look at the sad consequences of such a position. In Kharkov, the former capital of the Ukraine, only just over 1 percent of all the schools are Ukrainian. In 1987 the republic-wide competition of original songwriting was held here. Of the three thousand participants, *three* people performed Ukrainian songs. That's how Ukrainian song and culture are gradually fading into oblivion; incidentally, they were an inspiration to great Russian writers—Pushkin, Gogol, Chekhov. It's frightening to think how much poorer humanity's culture will be in the next century if this apparently unnoticed destructive process is not stopped.

As Mark Vilensky did, let me tell you briefly about myself. Although my parents are indigenous Ukrainians, we spoke Russian at home. Just like Mark, I went to a Russian school and speak and write Russian. And I don't regret it. But unlike Vilensky, in recent years I have become aware of the fact that I am an accomplice in a crime: having become completely involved in daily cares, I did not think about the fact that the cultures of the national minorities must also develop along with the great Russian culture, and not be allowed to die out.

We have created the *Red Book,* which protects every insignificant little flower so it does not disappear. We fine an old lady severely if she picks it and takes it to the market. But there is no *Red Book* for disappearing peoples. And no one fines me—for doing nothing—or Mark Vilensky—for being an apologist for the assimilation that leads to the destruction of nations.

> Z. ZALIVADNY
> Journalist
> Kharkov
> Received by *Ogonyok* May 1989
> Unpublished

HONEST, UNBIASED JOURNALISM?

I have no intention whatever of dragging you into a discussion of Jewish subjects. But I do want to give you my views on a certain issue which has been raised again and again recently in the pages of your magazine—usually in passing, in articles on other subjects, but sometimes more directly. There is no need to list all these articles. The situation is quite clear from one example: the letter from journalist Mark Vilensky, "a Jew by passport but a Russian urban intellectual" by his own definition.

In his letter, the author tells everyone who needs to know the reasons he considers himself a Russian, not a Jew. May God grant him good health and much success, and "dreams in the Russian language" (again, I am quoting the author's own words). But *Ogonyok*'s position in publishing such outbursts seems to me biased and dishonest, from the point of view both of journalism and of simple human ethics.

Understand me correctly. I am by no means questioning the right of Vilensky and those like him to express their thoughts in print. I merely think it is unfair that they are the *only* ones who get to speak. All of us remember only too well the spectacles of the seventies, when on TV and in the newspapers, frightened "Soviet citizens of Jewish nationality" were trotted out with instructions to denounce Israel and "international Zionism," and to declare that they were just as much a part of Russian culture as anyone.

All right, fine, that was the "stagnation" period, but what about now? Well, you may say, unlike those people, Vilensky is writing what he really feels. I won't argue with that, but so what? Imagine this situation: a respectable foreign newspaper from time to time publishes the views of former Russians who—while emphasizing their Russian origins—say that there's absolutely nothing Russian about them, and that in spirit they are, say, French, "and proud of it." If you were honest, you'd have to admit that you'd assess the position of that newspaper as deliberately anti-Russian. And what if the author of one of those letters also swore that he was speaking for the majority of Russians? What would you say then? Your Vilensky, though, has the effrontery (and stupidity) to assert that more than 80 percent of the Jews—that is, all Russian-speaking Jews in the Soviet Union!—are "like him"; in other words, that they renounce their own people. Now, cross your heart: would you dare print a letter that made a similar insulting statement about any other people, even if the bulk of them spoke Russian?

When the magazine *Nash Sovremennik*[1] (issue no. 3 of 1989) reflects on the inherently flawed nature of Jewish national culture (citing, for extra insurance, quotes taken out of context from the "classics of Marxism"), and offers the thought that the only solution to the Jewish question is for the Jewish people to disappear, I have no qualms with the magazine: why not let it express its opinion, especially in an editorial? But when *you* print essentially the same thing, offering it up as the opinion of an entire people, and throw in, as a mouthpiece, someone with a Jewish last name—that, gentlemen, cannot be called honest journalism.

A. YUROVSKY
Jerusalem
Published December 1989

---

[1] *Nash Sovremennik* [*Our Contemporary*] is a monthly magazine noted for its advocacy of right-wing Russian nationalist ideals.

THE "GIFT" OF AN ALPHABET

I have carefully followed what's been published about the victims of the Stalinist repressions, but nowhere have I found any mention of one category of victims—those who were called "Arabists"[1] in the camps. And there were quite a few of them (although I must say it seems immoral to talk about numbers when you are dealing with the taking of innocent lives). The entire guilt of these people consisted of the fact that they were *literate*—that books written in the Arabic alphabet were found in their possession (and barbarically destroyed).

The national press sometimes makes brief mention of how the peoples in the Turkic linguistic group—the heirs to a great and ancient culture—were forced to abandon their traditional Arabic writing system, first for the Latin alphabet in the 1930s, and then, in 1940, for the Slavic one. From the articles on this subject, one can judge the catastrophic consequences of the alphabet reform for many peoples whose culture was thereby torn from its centuries-long national roots. But even here, one never reads about the fact that the alphabet reform in the 1930s was accompanied by massive repressions. These repressions were directed not only at the intelligentsia, but at peasants as well, and they took place not only in cities, but among the most remote populations in the mountains and steppes. Simply for having a book of poems by Navoi[2] or an ancient treatise on herbs, carefully preserved and passed on from generation to generation, thousands, including old men and women, became prisoners in distant northern camps and were, for all practical purposes, condemned to die. (To justify this, a propaganda myth was created about the illiteracy and backwardness of the inhabitants of the southern republics, to whom the kind "father of all peoples"[3] gave the gift of an alphabet.) Their national culture was crushed spiritually, and those who could have passed it on to their descendants were destroyed physically.

---

[1] The writer is referring to the peoples living in Soviet Central Asia—the Kazakhs, the Uzbeks, the Tadzhiks and the Turkmen people.

[2] A Persian poet.

[3] i.e., Stalin.

Their tragedy should be remembered not only by their descendants, but by all of us.

A. ANTIPOV
Leningrad
Published June 1989

LANGUAGES IN A "STATE RULED BY LAW"

Lev Gushchin writes: "The question of language, which is now recognized as a matter under the jurisdiction of the individual republics, has become one of the most sensitive issues facing the Russian-speaking population.

"It is no secret that many Russians who live in the national republics do not know the local language. Now this is hampering them in finding a job.

"A second troublesome issue for such Russians is the 'residency requirement,' i.e., the minimum time one must have lived in a given republic before one is eligible for election to a governing body.

"These two problems have led to mass demonstrations by the Russian population and the creation of special 'international fronts'—movements in defense of the interests of the non-indigenous population."

As you know, several republics have recently published draft laws concerning language, according to which the language of the indigenous population is proposed as the only official state language. Let me say right off that this kind of decree has its justifications, which are often very important.

However, the change in the status of the Russian language presents the *non*-indigenous population of the republics with a whole series of unexpected, sometimes even painful, problems. Of course, the draft republic laws about language provide for measures to assist the Russian-speaking population in learning the new official state language. But it is not hard to imagine that part of the population will look for a way out of the newly created situation by moving to another republic with an official state language more convenient for it. This process is already taking place, and it is completely natural.

We believe that this migration should not be viewed exclusively as the personal business of individual citizens. After all, we have all been living according to the existing laws, and many people became residents of a given republic as part of national plans for developing the economy, etc.

This raises the question: doesn't it make sense, parallel with the drafting of new laws about language, to develop a single, national socioeconomic program to manage the migrations arising out of changes in republic legislation? This program is needed to guarantee balance in observing the legitimate interests of all the citizens of our country. It should cover the legal issues involved in choosing a place of residence and finding work, as well as many other things. Adopting such a program would enhance protection of the legal rights of the citizens of the USSR, and would be a concrete step on the road toward building a state ruled by law.

A. ROVSKY
V. AZIN
B. AIRAPETYAN
E. FYODORCHUK
Tashkent
Published September 1989

MILITARY COMMUNICATION

With great concern, I have been following the furor in the press over national cultures and their integral element—language. I understand that what the press is saying is an echo of public opinion, and of the things that are going on in the provinces. And I get the impression that we are rushing headlong from one extreme to the other. If, in the past, we used to ignore anything national, today we are raising it to the level of a cult, exalting it and singling it out. And, from there, it is only one more step to nationalism.

Do you really have to experience something yourself in order to understand it? Is it really not enough to see the national hatred in Yugoslavia and other countries, where people gave in to what appeared at the beginning to be well-founded and moderate demands, only to see such demands grow, in time, into nationalism? Why do we always seem to learn only by making mistakes, which we pay for with our blood?

The Army is a good indicator by which to gauge nationalist processes taking place in various localities, because it brings together, side by side, representatives of all the republics and peoples in the country.

Due to the nature of my military assignment, I have occasion to observe many different units. And this is what I see: open hostility toward everything Russian (including Russian soldiers) is growing and becoming more and more glaring. And this process is particularly strong and pronounced in the area of language. In the last two to three years, the situation has become especially tense. At times it is so absurd you don't know whether to laugh or cry.

In the company where Lieutenant S. Mustyats is deputy commander of political affairs, new recruits have come in. Among others, there are four Armenians who don't understand a word of Russian. No matter how hard the officer tried to communicate with them, it was useless. Then, suddenly, he had an inspiration: try speaking in English.

Well, guess what happened? Soon they began to understand each other. The four Armenians spoke English (not Russian!) perfectly well.

Recently, more and more soldiers have been coming into the Army who don't know Russian. Very quickly, they master only those expressions which—in their opinion—are the most necessary: "My foot hurts," "My stomach hurts," "I have to go to the doctor." They use words in combination with "I want" a lot: "I want to sleep, eat, smoke, go to the store. . . ." And another expression has become very popular, and every one of them knows it: "No way!"

It's very hard to command units containing these kinds of "mutes." Lots of problems arise even when there are only a few in the group. And what is someone like Captain N. Kanyshev supposed to do? In his company, a full third of the personnel doesn't know Russian. And I don't mean they just understand Russian *poorly;* they don't speak it at all!

What do you do? How do you command, direct and run mil-

itary training with such a company? Well, the commander of the
unit and his deputy for political affairs, Senior Lieutenant S. Chel-
nokov, have tried to teach the soldiers Russian. But so far the
results are . . . forget it!

The senior officer in the company long ago gave up on this, in
his words, "useless idea" and took a different tack. He learned to
speak "their language." And now he easily makes himself understood by his soldiers. But is this the answer? Is every commander
able to master a "bouquet" of languages? I don't think so. There
aren't very many polyglots around. I think the solution is to give
back to the great Russian language its function of communication
between the nationalities. Not in word, but in deed.

Yuri Anatolyevich KRAVCHENKO
Military officer
Village of Goryachie Klyuchi,
Sakhalin *oblast,* Kurilsk region
Received by *Ogonyok* March 1989
Unpublished

THE FATE OF EMPIRES

To: People's Deputy of the USSR E. A. Gaer, Member of the
Commission of the Council of Nationalities on Nationalities Policy
and Inter-Nationality Relations
cc: Editorial Offices of *Izvestia, Pravda, Ogonyok, Literaturnaya
Gazeta, Argumenty i Fakty, Soglasie*

Recently the central press has been writing about a dispute
between Japan and Russia (USSR). The main object of the dispute
is to whom the four southernmost Kurile Islands[1] should belong.

---

[1] A chain of small islands extending from northern Japan to the southern tip of the
Kamchatka Peninsula.

Basically, the issue boils down to who was the first (Russia or Japan) to occupy the islands.

I believe that this is a dispute between two plunderers: which one of them was the first to plunder their hapless victims—the Ainu people? If one goes by the logic of the central press, by the same right South America should belong to Spain and Portugal, and North America to England and France. The same could be said for Africa, Asia and the South Pacific Islands—all of which at one time were occupied by colonizers. But time does not stand still, and the majority of the colonies won their freedom and independence. The last major colonies nowadays are held only by Russia and China (I mean Tibet, Inner Mongolia, Xinjiang and a few other areas).

In Russia, the colonizers are hailed as "pioneers," despite the fact that these "pioneers" conquered Siberia, paving their way with the corpses of the local peoples, now vaguely called the "small peoples of the North." I think these peoples would not have become so "small" (i.e., small in numbers) if the Russian colonization had not destroyed (through assimilation) most of the local population and their cultures.

All empires have acted similarly: the Russians, Japanese, Chinese, German, French, English, Dutch, Spanish, Portuguese. . . . All of them destroyed the local population and local cultures, replacing them with their own colonists and their "more developed" culture without asking the indigenous peoples for their consent.

As for the Kurile Islands and Southern Sakhalin Island, historical justice demands the creation of an independent state for the Ainu, whose descendants (about 20,000 people) to this day live on a Japanese reservation on the island of Hokkaido. At the end of the war they were relocated there from Southern Sakhalin and the Kuriles by the Japanese.

Any people, regardless of its numbers, has an inalienable right to create its own state on its own land. Otherwise, it will disappear— be assimilated—as a people and forget its native language, customs and culture. This is what the "theory of the fusion of nations" proclaimed for so many years in the USSR has led to (and still leads to). The goal of this theory is obvious: to strengthen the collapsing empire by creating one large (Russian-speaking) "Soviet people."

I am sending this letter not only to you, Comrade Gaer, but to many central newspapers and magazines as well, although I am absolutely certain that none of them will print it. There has never been an empire in the world that voluntarily returned land and freedom to the peoples it enslaved, and Russia has remained the Russian Empire it was, only it has changed its outward appearance for decency's sake. The interests of the Empire have remained paramount, above historical truth, justice, morality or law. For example, the occupation of Lithuania, Latvia and Estonia in 1940 is justified by the need for warmer-water ports on the Baltic Sea.

However, the Russian people need to think about what awaits them if they continue to be conquerors and colonizers of other peoples. We Lithuanians once conquered all the land from the Baltic Sea to the Black Sea, and subsequently we finally lost not only the territory we had conquered, but even most of our own native land and our statehood. As world history shows, this is an historical law. The same fate awaits all empires.

Kyastutis CHEPONIS
Researcher, Institute of the Academy of Sciences of Lithuania
Vilnius
October 26, 1989
Unpublished

FOR RESIDENTS ONLY

Recently we were on a trip in Estonia. We had some free time, and, like all other women in the world, we wanted to take a look at what they had in the stores, especially since we've always been very pleased with the excellent service offered by the Estonians. In a fine-goods store in the village of Ust-Narva we saw two shop windows: one had goods for sale to visitors, and the other, which was nicer, had products for residents. When we tried to buy some hand cream, the saleslady asked us for our passports, referring to a decree that certain goods were to be sold only to registered residents of Estonia. Because the local residents were so ashamed of that decree, they offered to lend us their own passports. But our mood was spoiled, and all we wanted to do was go home.

We are neighbors. No one has stopped the trains and buses

coming from Estonia; a lot of Estonians sell things in the markets here. They come to Leningrad in their own cars. But it's hard to imagine that Leningraders would demand that they show a passport with a Leningrad residence permit.

I. A. MARKOVA
and eight other employees of the Scientific Research Institute
    of the "Elektrosila" Electronics Plant
Leningrad
Published May 1989

"AN IMMIGRANT AND AN OCCUPIER"

To: Comrade Korotich, *Ogonyok* magazine

Try to express the idea in the pages of your magazine that the Estonians should give part of the money (some 16,000 rubles) they receive for each Russian worker who comes here to those of us who want to go away from here and leave our apartments.

At least 4,000 for each empty apartment we leave behind. After all, how long are we going to have to suffer in rented little corners until we get a new one in a new republic?

Then the words, "Our borders are open, and everybody who wants to leave can do so," will have some meaning. It's one thing to want to, and another thing to be able to.

Let the Estonians be the lords here, for God's sake; let them live here in wealth and be happy.

I personally very much want to leave here, but I can't. I have no money and no place to go. And I don't want to be "an immigrant and an occupier" here.

Now, literally everywhere, you hear that no one asked us to come here. I can calmly say that someone very much asked us (specifically, my former husband and me) to come here and spent several months convincing us. Otherwise we wouldn't have come. What for? And we got this stinking apartment full of dead rats

Reuters: Dominique Dudouble.

Flag-waving Estonian nationalists, in traditional dress, participate in a human chain from Tallinn, Estonia, to Vilnius, Lithuania, as the three Baltic republics commemorate the fiftieth anniversary of their "illegal annexation" by the USSR.

instead of the wonderful apartment on the second floor that we gave the state when we moved.

In short, I don't want them to say, "Whoever wants to go, can go," until they're willing to help everybody who leaves an apartment here without exchanging it for a new one. That would only be fair—to compensate those people who have spent half their life here working and who have now turned into "occupiers," for their moral insult and material loss.

If huge crowds want to join hands and scream "freedom" (*vabadus*), then let them help free themselves of our presence by giving us money. Especially since it isn't their money, but money sucked out of enterprises who don't have enough workers.

After all, the Estonians don't want to work. Every last one of them wants to be a boss and live rich. I myself am a worker, and I know what I'm talking about.

I'll never get used to things here. I very much want to leave, but I can't. There's nowhere to go. I understand that neither *Ogon-*

yok nor Korotich personally can help me. But at least let them give those creators of the second bourgeois revolution the idea of how painlessly they could get rid of us occupiers. And, to boot, they would have to build less housing.

> G. H. ANSHUKOVA
> Rakvere, Estonia
> 20 September 1989
> Unpublished

"PLEASE QUIET DOWN . . ."

On January 10, 1990, Mikhail Gorbachev paid a "diplomatic visit" to Lithuania, whose Communist Party had just voted to secede from the national party. For three days he begged the Lithuanians for patience in their move toward independence from the USSR, although he held out the vague promise that a "mechanism" might be set up to "permit a republic to leave the Soviet Union." Gorbachev's remarkable face-to-face encounters with huge crowds of nationalist demonstrators in Vilnius were televised across the country.

Last night's TV program, on which Gorbachev spoke from Lithuania, moved me to put pen to paper. I'm not talking about all Lithuanians, but to those who are not satisfied with their lot I would like to say, "What do you have to complain about?" After the years of the war you didn't help rebuild Russia. On the contrary, you milked Russia dry to meet the needs of your own region. Just try to deny it.

Meanwhile, here in the Crimean steppes, we've had to try to build everything ourselves from what our own countryside offered us. You can come down here and have a look at the town of Zelenaya Niva and the other towns around it. The people here have given their whole working lives to the collective farms. And what did they get? Huts with iron furniture. Not like your little houses with their soft couches. And there's no smoke in your houses. In ours, smoke billows as though from an engine. In huts like these, veterans of the Great Patriotic War and their widows are already beginning to die. And the roads! Forty-five years of peacetime and they still haven't fixed the roads. In the winter you sink down in the mud—in the summer you choke in the dirt.

But the Russian people don't complain. They endure. They endure everything. As long as Russia has existed they have endured.

And where else have you Lithuanians seen a head of state come to talk with people such as you? Who else would have ever spoken to you in such plain Russian—spoken from the heart—as did Mikhail Gorbachev? He looked at you as though he was conversing with kind people and you maliciously and mean-spiritedly insulted him. We saw all this on TV. In our village, Krasnoperekopsk, in 1954, we citizens ourselves built the water works. We ourselves dug the ditches and laid the pipes. This was all our own labor and effort. In 1989 we ourselves laid gas lines into each house and no one helped us or gave us so much as a kopeck. We were put on pension and good-bye.

So back to your complaining and whining. Think about this a little and please quiet down at last. A Russian proverb says, "The fat dog gets lazy." If your life is so bad, well, what do you think ours is like? Or do you want to make other people angry? Do you want to create even more divisions in our country?

K. I. MOROZ
Krasnoperekopsk, Crimea
Received by *Ogonyok* January 1989

———

On February 24, 1990, in the first true multiparty elections held in the Soviet Union since the Bolshevik Revolution, Sajudis, the Lithuanian nationalist organization, won a majority of seats in Lithuania's Supreme Soviet. Two weeks later, on March 11, the newly elected legislature formally declared its independence from the USSR.

Mikhail Gorbachev immediately proclaimed the Lithuanian resolution "illegitimate and invalid." He also announced that secession would not be negotiated with Lithuania or any other republic. "We hold talks only with foreign states," he said. Thus began an escalating war of nerves between Moscow and Vilnius.

In the meantime, the Congress of People's Deputies, in session in Moscow, began drafting a law specifying the requirements a republic would have to meet before being allowed to secede from the Union.

MARKET RELATIONS

Ogonyok writes a lot about market relations. Well, as far as I'm concerned, there's plenty of that . . . just go to any market. Behind the counter you find rude, greasy, ugly faces with telltale southern suntans. And they just lawlessly rip people off! You don't plan to give *them* power, do you?

No doubt, we need markets, but the traders in them should be our people, Russians. They don't have any inbred insolence and scorn for all things Russian. And they especially don't have that money-grubbing quality that is so characteristic of Armenians and Georgians.

I have been in retirement for many years now, and I often go out for walks. I have started to notice that I see fewer and fewer kind Russian faces. All I see is Tatars or Uzbeks . . . Jews . . . and now these Vietnamese. . . . The streets are filthy with former "quota-fillers"[1] who settled down in the capital. If things are so hungry and empty here, what do they all come here for? Everybody knows that a fish rots from the head, so the first thing we need to do is cleanse Moscow of all this filth.

L. SHAKRINA
Moscow
Published October 1989

---

[1] i.e., settlers who filled the Moscow immigration quota for one nationality or another.

HOW FASCISM STARTS

May 14, 1989, was a bright Sunday morning. The birds were singing and the smell of lilac was in the air. That day I understood for
the first time how fascism starts. I'm talking about the meeting of
the Pamyat Society[1] in Luzhniki Stadium in Moscow. Did I know
where I was going? Without a doubt. My curiosity was heightened
by rumors and coverage in *Ogonyok,* the "Vzglyad" ["Glance"] TV
program, etc. To be honest, I was expecting to find nothing more
than a bunch of people who had a certain position—albeit one that
was sickening to me—and weren't afraid to express it out loud.
After all, there is the article in the Criminal Code against fanning
nationalist hatred; there is public opinion, and finally, the moderate
traditions of the Russian intelligentsia.

While I was still on my way up to the square, microphones
amplified to a shrill whine screeched out slogans:

"End the power of the Jews over Christians!"
"Tell the officials holding secret negotiations with Israel to
straighten out!"
"Give us de-Zionization!"

And so on, and so forth.

The crowd responded with approving roars. Above them hung
banners with crossed-out Stars of David and slogans. Pins, em-
blems, flyers, and lists of the society's enemies were flying wildly
about. An excited woman was collecting signatures to demand that
all the Jews be sent out of Moscow. Among the participants in the
meeting were veterans and young people; Palestinians with flags
and official "observers" in street clothes; Pamyat fanatics and children. Next to me a pleasant enough woman told her eight- or
nine-year-old daughter, "Let's go, Lenochka. Once again they're
not telling us anything concrete about how to fight Zionism."

The crowd, whipped up to the limit, applauded poems more
noteworthy for their zoological than their literary merit:

---

[1] An ultranationalist organization, whose name means "Memory." The Pamyat Society's stated purpose is the care and restoration of antique Russian buildings and artifacts.
In reality, it is a virulently antisemitic paramilitary organization, many of whose members
sport black T-shirts or Nazi-style greatcoats.

". . . For the vermin, there will come a time . . .
"We'll pulverize that filthy reptile slime."

A short distance away our strict, but fair, police observed this orgy with democratic calm. Well, what's wrong with it? We have *glasnost* now, you know!

I don't want to list what else the demonstrators bellowed, sometimes with, and sometimes without, the microphone. It's disgusting to remember the antisemitic slogans and those faces twisted with hate. I captured it all on my slides and recorded it on tape. What my friends and I witnessed constitutes a real threat; to ignore it would be a crime. I will never forget how a very young redheaded boy yelled at me how he dreamed of bashing in the head of at least one kike kid.

About myself: I am a twenty-year-old Jewish woman. I was born and live in Moscow. I am terrified about having children.

Sasha KALNER
Moscow
Received by *Ogonyok* June 1989
Unpublished

"DON'T HIDE YOUR HEAD UNDER YOUR WINGS"

To: First Secretary of the Novosibirsk *Oblast* Committee
  of the CPSU
Deputy of the Supreme Soviet of the USSR
Comrade V. V. Kazarezov

Copy: *Ogonyok* magazine

Dear Vladimir Vasilyevich:

Today, August 13, 1989, I accidentally came upon a meeting of the Pamyat Society in Narymsky Square.

Ogonyok: Vladimir Uborevich-Borovsky.

Рисунок
Владимира
УБОРЕВИЧА-
БОРОВСКОГО

It is difficult to describe all the filth they uttered there about Soviet power, about V. I. Lenin and about the Jews. Everybody knows that the Pamyat Society has it in for the Jews. Insulting and labeling an entire nationality "kikes" is indeed an insult. Your name was also repeated many times. They accuse you of not taking decisive measures against Jews who, allegedly, have brought Russia to a crisis.

I am a Jew by nationality. I was at the front in World War II, was wounded twice and received government medals. I don't know Hebrew; I speak only Russian. All of my friends at the front were Russian. We saved each other's lives. To this day, one of them, whose life I saved at the risk of my own, still writes to me.

I don't have the strength to listen to all the filth that the Pamyat people are pushing. Of course, I got into a discussion with them. But what can I do alone? The Pamyat Society is an organized mafia. They attract young people, and that is particularly dangerous. Pamyat organizes meetings on Narymsky Square every Sunday from 2 to 6 p.m. They have their own printers and are about to open their own bank account. They are allowed to do everything! Where are we headed? Is this really what we veterans of the front dreamt about? Isn't the nationalist violence in Abkhazia, Uzbekistan[1] and other places enough? There will be butchery in Novosibirsk, too; it will happen with your compliance. There is a new law that gives you the right to make people criminally liable for instigating national hatred and for insulting a nationality. Why won't you act? Your failure to do so encourages Pamyat. They are getting more and more insolent not by the day, but by the hour! Soon it will be too late!

I think that if there is a pogrom—and there will surely be one—no one will forgive you for it. You should come yourself to Narymsky Square on Sunday at 2 p.m. (you could come incognito). You will see that there is more than enough evidence to bring them to criminal justice. Incidentally, Kazantsev, the leader of Pamyat, has asked more than once, "Why doesn't this Kazarezov take us to trial? He's afraid!" Kazantsev thinks that you are a coward, a do-nothing. If only you could hear how much filth they say about you. You have to know your enemies! Don't hide your head under your wings! It will cost you dearly!

Respectfully,
N. F. ZUBKOV
Veteran of World War II, disabled
Novosibirsk
August 13, 1989
Unpublished

[1] Abkhazia is an autonomous region in the northwestern portion of the Soviet Republic of Georgia. Uzbekistan is one of the constituent republics of the USSR. In 1989, both were the scene of ethnic violence.

A MONEY-SAVING IDEA

Your magazine really is a hotbed of Zionism and pharisaism—a bunch of kikes of all breeds. But there is something useful in that. The situation in this country is developing in such a way that you will all have to answer. If you live that long. Provocateurs and instigators always get what they deserve.

The important thing, when the time comes, is not to let your gang take off abroad, so that later we don't have to waste time looking for you—the way we did for Trotsky, for example. We'll save money that way.

S. KAZAKOV
Rostov-on-Don
Published October 1989

"I DON'T WANT TO LEAVE MY HOMELAND"

I am writing because I am ashamed to live in a country whose citizens are forced to run away abroad because the state they live in cannot guarantee their safety. What is going on in our country, comrades? Why do belligerent thugs from the notorious Pamyat Society walk around the streets of Moscow with antisemitic slogans on their T-shirts? Who gave them the right to speak for the whole Russian people?

During the Great Patriotic War (we lived in Kiev then) a Jewish boy named Yasha lived with our family. His father had gone to the front as a volunteer, and his mother and grandmother were shot by the Nazis. My father was also at the front, and my mother, a simple *Russian* woman, was raising us, so that Yasha became our brother. Many years passed, and last year Yasha was granted permission to emigrate. When he was saying good-bye to our elderly mother, he said, "Forgive me, mama. I'm leaving because it hurts me that the Soviet State, for whom my grandfather fought in the Civil War and my father in the Great Patriotic War, can't—or doesn't want to, which is even more terrifying—protect me the way my father and grandfather once protected it. Where is the guarantee that my children will be alive tomorrow? And I desperately don't want to leave my homeland. . . ."

What can I add to that? Some people may object by saying that we now have democracy, and everyone can express his opinion. I agree. But if it involves sowing nationalist hatred, how can there be any talk of democracy? Why don't the authorities say something? Or is what is going on in the country serving their purpose?

I am Russian and proud of it. Let every Jew, Georgian, Tatar or Kazakh be proud of the fact that he is a Jew or Georgian or Tatar or Kazakh. Only respect for people of all nationalities, only the friendship and brotherhood of all peoples will save our country from the difficult situation it is in. And, as a true Russian, as a genuine Communist, I demand that the wild outbursts of those thugs from Pamyat and their ilk be stopped! I am sure that all honest people will support me.

V. L. SERGACHEV
Received by *Ogonyok* Autumn 1989
Unpublished

INCIDENT IN TBILISI

Dear Editor-in-Chief:

At 4 a.m. on April 9, 1989, in front of the Government House in Tbilisi, participants in a peaceful demonstration were dispersed with unprecedented cruelty. Punitive Soviet Army brigades were armed with clubs, shovels, tear gas and nerve gas. All of these were used against unarmed, peaceful residents of the city. As a result of this bloody action, eighteen people died, primarily women, and scores were severely wounded.

Central Television and the central press are covering this event extremely unobjectively. The information they present has nothing to do with reality.

We ask that you present truthful and reliable information in your magazine about this horrible event.

> Employees of the Trauma and Orthopedics Center of the
> Ministry of Health of the Georgian SSR
> [twenty signatures]
> 17 April 1989
> Unpublished

"WHAT HAPPENED TO *GLASNOST?*"

Dear Comrade V. A. Korotich:

You surely know about the events in Tbilisi at dawn on April 9. How is the central press and television reacting to these events? What happened to that noble slogan *Glasnost?* Can we really only criticize the dead, and people who are not in power anymore? The entire central press and television not only is not telling the truth but is distorting it out of shape. Everyone knows that the participants in the peaceful demonstration, even as they uttered the words "Our Father, let us die as Christians," were brutally and barbarously killed by soldiers, using sharpened shovels, poison gas and clubs.

Denying this is, at the very least, stupid because everything has been thoroughly documented. Several thousand people saw everything with their own eyes, including *Literaturnaya Gazeta* correspondent Yuri Rost. He took pictures of everything, but his article was not published in *Literaturnaya Gazeta*. It was published in the Tbilisi newspaper *Molodezh Gruzii,* which was then confiscated. I am amazed at the stupidity of the person who gave the order to hide the complete truth from the population. After all, everyone will find out about it anyway. Very soon, history will judge today's executioners, who are no better than the Nazis. I am a veteran of the Great Patriotic War and participated in the storming of Berlin. Nowhere did I see such brutality, not toward peaceful citizens, not even toward prisoners.

I am interested to see whether you will put this letter in your magazine. If not, so much the worse for our press.

Vakhtang Konstantinovich CHICHINADZE
Academician of the Academy of Sciences of the Georgian SSR
Veteran of the Great Patriotic War
18 April 1989
Unpublished

AN OPEN LETTER TO MINISTER OF DEFENSE OF THE USSR YAZOV

Comrade Minister:

"The Red Army is the strongest." We've known that for a long time, but we never imagined how strong it could be against unarmed people (we've seen how strong it was against *armed* people in Afghanistan). By killing women with shovels, your soldiers showed true heroism.

I'm sure that if my people have the strength to start a civil war, you will fall face first into shit, just like in Afghanistan.

I. ARTILAKVA
Tbilisi
10 April 1989

A SILENT CONSCIENCE

On May 30, 1989, during an emotional debate on the events in Georgia, General Igor N. Rodionov, military commander of the Transcaucasian Region, addressed the Congress of People's Deputies. In his speech, he staunchly defended the use of military force against the Tbilisi demonstrators.

Comrade General! Since I doubt that I will ever have an opportunity to meet you, to look you in the eyes, I will try—presumably in vain—to reach your conscience through the press. In your speech at the session of the Congress of People's Deputies, where you explained the tragic—not only for the Georgian people, but for all our peoples—events, you shook me deeply, not so much by *what* you said, but *how* you said it. I will not take it upon myself to judge the reasons for the events of April 9. I, like millions who listened to you, was not there. Let us say that, although you were a direct participant in the tragedy, you are not even guilty (I will grant you that you are a military man and were only carrying out the orders of someone whose name you cannot now reveal). But how could you—how *dare* you—report on it so haughtily and calmly to the Congress!!! That is what shocked me; that is what made me take up my pen and try to get through to you, to penetrate to the place where most normal people have a heart.

I do not want to discuss with you what or who forced you to use armored personnel carriers and shovels against unarmed people. I am talking about something else. The death at the hands of soldiers of even one pregnant woman would make anyone shudder. But you informed the Congress with Olympian calm about a mere sixteen(!) bodies of, in your words, "people whose cause of death is unknown." As for the unprecedented use of chemical weapons against peaceful civilians, which the whole world is now talking about, you treated it as if it were a trifle, or a misunderstanding or, in any case, a perfectly ordinary thing. I want my voice to reach you so you will understand that all of your explanations and justifications cannot be accepted by a single sane person—if for no other reason, because of your apparent lack of conscience. How can there

TASS from SOVFOTO: I. Shlamov.

Georgians, holding wreaths and portraits, mourn the victims of the April 9, 1989 incident in Tbilisi.

be any talk of charity and humanity in our society if you, a primary participant in these events, do not feel a sense of personal guilt. Not only did you not lower your eyes when you mentioned the human victims; you left the podium convinced that you had done your duty!

People (I am sure I am not the only one) expected from you some comprehension that a tragedy had occurred, and that you were the witting or unwitting instigator of it. People expected repentance. But, instead, you showed inhumanity, which may have been received just as insensitively by some of your audience, but which, I am convinced, made everyone with a living conscience shudder. And if one's conscience is silent (the way yours is), then what is the point of all our laws and our amendments to the Constitution? How will they help anyone?

> G. KONOVALOVA
> Actress
> Vakhtangov State Academic Theater
> June 6, 1989
> Unpublished

WHO IS SUPPOSED
TO PROTECT US?

I would like to address a problem that has become a topic of controversy and a source of wild outbursts of emotion, namely the role of military units of the Ministry of Internal Affairs of the USSR.

More than once now, while performing my duties maintaining public order, I have had to endure responses like, "And where are your shovels?" For us, the people who work for the Ministry of Internal Affairs, it is obvious that we are not the only ones affected by the "Tbilisi syndrome." Incidents of insults and direct attacks on soldiers and cadets have increased. In the clash between the processes of democratization of society and the activities of the Internal Affairs agencies a definite role has been played by the media, as well as by the not always carefully weighed statements of individual leaders.

Yes, there are facts we who work in the organs of the Ministry are ashamed of. And believe me, they are painful. No doubt, we have our degenerates and our petty autocrats. No doubt, we have not always been given reasonable orders to carry out. But these diseases have afflicted and continue to afflict many, many other agencies and organizations. The Ministry of Internal Affairs developed and took shape in our country, and suffers from the same illnesses as our society as a whole. Like society at large, we are trying to get rid of them.

None of us gets the malicious urge to ask the first doctor we meet, "Well, where's your syringe infected with AIDS?" or to ask a construction worker, "Let's see those little hands that made the gas pipeline!"[1] and so forth.

The crux of the matter is this: it is painful for me, an officer and a political worker, to see our young men—many of whom, at the risk of their own lives, did their international duty in the Democratic Republic of Afghanistan, or were among the first participants in the cleanup of the Chernobyl disaster, or put a stop to the slaughter in Sumgait[2] and Fergana[3]—called enemies of democracy and *perestroika*.

Comrades, let's ask ourselves this question: if we are not going to close our eyes—in other words, if we do not consider the increase in crime and the wave of extremism that has overwhelmed the country a normal thing—then who is supposed to protect us? And what should society's attitude toward these young men be?

I. GALYUK
Senior lieutenant
Internal Service
Kharkov
Published September 1989

[1] On June 3, 1989, approximately four hundred people were killed when a huge gas pipeline explosion engulfed two passing trains. The accident occurred near the city of Ufa, in the Ural Mountains east of Moscow.

[2] A city in the Republic of Azerbaijan. On February 28, 1988, it was the scene of massive disorders, during which crowds of Shi'ite Muslim Azerbaijanis reportedly beat, raped and killed members of the city's Christian ethnic Armenian minority on sight. The official death toll from the incident was thirty-two, but Armenian nationalists insist that the number killed was at least ten times higher. Eight Soviet Army soldiers also allegedly died as they attempted to restore order, but this fact was not confirmed by state sources.

[3] A city in the Republic of Uzbekistan. On June 3–4, 1989, mobs of Uzbeks, avenging an insult made by a Meskhetian Turk to an Uzbek woman peddling fruit in the nearby town of Kuvasai, killed forty Meskhetians and ransacked hundreds of Meskhetian homes and businesses. At least ten Uzbeks also perished during the rioting. Later the same week, when Uzbek youths tried to storm a refugee camp that had been set up for the Meskhetians, five Uzbeks were killed by Soviet troops.

A MATTER OF PRIORITIES

The events of April 9 in Tbilisi and their coverage in the press were a shock to us, two military school instructors, especially since our work involves training young people for service in an Army which is now stained with the blood of our fellow citizens. There was a hope that this was a tragic accident, that harsh punishment would befall the guilty parties. However, these hopes remained unfulfilled: neither the killers nor Major-General Rodionov, nor the criminals empowered by the Party who sanctioned the slaughter, but only the leaders of informal organizations[1] ended up behind bars. And the central press responded not with pain and anger, but with cowardly silence. People are understanding more and more that this barbaric annihilation of people's lives, aimed at deterring popular movements, was not the independent action of a general who disgraced his uniform, not the brazenness of local Party gangs, but an action sanctioned by the highest military and Party leadership of the country—genetically linked to and deriving from Lenin's "Red Terror" and Stalin's struggle against "enemies of the people." These events opened our eyes to the fact that the young people we are training for the Army may end up either as unwitting instruments of genocide, as in Afghanistan, or as executioners, as in Tbilisi. And so, we left the school.

We would like to address the Minister of Defense of the USSR, General D. T. Yazov, from the pages of *Ogonyok*. As citizens of the USSR, we are not shirking our constitutional duty to defend our homeland, but we do reserve the right not to consider this or that commander the personification of its will; consequently, we reserve the right not to carry out orders which turn us into executioners. We reserve the right to remain first and foremost human beings, even if this means disobeying the Army Rules of Conduct.

---

[1] Nongovernmental political organizations. In this case, the writer is referring to the Georgian nationalist group which led the Tbilisi demonstrations.

And finally, since we categorically refuse to train pogrom fighters and killers, we are petitioning that each of us be demoted from reserve officer to the rank of private.

Former military leader
Senior Lieutenant (Reserves) Ya. M. ZOLOTAREVSKY
Vorkuta, Komi ASSR

Former military leader
Lieutenant (Reserves) V. O. VASILIEV
Vorkuta, Komi ASSR
October 20, 1989
Unpublished

Early in 1988, Christian ethnic Armenians living in Nagorno-Karabakh, a predominantly Armenian autonomous oblast *located totally within the borders of Muslim Azerbaijan, began demonstrating for their republic's "reunification" with Armenia. Yerevan, the capital of Armenia, was also the scene of huge demonstrations in favor of reunification.*

The Azerbaijani response to this display of nationalism was quick and decisive. On February 28, mobs of Azerbaijanis, allegedly reacting to rumors of Armenian violence against their kinfolk during the demonstrations in Nagorno-Karabakh, rampaged through the Azerbaijani city of Sumgait, reportedly beating, raping or killing virtually every member of the city's minority Armenian population whom they encountered. The Soviet government eventually announced a death toll of thirty-two, but Armenian nationalists maintained that the real figure was well over three hundred, and accused the government and national press of being "criminally quiet" about the incident.

As the Soviet Central Committee debated the issue of reunification—finally voting not to permit it—the ethnic strife between Armenians and Azerbaijanis continued to escalate. Thousands of refugees streamed out of the Caucasus region; strikes spread in Nagorno-Karabakh and in Armenia itself; the Azerbaijanis instituted a blockade of food and materials slated to pass through their republic on their way to Nagorno-Karabakh and Armenia; reports of "pogroms" against Armenians—most notably in the Azerbaijanian capital of Baku—proliferated; the number of violent incidents along the border of the two republics grew rapidly; and Armenians began to take up arms in "forced self-defense." Finally, as 1989 drew to a close, Armenia and Azerbaijan stood at the brink of civil war.

STOP THE GENOCIDE!

The cover-up of and the distortion of the true history of the Armenian and Azerbaijani people artificially created the political situation for the genocide of the Armenian people—between 1905 and 1920,[1] and in 1988.

The Armenian population in Nagorno-Karabakh was threatened with "bloodless" genocide.[2] They did not give in and were subjected to a blockade that went on longer than the one in Leningrad. And now the entire Armenian people is being threatened with "bloody" genocide because the Azerbaijanis are attacking Armenia. There have already been victims.

The impunity of the organizers of the Sumgait genocide has led to total anarchy. All of this is incompatible with the idea of a state ruled by law, and one on the eve of the twenty-first century at that. I submit that the state should not be interested in destroying the Armenian people, and their forced self-defense should not be equated with the actions of their attackers.

Ida A. BABAYAN
Candidate in art history
Yerevan
September 4, 1989
Unpublished

---

[1] A few highlights of this "true history":

Between 1893 and 1920 there was a continuing wave of massacres of the Armenians by the Turks which, in the words of one historian, seemed nothing short of a "systematic plan for the elimination of the entire Armenian race." In 1915, for example, the Turks, in an effort to keep the Armenians from aiding the Russian Army during World War I, drove the majority of the Armenian population into the Arabian desert. As many as half a million of them died.

In March 1918, a few months after the Bolshevik Revolution in Russia, the Red Army used Armenian fighters in a successful assault on the oil port of Baku; thousands of Azerbaijanis were killed. The Turkic-speaking Azerbaijanis, fighting to retain their independence from the Bolsheviks, then struck an alliance with the same Turkish government which had been routinely massacring the Armenians. But, in 1920, the Bolsheviks reached their *own* agreement with Turkey, thereby removing the last obstacle to the Soviet annexation of Azerbaijan. A few months later, Armenia, weakened still further by yet another mauling at the hands of the Turks, also capitulated to a Communist ultimatum.

[2] i.e., the repression of their language, culture and religion.

STOP THE PROVOCATIONS!

AN OPEN LETTER TO VITALY ALEKSEYEVICH KOROTICH,
EDITOR IN CHIEF OF OGONYOK

Dear Vitaly Alekseyevich:

The multinational collective of workers in a Baku shoe factory warmly congratulate you on being elected as a People's Deputy of the USSR.

Vitaly Alekseyevich, all of our people have been following the events going on in and around the Nagorno-Karabakh Autonomous *Oblast* (NKAO) with great concern and worry. We were prompted to write to you by A. Golovkov's article in *Ogonyok* (issue no. 18), entitled "A Special Area."

We were puzzled and disappointed by this article. The more you read, the more inaccuracies, vagueness, unverified rumors and assumptions you find there—all stated as obvious fact.

A. Golovkov was not in Baku last winter, or he would have seen that by no means did a "throng of several thousand go wild under the green flags of Islam." More than 500,000 people of various nationalities and, incidentally, religions gathered every day on the square during that period. People talked about what was troubling them, and the agenda included not only the Karabakh question, but also the environment, the preservation of the language, the restoration of ancient monuments and, many other sore points. The flags of the Soviet Union and the Azerbaijani republic and many, many posters with Lenin's portrait fluttered in the square. Yes, there were some religious flags. After all, religious believers had something to say about all these problems, too. But to infer from this fact that the real, underlying cause of the conflict was religious is laughable and absurd.

Who needs that kind of so-called truth?

If A. Golovkov wanted to stir the reader's imagination with something unusual, he should have dug into the facts, instead of relying on everyday fabrications. And the facts are these: that the demonstrations in Yerevan—which the author shamefully fails to mention—flags of the Soviet Union were trampled underfoot, people called for bloodshed and Party and Komsomol cards were burned. And if you ask whether any individuals have been held responsible for this, you won't find an answer anywhere. Apparently, *that* truth is not for us. . . .

And incidentally, since we are saying that we need the truth, let's finally tell the truth about Sumgait, too. It is perfectly true that the tragedy of Sumgait is the tragedy of the entire Soviet people. And since the newspaper *Sovetsky Karabakh* is saying that we should put to shame the people who organized the mass killings in that city, let's just ask ourselves, well, who? Who has even once mentioned in the press that before the tragic events in Sumgait, the militant Armenians were collecting money from the Armenian population of the city? After all, that isn't a secret even to us. And everybody knows that the militants then advised the Armenians to take their deposits out of the savings banks, and that they also told the rich Armenian "underworld businessmen" to leave the city. What else can this mean, but that a provocation was being planned? Yes, the Sumgait tragedy was very carefully planned by Armenian nationalists.

Several hours before the tragedy, Armenian photo correspondents secretly got inside the city. The first criminal act was committed by a certain Grigoryan who, under the guise of being an Azerbaijani, who personally murdered five Sumgait Armenians. And after that, the huge crowd could not be stopped. And the next—the *next!*—day in Stepanakert[1] they were already raising an obelisk to the "victims of the Sumgait genocide." So, maybe we should open our eyes to the truth, no matter how bitter it is? Or is that truth not to someone's advantage?

What does the summer of 1989 have in store for us? Another "war of strikes"? And what if someone somewhere again deliberately prepares a provocation? Then the nationalist hatred will rise to new heights. And again blood will be shed, and women and children will suffer. Maybe it's better to stop all of that right now, when events have not yet gathered steam?

> [Hundreds of signatures]
> Baku
> Received by *Ogonyok* June 1989
> Unpublished

---

[1] The capital of Nagorno-Karabakh.

A TELEGRAM FROM DZHERMUK

TELEGRAM

To: V. A. Korotich, Editor in Chief, *Ogonyok* magazine

We are the workers of the Dzhermukstroy Construction Trust of the Armenian Republic. On September 17, the television program "Vremya"[1] broadcast an interview by Central Television correspondent Zubkov with the First Secretary of the Communist Party of Azerbaijan, T. Bezirov. The First Secretary told the entire Soviet people, hand on heart, about the brotherhood and good will of the Azerbaijani leadership toward the Armenian people. Eighty-seven percent of the shipments to Armenia come through Azerbaijan, but for the past two months now Armenia and the Nagorno-Karabakh Autonomous *Oblast* have not received a single railroad car of goods, and the goods that arrived before that had been pilfered or broken and arrived in unusable form. Is aggression in the form of a two-month economic blockade brotherhood? Is it good will that construction sites are idle because of the lack of construction materials? If there is no fuel to transport a woman in labor to the hospital or bread to a kindergarten, is that brotherhood in the opinion of the First Secretary?

The print media writes and television talks about chaos and the work stoppage in Armenia. But who is responsible for this situation? Not a word about that, in the end. Whom can we turn to for faith and help? So far, we trust your magazine. Perhaps one of your correspondents could personally witness the "sincerity" of the Azerbaijani leadership's statements by coming to Armenia personally and seeing all of this with his own eyes.

Council of the Workers' Collective,
Dzhermukstroy Construction Trust
Dzhermuk, Armenian SSR
September 19, 1989
Unpublished

[1] "Vremya" is Soviet Central Television's nightly news program, broadcast every evening at nine o'clock.

FOR NOW, THINGS ARE QUIET . . .

In Baku, Armenians continue to be persecuted. They are being fired from their jobs, beaten up, chased out of the republic and out of the city. Along the way, the storm troopers who call themselves the "Popular Front" are beating up Jews, Russians and even Azerbaijanis themselves. They are attacking girls who, in their opinion, must wear "modest" skirts (even in summer), not sleeveless dresses.

The beatings take place on the streets and in the marketplace. An ultimatum drove the Armenians out of the Apsheron spa clinics. For now, as the fascists say, just the Armenians. At a meeting Musavat[1] flags were raised. Half a century has passed, and the crimes of the Musavat have been forgotten. Young kids with wild eyes don't know history and idealize Azerbaijan's dark past. And they are encouraged and helped by "intellectuals." At the train station there are inflammatory posters. And at the session of the Supreme Soviet of the Azerbaijan SSR, Secretary of the Central Committee Vezirov made some kind of behind-the-scenes deal with "functionaries" from the notorious Popular Front. This "organization" has only Azerbaijanis in it, although traditionally people of many nationalities have lived in Baku, and they are now completely unprotected against sudden attacks, displacement and dismissal. Traditionally, any firing of a person is very well documented, but now the document doesn't say who quit and who was "asked" to leave while he was still in one piece. If the director of an institution says that he can't guarantee your safety or even your life if you don't leave, well, you can imagine, that is genuine terror—apartheid.

Find the people who have moved to Moscow from Baku. They are already safe. They will tell you everything. Local residents will lie because our lives, especially the lives of our children and families, will not be worth a thing if we tell the truth.

All the residents of Baku agree that Nagorno-Karabakh should stay in Azerbaijan. But still, non-Azerbaijanis are being persecuted. They feel uncertain about tomorrow. For now, things are quiet, but there's no guarantee that tomorrow everything won't change. We've seen it before. Roughnecks are taking advantage of the fact that Armenians were insulted at the Congress and called murderers (of

---

[1] The Musavats were pan-Islamic activists opposed to the Bolshevik Revolution.

murderers!). Now the Army is staying out of it—and these rough-necks are getting bolder by the day.

For God's sake, please help us. Let the central government bang its fist on the table. You can't just put bandits like this in the corner for being naughty. They have to be put in jail or shot. Has Moscow betrayed us internationalists? We are Azerbaijanis, Armenians, Russians and many others who live in Baku.

If the Army (you can't depend on the Baku Ministry of Internal Affairs) and Moscow have stepped out of it, then we will be forced to take up arms ourselves. And the entire responsibility will be on Moscow's shoulders. What are we supposed to do if the state has rejected us? We don't want that. That will obviously mean more victims.

Please, Muscovites, fellow countrymen, help us.

> The residents of Baku
> October 6, 1989
> Unpublished

GET THE RUSSIANS!

For almost two years now we've been living in constant fear for our lives and the lives of our children and grandchildren. We are Russians living in the capital of Azerbaijan, Baku. We're very tired of the situation in the republic, where two once-brotherly peoples are now enemies to the death. There are two in this fight, but apparently a third is to blame. The third one, of course, is the Russians. And how! When someone has to help, get the Russians; when something has to be built somewhere, get the Russians; when someone needs to be taught something, get the Russians. But as soon as you need a culprit, get the Russians again. That's why the most dumped-on, insulted people is we—the Russians.

There are two in this fight—but a third one is dying. It's so painful to read in the newspapers about the deaths of Russian boys on Armenian and Azerbaijani soil. I don't think you would like having to bury your own child killed by those hands. I'm sure you have never been made to feel like a second-class citizen, where at every turn you hear, "Go back to that Russia of yours!" We'll be glad to go back to our homeland, where our roots are, where from morning till night we can hear our native Russian language. Right now the refugees are Armenians and Azerbaijanis. But when the Russians' turn comes, who'll take us? Who'll protect us? Russia is enormous; is there really no corner where we can settle? They don't want us here on Azerbaijani soil. We're useless here. Everywhere you go, it's the "oppression by the Russians." Do you think it's nice to hear words like "We'll kick out those Armenians, and then we'll go after the Russians?"

We're afraid to go out into the city, where they might ask us for our passport. We're afraid to walk down the street after seven at night because the worst things could happen to any one of us.

We Russians want to live and work in peace. How many Russian men are we going to lose? Why do they, our children, have to use their bodies to stop wild crowds? And who cares? In Armenia and Georgia there have been nationwide funeral marches, but the Russian victims are ignored; after all, they're the "occupiers"!

We are tired; why isn't anything being done "up there" to stop all this? Enough victims and blood! It's time to move from lofty words to action.

We Russians are asking the Soviet Federation for political asylum in Russia so that we, the Russians in Azerbaijan, can resettle in Russian cities, where we can peacefully raise—and not lose—our children, live a normal, full-fledged life, and die a natural death.

The Azerbaijanis are chasing us out. Why should they live calmly in Russia? Look how many of them have settled all over Moscow!

From the rostrums they're calling two hostile people to reconciliation, but that call goes unheard.

Russians! Unite and help us who live outside Russia!

If they don't want us anywhere and are chasing us out, we'll come back to Russia!

[Twenty-five signatures]
Baku
October 18, 1989
Unpublished

THE ENEMY WITHIN

Our M. Gorbachev, as a political leader, enjoys great popularity in the international arena. That's all very well, but meanwhile, within our country, such unbelievable events have occurred that it simply breaks my heart. I would like to touch upon just one such event. Yesterday, the second of January, on the informational television program "Vremya" ["Time"], everyone heard about what had taken place from the thirty-first of December to the second of January on the border between Azerbaijan and Iran, in the region called Na-khichevan.

This border holds a special significance for the mothers who are sending their sons there to defend our country. They pray constantly that on the border there will be peace, quiet and seren-ity. They foresee danger, it stands to reason, not from their own countrymen, but from enemies across the border.

And yet, what happened? Hooligan thugs, young people, openly attacked the border guards—our children—and their com-manders, attacked the families of the commanders, and brought upon our country a tangible outrage. It's clear that these hooligans did not expect to be punished. There are no words to describe this incident.

As the mother of a border guard and as a citizen of the USSR, I decided, through the forum of the journal *Ogonyok,* which is so respected in our country, to ask our President, esteemed Mikhail Sergeyevich, to apply his political wisdom and learning and deci-siveness to the question of maintaining order, specifically, *within* our country. It's shameful to have disorder within the country in front of the whole world.

My son is serving in Astar. He is in the border guard station no. 17, and he's been there a year already. Twice I have gone there, to Azerbaijan. I should add that each time, I went there at the exact moment when there were strikes and disorder, when extremists were especially vicious. They were smashing windows in the trains; they were overturning buses. I went there then ready for anything. No force could have kept me away—I went there precisely because there was such disorder there, and my son was in the middle of it.

But I was, in the full sense of the words, "warmly welcomed" by the well-meaning, honest, frank attitude and the hospitality of simple Azerbaijanis. Not one menacing look or nasty remark was directed at me. Far from it! A completely unknown Azerbaijani woman who spoke very little Russian tried to strike up a conversation with me on a bus. She treated me to some cottage cheese and snacks she had with her. And in Astar, when I was standing at the brink of all the strife, an old Azerbaijani man welcomed me very warmly into his home for a cup of tea and sat with me. This is the true face of the simple working people. And yet, these hooligan thugs are everywhere, and it is not out of the question that another incident like this will take place along the Soviet–Iran border.

It's very frightening for me to imagine that the extremists even fell upon border guard station no. 17, where ideal order, discipline and a reverence for a soldier's duty reign supreme. And it's even *more* frightening to imagine that my son, in the line of duty, might be called upon to shoot at one of his own countrymen—at the son of a mother just like me! What could be more cruel?

I understand the great importance of our President's international standing. But, as a mother, I plead with him to undertake the unavoidable task of restoring order along the Nakhichevan border. In peacetime, we do not want to lose our sons to the hands of warlike hooligan thugs. Please help me. Can you even *hear* me?!?

Nelli Ivanovna NIKITENKO
Nalchik, Kabardian Autonomous SSR
January 3, 1990
Unpublished

On January 9, 1990, the Armenian parliament passed a law permitting residents of Nagorno-Karabakh to vote in Armenian elections. On the tenth, the Presidium of the Supreme Soviet declared this law unconstitutional. On the eleventh, the Armenian legislators voted themselves the right to override national laws that affected the republic, including the Presidium's ruling of the day before.

This proved too much for some Azerbaijanis. On the eleventh and twelfth, they barricaded off the Communist Party offices in Baku and seized the local radio station. Then, the next night, extremist mobs went on a bloody rampage through Armenian sections of the city, beating, stabbing and shooting the residents and burning their homes and shops.

Meanwhile, both Armenian and Azerbaijani "volunteer" groups were raiding Soviet military supply depots, arming themselves with automatic rifles, grenades and—some said—even helicopters. Reports also circulated that, with the Nakhichevan border stations in ruins after the December 31–January 2 rioting, Iranians were now openly supplying Azerbaijani extremists with weapons from across their common border.

Against this background, President Gorbachev finally acted. Dismissing as "rabble" the growing chorus of conservatives who blamed everything on perestroika, he signed a decree on January 15 sending 11,000 Soviet troops to the Transcaucasus region to restore the peace. Using tanks and armored personnel carriers to smash through Azerbaijani barricades, artillery to shell oil tankers that had been seized by the rebels to blockade the Baku harbor, and masses of troops to reseal the Nakhichevan border, the Soviets finally imposed an uneasy calm. Scores of demonstrators, soldiers and civilians lay dead.

WHAT KIND OF FREEDOM
DO WE NEED?
An Afterword by Olzhas Suleimenov

The first Congress of People's Deputies took place on the crest of a wave raised in society by a drawn-out electoral campaign, and in the heated atmosphere of clashes between nationalities in Azerbaijan, Nagorno-Karabakh and Fergana, and growing unrest in Moldavia, Georgia and the Baltic republics. . . .

The situation itself somehow ordained the basic subject for the first Congress: DECOLONIZATION.

It was not noted on the official agenda, but it was present in nearly every speech by the Deputies from the republics.

No revolution has ever been guided by carefully considered scientific theory, and that includes the Leninist one. Marx's theories for constructing socialism did not fit Russia. According to Marx, socialism was capitalism's highest stage of development. But in Russia, where capitalism had just been born, the situation was not ripe. The result: tens of millions of lives lost, the destruction of entire peoples. In this situation, could the nationalities question— which, besides tact, requires deep analysis of conflicts and problems that have been simmering for centuries—be solved properly? It was easier for the state to suppress "nationalist" phenomena: adherence to national traditions and love for one's native language.

What is to be done now? The issues of the nationalities and the economy will be the key factors in determining the contents of the current period of our history. But we cannot ignore the decolonization experience other countries have had. All national liberation movements have made independence their final goal. But why did independence not make the people in the liberated countries completely happy? The euphoria of long-awaited freedom passed quickly, and masses of new problems arose, which in turn led to bloody power struggles, civil wars and interethnic strife. The reaction of shatteringly swift decay releases shattering energy. "Freedom is no benefit"—what could be more blasphemous than this paradox? But real history forces one to consider at least the possibility . . . .

At one of the UN conferences in Geneva I proposed for discussion a formula for a national liberation movement, wherein independence was regarded not as the final goal, but as a transition stage from centuries of colonial DEPENDENCE through a period of INDEPENDENCE into an era of conscious INTERDEPENDENCE.

But can there be a full-fledged period of independence in a still-united federation? Today we are looking for an answer to precisely that question.

The second Congress has ended, but the optimal road has not yet been found. The issue is too complex. The national movements in the Baltic republics, Nagorno-Karabakh, Central Asia and the Transcaucasus are consistently growing. That may be the only thing they have in common. In everything else, because of differences in religion, ideology, level of economic development, and racial and ethnic affiliations, there is little that is similar. Every nation is striving for its own model of independence which arises out of its own conception of happiness for its people.

But now one thing is clear—for better or for worse: every nation wants to find out who it is. And to do that it wants to live for a certain period of time on its own. There are probably no officials now who would call for complete, permanent isolation from the world. They want to go toward unification—through separation.

The dangers of the course of events connected with peoples' efforts to achieve genuine independence through bloodshed are all too obvious to us. We need careful consideration and caution. Reckless radicalism is more dangerous in our circumstances than, let us say, in East Germany. We are beginning to understand that a multifaceted national power, with no experience at democratization and where destructive forces are already beginning to predominate, is reminiscent of a fuel depot, where it is very dangerous to light the

torch of freedom to point out the holes in the storage tanks! First
ventilate the place, open all the doors and make some windows.
And open a few of those windows out into the world!

Olzhas SULEIMENOV
Poet, first secretary of the Union of Writers of Kazakhstan
Member of the Supreme Soviet of the USSR
Member of the Interregional Group of
    People's Deputies of the USSR

THE LESSONS
OF HISTORY

Ogonyok.

WRITE THE TRUTH!

I would like to declare my love for you, comrade journalists, and to *Ogonyok,* which has become so interesting from cover to cover. Personally, I find the most striking pages are the ones where you publish letters from readers and material about historical subjects.

I don't agree with those readers who demand that the difficult subject of the thirties be "closed" and that you write only about our victories. Apparently, they are living by inertia. Living the modern way means writing the truth. I was born in 1953 and grew up in the countryside. When I read today's *Ogonyok* I never cease to be amazed at how little I know my own history. You probably read a confession like this in practically every other letter. This is what is surprising: articles and books abound about some kingdom across the seas—whole centuries lie before us; but we write the story of the country in which we live and work in such a way that no one wants to read it, and we forget about folk heroes, events and tragedies along the way. And if one book reveals some interesting facts, in the next "updated" edition they are gone.

For example, take the three volumes of works by M. A. Suslov.[1] It is a very interesting collection, but you won't find his speech at the February Plenum of the Central Committee of the CPSU in 1964, in which he spoke about the Cult of Personality. And there are lots of such examples. I think that the revelations about the Cult of Personality have recently been stopped by people who themselves helped create it, and who have stayed in power for many years.

In our village library—with great difficulty—I managed to find the materials of the Twentieth, Twenty-first and Twenty-second Party Congresses.[2] Reading them I found answers to a lot of questions. And once again I was convinced that, yes, we have to

[1] For years the Communist Party's chief ideologist, Suslov was a leading Politburo member under Khrushchev and Brezhnev. Suslov is rumored to have been the principal architect of the overthrow of Khrushchev in 1964.

[2] The Twentieth Party Congress, held in February 1956, was the one in which Nikita Khrushchev made his "secret speech," itemizing many of Stalin's "crimes," and condemning him for having established "a Cult of Personality."

write about Dneproges and Magnitka,[3] but we can't *not* write about the fear of thousands of people waiting for the doorbell to ring in the middle of the night. These things are part of our heritage, as is the history we are making today. And if we are not "cogs," but "knights of *perestroika*," as the journalists say, then we must know who it is that is putting sticks in the spokes of our wheels, who is putting the brakes on the process of democratization.

I won't bore you with my examples and opinions. I will only say that it is *Ogonyok* itself that forced us to look at life more broadly and brought out the urgent need for us to participate in the social reconstruction of our society.

N. I. KRASNOBORODKO
Village of Chersky, Yakut ASSR
Published January 1988

"GOOSEBUMPS"

I am a constant *Ogonyok* reader. But recently I've gotten very upset by your publication of the ill-considered opinions of your readers, especially when they speak about Stalin.

After all, people like Stalin are needed for today's *perestroika*. He used to hand out harsh punishment for violations and crimes against society. And he was quite right to do so. That is what is needed. So much is going on in our country today: more and more violations and crimes, including even prostitution and drug abuse. And zero attention is being paid to it. Under Stalin there was none of that.

It would be interesting to know, why do people today rail so against Stalin? My answer is that the very mention of his name gives people goosebumps. Answer me this, please: would Joseph Stalin have allowed a nineteen-year-old boy to land his airplane here on Red Square? Never! Not for anything in the world!

---

[3] Dneproges and Magnitka were major Soviet construction projects.

The extent of the respect people have for Stalin is also clear from the fact that most of the citizens of the Soviet Union are carefully preserving portraits of him. Meanwhile, the portraits of other former leaders lie around any old place. Doesn't that show the people's love for Stalin?

K. G. MALLAKURBANOV
Teacher of Russian and literature
Village of Lyakhlya, Dagestan ASSR
Published December 1987

THE FAMINE OF 1933

Today's generation should know the truth about what their fathers and grandfathers went through. But people now are either ashamed and silent about many things in history, or they talk about them only in passing. Take the famine of 1933, for example. I cannot remember it without shuddering. That summer I was still a young boy, and I had to lead the half-dead cows that were still left out to pasture. In the meadow I would collect clover, dry it and crush it into a powder. My mother would mix the clover "flour" with buckwheat chaff and that is what we would eat, along with a nettle gruel. To the end of my days I will never forget the eyes of the people who were dying of starvation.

When I grew up, I started to ask myself, how could it be that Lenin (his death was my first strong childhood memory) was able to feed the people very quickly after the Civil War, with all its destruction, but only a few years later wholesale death fell upon our land? I remember very clearly that there were no natural disasters then.

The writer M. Alekseyev, in his short story "The Ruffians," drew chilling pictures of the famine in the Saratov *oblast*. The people were so exhausted that they did not even have the strength to bury the dead. He described very well what I myself witnessed. The writer was at a loss for any kind of convincing explanation of this and said frankly that he was trying to understand the reasons for this famine.

I am trying to do the same thing. Was the famine a fatal inevitability, or was it someone's fault and could it have been avoided? As far as I know, no one has even attempted to give a comprehensive answer to this question. Keeping silent about it is, at the very least, immoral. After all, in terms of the number of victims of Stalin's repressions, the year 1933 exceeds others.

M. E. GALUSHKO
Sumy, Ukrainian SSR
Published January 1988

Mr. Galushko's letter is a graphic illustration how little had actually been publicly written or said—even as late as the beginning of 1988— about the famine of 1933 in the Ukraine, and the degree of Stalin's responsibility for it. Only in March 1989, in a major article in Pravda *by historian V. P. Danilov and economist N. V. Teptsov, did an organ of the Party admit that the famine had actually been instigated by Stalin in order to force the collectivization of the region's farmland, and to break Ukrainian nationalism. At least three million, and possibly as many as thirteen million, Ukrainians died, many because they were forcibly prevented from leaving the hunger zone. Danilov and Teptsov called the famine "the most terrible of the crimes committed by Stalin and his group."*

SONGS OF "OUR HAPPY CHILDHOOD"

After the Civil War, my father actively participated in the consolidation of Soviet power in our village. He was an organizer and the first head of the collective farm in the village of Sukhoe-Solotino in the Ivnyansky region of the Kursk *oblast*. At the end of 1932 or in early 1933 (I don't remember exactly) he was arrested after a false accusation. Soon they came for us, too. I remember very well that cold winter day (I was seven then) when two carts came for us with two guards. We were all put on them in what we were wearing and taken to the town of Oboyan, thirty miles from the village. Counting mother, there were seven of us, but they took only five (my youngest brother was three then, my oldest sister eleven). . . . Along the way people threw things on the carts for us—either a worn jacket or an old blanket—and mother would cover us from the cold. In Oboyan late at night we were put in the church, where there were already a lot of us "enemies of the people." The next day we were loaded into railroad cars with the "bourgeois." Each car received one metal can for our natural needs, and we were taken north.

I don't know how many people were in each car, but I remember that we slept in turns. We traveled for a whole month. The guards opened the car doors only according to schedule, when it was time to empty the toilet buckets. Women cried, begging the guards to permit the buckets to be taken more often, because the children were suffocating. But their entreaties were fruitless— the schedule was kept unerringly.

They brought us to the White Sea–Baltic Sea Canal and housed us in barracks. Then in the woods they built the Karb Lake camp, Medvezhegorsk region, which was guarded by a military garrison. Each family, no matter how many children there were, was given one room. Our whole family, for example, slept on the floor, summer and winter. In the winter the stove was going round the clock. We didn't economize on wood, because the forest was right next door and that was our only salvation from the cold. But in the summer we didn't sleep at night. The bugs and cockroaches took over. There was no escaping them. And considering that we, like many other children, would often lie for weeks hungry and swollen without moving, we just didn't feel the bites. Everyone over fourteen years old worked chopping trees into logs. . . .

The camp village also had an elementary school, where people from the old intelligentsia taught. They had been sent into exile along with us and shared our plight and our deprivation. They also got sick, went hungry and died. All the children (who could move) went to school since the parents believed that someday this nightmare would end and a new time would come. And so, they thought, it doesn't matter how hard it is—the children must not miss class; they must study. The only thing we were afraid of was going to class in the second shift. Most of the children suffered from night blindness, and in the evening, after classes, we could not get to our houses alone, because there were stumps, branches and snow everywhere, and injuries were unavoidable. To solve this problem, parents would have to go out into the street in the evening after classes and scream their children's names at the top of their lungs— all the while not going too far from their homes, because many of *them* couldn't see anything either. And so, orienting ourselves by our family's voices, we could get home. Whoever did not have someone to call him or her would wander around the camp village for a long time until someone who could see would hear their cry and take them home.

That was how we grew up. And in singing class, every time, we sang songs about Stalin, Voroshilov, Budenny and about our happy childhood.

V. J. BULGAKOV
Kharkov
Received by *Ogonyok* Spring 1989
Unpublished

"BY SOME MIRACLE, I STAYED ALIVE . . ."

In 1942 I was arrested on a false denunciation. At that time, there were no courts, just punitive agencies. There were exhausting interrogations and tortures, and then I was given my sentence: five years' imprisonment without the right of correspondence, according to Article 58, for being an "enemy of the people." I was sent to the Narovchat[1] prison. From there, three hundred of us political prisoners were hauled off to the city of Saransk to build an airfield. Our grave had already been prepared for us—a ditch about two meters deep. There were bunks in the ditch covered with straw, and a straw roof, no windows, no walls. And, in November 1942,

---

[1] A city near Penza, in the middle Volga area of the Russian Republic.

we were shoved into that pit and forbidden to come out. The roof started to burn, and then the people. I didn't want to die, and with six other women, I managed to crawl out of the fire. We were left with enormous burns. The city hospital didn't want to admit us political prisoners, so we were put in another place with no medical facilities. No one gave us first aid. A doctor who was also a political prisoner came in, told us he had no medical instruments, and cut off the burns with a razor blade, and that was the end of the entire treatment. By some miracle, I stayed alive, even though the burns covered two thirds of my body.

In March 1943, the Penza *oblast* court vindicated us, and an NKVD[2] man came up to me and warned me that if I ever talked about that fire, I would be destroyed without a trace. All my life I have lived in fear, but now my life is coming to an end, and I'm not afraid of anything anymore.

In 1979 I started to write inquiries to find out the truth about that tragedy, but over and over again I received official denials. Finally, after an inquiry made to the Procurator's Office of the RSFSR[3] on April 13, 1989, I was told that, yes, there had been a fire and that the culprits had been found. But to this day, they will not issue a list of the victims.

I propose that the site of the tragedy be made into a common grave for the victims of Stalinism. After all, women, young mothers and young girls were burned to death in that pit.

A. KOSINOVA (Podboronova)
Aleksin, Tula *oblast*
Published October 1989

[2] The Soviet secret police were known as the NKVD from 1935 until 1943, when the agency was split into two commissariats and renamed the MGB. In 1954, the KGB was separated out from the MGB.

[3] The abbreviation for the Russian Soviet Federated Socialist Republic, the largest constituent republic of the Soviet Union.

AN "INNOCENT EXTINGUISHED LIFE"

In the spring of 1989, a mother and daughter wrote a joint letter to Ogonyok *in which each of them recalled their family's experiences during the Stalinist repressions.*

I consider it my duty to the holy memory of my father to enter his name, Friedrich Karlovich Gesse (born 1894, a Saint Petersburg German by nationality, by profession an assistant professor, head of the Foreign Languages Department of the Agricultural Academy in Pushkin) into the millions-long list of innocent extinguished lives.

On February 26, 1938, my birthday (I was one year old) evil people broke into our house and took away my father, a forty-three-year-old man in the best of health and happiness—forever.

My mother, Serafima Pavlovna Sokolova, born in 1905, is a remarkable person for her strength of spirit, courage, love of life and her happy, optimistic nature. . . . After working two shifts at the Lenmetrostroy night school, she would sit down in the evenings at the piano and always said, "Now, girls, my private life starts." And her pleasant voice began to sing, her fingers gliding along the keys; we would fall asleep to the sounds of old Russian romantic songs. She would often say, "Sing what your father loved, learn it, sing and remember!"

I. F. GESSE-TATEOSOVA
Leningrad

Against the background [of Stalinist terror], my husband, Friedrich Karlovich Gesse, was an honest man, physically and spiritually pure. . . . He loved to ski and ride a bicycle. In the forest he could distinguish with a hunter's eye all the nuances of the world around him. He loved to ride to the villages in the Russian hinterland, to the Valdai plateau. There we would marvel at the wonderful forests and lakes, since ruined during the recent years of "stagnation. . . ." Looking at the clear blue sky and following the airplanes, he was sorry that he didn't become a pilot. What attracted him to that profession was the freedom of movement, the possibility of seeing the entire earth from above. He loved my older daughters as his own, bought them presents, worried about their shoes, clothing— something that always touched me. And how joyous he was at the birth of his only daughter, Inga. In premonitions of the coming tragedy (arrests were taking place everywhere), he would say that he probably would not see his daughter as an adult.

That horrible evening of February 26, 1938, three men came from the "Grey House." Among them was a middle-aged military officer, a colonel. The interrogation was long; the search took all night. They took all our valuables (his father's gold watch, ring, etc.). They sealed the room, filled with books collected over a lifetime, and confiscated a valuable library of art books.

They took him away on the morning of February 27, 1938—as it turned out, forever. For many years I did not believe that I would never see him again. What saved me in those years was my maiden name, Sokolova, and nationality. Apparently someone did have pity on a mother of three; I was not arrested.

In the 1940s the procurator of the Dzerzhinsky region summoned me to his office on Belinsky street. He gently urged me to start my own life anew, get remarried, since Friedrich was supposedly never going to come back to Leningrad. Now I understand that he knew about Friedrich's execution, and I am grateful to this young man with the dark eyes for his concern about me and his pity, because at that time it was a remarkable thing.

During those years I never even dreamed Friedrich could be dead, but dreamt about going to see him at the first opportunity. The books and things, everything that reminded me of him, were confiscated (it required a three-ton truck). The sentence, according to Article 58, was ten years without rights of correspondence, and I did not believe the certificate of death in the camps. I always hoped that my husband would come home.

Serafima Pavlovna SOKOLOVA
Leningrad
Received by *Ogonyok* Spring 1989
Unpublished

THE "MEMORIAL" SOCIETY

Recently in Moscow, and in other cities around the country, there has been broad development of a public movement to honor the memory of the victims of Stalin's repressions.

One result of this movement has been the formation of the "Memorial" society. This society sees as its main objective the establishment—through volunteer contributions—of a monument to the victims of Stalinism, and also of a "Memorial" information, research and educational center, housing a museum, archives and library open to all.

To receive legal status, according to the existing regulations, the voluntary historical educational society "Memorial" must be sponsored by "founding organizations."

We hereby request that the editors consider the possibility of the participation of the magazine *Ogonyok* in the work of the "Memorial" society, as one of its founding sponsors.

> Ya. Ya. ETINGER, doctor of history
> L. A. PONOMARYOV, doctor in physical and
> mathematical sciences
> Yu. V. SAMODUROV, candidate in geological
> and mineralogical sciences
> and A. S. TOKAREV
> Members of the Initiative Group to Found the
> Voluntary Historical and Educational Society
> "Memorial"
> Published August 1988

Ogonyok's reply: The editors and the staff of *Ogonyok* support the proposal of these scholars. *Ogonyok,* together with the Union of Architects of the USSR, The Union of Cinematographers of the USSR and The Union of Theater Performers of the USSR, will become one of the founding sponsors of the National Voluntary Historical and Educational Society "Memorial," whose objective is to honor the memory of the victims of Stalinism.

We should like to inform our readers that a bank account has been opened to collect funds for the construction in Moscow of a monument to the victims of Stalinism. The account number is 700454. Any individual or organization may make voluntary contributions to this account at any district branch of Zhilsotsbank [Housing Security Bank], Promstroibank [Industrial Construction Bank] or Agrobank [Agricultural Bank], or at any branch of the Savings Bank of the USSR.

The editors and staff of Ogonyok
August 1988

DON'T USE MY MONEY TO FAN HATRED FOR STALIN!

I read in *Ogonyok* no. 12 of this year a letter from A. P. Alekhnovich and A. S. Leikin, from Byelorussia, who proposed using money from subscribers to *Ogonyok* magazine "to build a memorial to the victims of Stalinism." I am one of *Ogonyok*'s subscribers and am against having even a kopeck of my money go to the construction of a "memorial to the victims of Stalinism." I think fanning hatred for Stalin is harmful and unfair.

We are being frightened with reports of "partridge hunts" (mass shootings of completely innocent people)—and it is being called the "Stalin terror." But it was NOT Stalin who called the shootings "a method of making a Communist humanity out of the human material of the capitalist era." It was NOT Stalin who said that "the *kulak*[1] . . . understands only the language of lead" (*Literaturnaya Gazeta,* March 8 of this year, page 2). And those who did propound such ideas were also not sadists or bloodthirsty. These remarks merely illustrate the boiling point the social struggle had reached. Life itself in that society was enough to form such views.

---

[1] The *kulaks* were independent peasant small landholders whom Stalin, as part of his policy of forced collectivization, ordered "liquidated as a class." The result was massive repression, bloodshed and chaos.

And if someone thinks that the liberal bourgeoisie or General Denikin[2] would have guaranteed "Russia's freedom," let him not forget that it was none other than General Denikin's "good guys" who filled up wells with the bodies of Red Army soldiers who had been shot. And if Denikin had won, then the "liberal" bourgeoisie would have enjoyed their *own* "bloodbath," fomented by a White Guard Terror against the workers and peasants. And if we are going to play this game of "alternative versions of history," then if Stalin had not been the leader of our country, there would have been "partridge hunts" anyway, only there would have been no socialism.

It was the "Stalinist version of history"—and none other—that guaranteed the successful construction of a socialist society in one country[3] and a defense of that socialism once it had been built. Therefore, I propose using the money that A. P. Alekhnovich and A. S. Leikin talk about in their letter to build a monument to the Victory of the Soviet people, led by Joseph Stalin, in the Great Patriotic War.

Yuri Trofimovich LYSENKO[4]
20 March 1989
Unpublished

---

[2] A leading commander of the White Army during the Civil War following the Bolshevik Revolution.

[3] "Socialism in one country" was Stalin's principal slogan when he was competing for influence in the Party with Trotsky, who called for "world revolution."

[4] The son of Trofim D. Lysenko. In the late 1940s, the elder Lysenko, whom historian Donald W. Treadgold describes as a "poorly educated plant breeder," became the chief ideologist for Stalin's agricultural program. Lysenko, who believed that heredity is not based on genes and chromosomes, and that acquired characteristics can be passed on from generation to generation, imposed his views on Soviet genetics and agricultural policy. Biologists and agronomists who disagreed with him were arrested, and, in some cases, liquidated. Many feel that neither Soviet science nor agriculture has yet entirely recovered.

"REMEMBER THE LIVING"

From the lofty rostrum of the Nineteenth Party Conference we have heard words confirming the need to create a memorial in Moscow to the victims of the unfounded repressions of the 1930s to 1950s. I hope that, this time, the decision to build such a memorial will be followed through. Nevertheless, I think that while honoring the memory of those who died, we must remember those who are still alive, those who survived the Stalinist camps and lived to be rehabilitated.

Today the press often raises the question of how to react to officials who actively participated in carrying out the policy of repression and to the rank and file who implemented it. Some propose that they be held criminally responsible. It seems to me that, whatever decision the sides in the issue come to—I, incidentally, am not a supporter of severe measures—one thing is beyond dispute: the victims of the unfounded repressions who are still alive should have living conditions that are at the very least no worse than those of the people who carried out the repressions. It seems to me it would be absolutely fair if those who have suffered unjustly and have been fully rehabilitated were given rights equal to veterans of World War II.

I am not talking about some sort of compensation. How can one possibly compensate for the death of a family, the loss of friends and loved ones or ruined health? I am talking about something else. In normal living conditions we could have made incomparably greater contributions to society than we did when we lived in circumstances we did not choose.

I must cite an example from my own life. Before my arrest in 1937 and my subsequent conviction as the wife of a "traitor to the homeland," I had graduated from Leningrad State University in 1930 and worked as a history teacher. Between being released from prison in 1943 and my rehabilitation in 1956 I did not have the right to work in my profession.

I cannot guess what my life would have been like had the terrible tragedy that afflicted our country in 1937–1938 not occurred, had I not had to live through my husband's arrest and the subsequent disruption of my life; but, apart from any accidents of fate, I think I could have devoted myself wholeheartedly and completely to my beloved profession.

I am not to blame that I was never able to work in a school again and therefore never earned the pension benefits to which I would otherwise have been entitled.

My fate is far from the most pitiful. There are people who are in a worse material situation than I am.

The measures that will be taken in the great cause of rehabilitating the victims of the unfounded repressions of the 1930s to 1950s will be incomplete if they are limited to a tribute to the memory of the fallen, and pay no attention to the living.

N. G. POYGINA
Moscow
Published November 1988

A MONUMENT TO A MONSTER?

Go visit the majestic State Stalin Museum in the city of Gori, and the guides will tell you that Stalin's genius saved the country and the entire world from fascism and determined the fate of socialism, collectivization and industrialization. The museum on a daily basis brainwashes hundreds and hundreds of tourists. It is a monument to subjectivism and to the Cult of Personality. Here people are deliberately fed an abridged truth, lies mixed with nationalism. How many words of praise are uttered by the guides at Stalin's statue?! Handy craftsmen openly sell homemade photo albums and pictures of Stalin. The stores sell color portraits of the generalissimo. . . .

Isn't it time to stop this mockery of the memory of those who fell during the time of Stalin's cult? Why, in these days of *glasnost,* do we allow this degradation of truth in the State Museum of Stalin? I am not proposing that the guides for this museum of tragedy pass strict exams or that we seek their objectivity (they are not capable of it). I am simply proposing that the museum be closed. It is worse than any church whose goal is to keep believers in the dark.

In Gori, they tell legends of how the Georgians fought to keep Stalin's statue from being torn down, and they tell them with such emotion! No, I won't say that it should be torn down. But how can one look at that seventeen-meter-high statue of Stalin atop that triumphal building? At the solemn ceremony honoring the Seventieth Anniversary of the October Revolution, Mikhail Sergeyevich Gorbachev clearly said, "Stalin and those around him are to blame for the mass repressions which took place and these violations are enormous and unforgivable."

Therefore, we should look at this as a monument to a monster, to an executioner. Is this, in fact, the goal of any monument?

I. V. SOFRONII
Journalist
Benderi
Published January 1988

"I WANT TO LIVE IN THE SEA"

Greetings, Comrade Stalin!

Someone born in 1966 is writing to you. Who am I? I am a son of the Ingush[1] people, a son of the Soviet people. I am a tiny particle in a single, great community. However, above all, Comrade Stalin, I am a human being. I have my own personality, my own notions about the world, my own view of life.

I want to ask you some questions, and please try to answer them.

So, my first question: what did you do with my people? There just is not enough paper to describe what you did with *all* the Soviet people. Let me be more specific. What did you do with the Soviet people called the Ingush?

[1] A predominantly Muslim people native to the Northern Caucasus Mountains.

Don't be too quick to accuse me of nationalism. Nationalism, as we usually define it, should not be confused with love for your roots. The concept of your homeland starts with small things—first and foremost the land of your ancestors.

And you deprived the Ingush for a long time of the most precious thing there is—the land of their ancestors. You condemned them to poverty, suffering and torture.

When the Great Patriotic War rolled back to the west, when the battles were already roaring on the other side of the Dnieper River, a special governmental decision was made to relocate the Ingush. Army units occupied their villages. Abandoning their households and homes to fate and grabbing only their hand luggage, the people were loaded under armed guard onto trucks and sent off to parts unknown. Then these unfortunate souls were stuffed into airless railroad cars. The very same convoys included former Red partisans from the Civil War, soldiers on leave and invalids from the front, and deserters and bandits. Now they were all the same. Now everybody was being specially relocated; they were all enemies.

This gives rise to a question for you, oh genius of the world proletariat: why did the entire Ingush people become victims of repression because of the antigovernmental activities of a handful of renegades, no more than a hundred people?

But let me continue. The people were kept in the railroad cars like cattle. There was not enough drinking water, bodily wastes were not cleaned up, disease was rampant. The trains moved along for months. Corpses rotted for weeks. The impoverished Ingush people, already very few in number, were thinned out still further.

Once they reached their destination, after an exhausting journey of many months, even greater hardships awaited them. The lifeless Kazakh steppes yielded nothing but cold and hunger. The hastily constructed barracks could not satisfy even the most elementary needs. The people literally ate dirt. A person could not go to the next village to visit relatives without the permission of the police. But, even here, the character of these mountain dwellers worked miracles. . . .

Tell me, father of all peoples, who will take hold of those black funeral kerchiefs and wipe the eyes of the old women and mothers? Tell me, oh greatest of the great, who will bring back my grandfather's brothers, who could not endure this hell? Who will bring back my grandfather who "earned" tuberculosis there and did not

live to see his grandson become an adult? Who will bring back my
mother's brother, who died from hunger as an infant at his mother's
breast? And finally, who will warm the hardened hearts of my
countrymen?

Let me ask you one of the most important questions: what did
you leave to me after you were gone?

Most of all, a huge country with a low standard of living and
high production figures for ore and rolled steel, pig iron and the
like. A country where for a long time the forces of production
counted for everything, where man was viewed merely as a participant in the production process, where the productivity of labor was
the criterion for relationships between people. A country bound up
by bureaucratic strictures. A huge army of bureaucrats who sucked
tremendous resources out of the state budget, decided for the producers how they were to live, what they were to breathe, what they
were to think and to whom they were subordinate. This entire
intricate network promised to take us to Communism and make real
people out of all of us. Higher bureaucratic agencies decided
whether I could live here or not, whether I could get something or
not, whether I could buy goods on credit or not, whether I had
rights or not, whether I could go abroad or not, whether I could
love this woman or not. Stay in your place; they will decide everything for you. You are a cog in a single, giant machine that produces
more and more and more. If you aren't able to do it, just be able to
do it; if you don't like it, just like it. A great builder of Communism
knows no weakness of any kind. The Party will lead us to Communism, to a happy life. The Party is the mind, honor and conscience
of our era.

What kind of people have you made, Comrade Stalin? They
say one thing, think something else and do yet a third thing. It's just
as if people are wearing masks. Here they don't like it when you are
your own person; you must always appear to be better than you
actually are. That is the general rule of survival in a collective.
Don't say what you yourself think; say what everybody thinks. The
universal sense of enslavement and the put-on front disappear, from
time to time, only with alcohol.

Integrity and sincerity in your society, oh great thinker, are a
weight that will, in the end, take you down. The huge aquarium
you built contains millions of little fish who look up to the surface
in the hopes of getting some food, and if there isn't anything up

there, they just eat each other. But I am a fish who wants to live in the sea.

Thank you, Comrade Stalin, for the "happy life" I have lived. I write this in the past tense, hoping to leave it all behind as a horrible dream.

I. I. GROYEV
Amur *oblast*
February 7, 1989
Unpublished

"EVEN THE SAINTS AREN'T SACRED!"

I had no problems with Stalin. Too bad that he had to go, that his life's work was defiled by the talentless boors who followed him, but what can you do? We'll muddle through somehow; maybe we'll live to see better times. But then along comes *Ogonyok*. . . .

With what you've started, even the saints aren't sacred! There is practically not a single issue where you don't sling rotten mud all over that dead man; you spew out frenzied malice and hatred. Sometimes it's just amazing: Well, it looks like you have slandered, spit and sh—— on every single atom of his dust. What more can you think up? Every time one opens another issue, there's sure to be something else in store. . . .

I don't know about anyone else, but it's finally had an effect on me. Your poison has aroused interest and just plain sympathy for that man. After all, a person can't be "completely black"!

And then, a dead person can't defend himself against your lies and slander. Stalin has not been convicted by any court, not even a people's court. And you have the nerve to try to be his court in history.

. . . Thinking people are completely against your blind ten-
dentiousness and hair-raising slander!

> T. GERTSIK
> Village of Petropavlovka
> Dnepropetrovsk *oblast*
> Published October 1989

"I'M PROUD TO BEAR MY FATHER'S NAME"— A LETTER FROM KHRUSHCHEV'S SON

The human memory is a strange mechanism. No matter how hard
I have tried, I cannot remember the evening my father left for the
regular session of the Twentieth Party Congress—which, for some
unannounced reason, was closed—to give a speech that in a single
instant transformed the fate of the country.[1]

None of us at home knew that the speech was being prepared;
our family was not in the habit of discussing Father's work. He
introduced this unwritten—but sacrosanct—law at the very beginning of his political career, and we observed it to the very last day
Father continued to hold the highest posts in the Party and the
government.

Incidentally, he did occasionally talk about some things himself. The day after he read his famous speech, I remember he came
to breakfast in a very animated state and told us that the day before
at the Congress serious abuses by Stalin had been disclosed: that
many innocent people had been subjected to repression, and that
the Congress had called for the immediate rehabilitation of the
victims.

---

[1] Nikita Khrushchev's so-called secret speech, in which he called for the eradication
of Stalin's "Cult of Personality," was delivered on February 24, 1956.

I cannot describe the amazement and shock we felt upon hearing those words. Coming from Father, who had been one of Stalin's closest aides—more than that, his loyal and fervent supporter, devoted to him with every fiber of his very soul—they sounded like a doomsday pronouncement!

Father dropped the subject and left the house soon afterward, but the words he had spoken were enough; it was clear that major changes were in the wind.

Such, indeed, was the case. But hardly anyone—even my father—could have imagined the horror of the picture of Stalin's orgy of terror that slowly began to emerge. Worse even than those mind-boggling numbers of human lives lost—the statistical record, incidentally, is still incomplete—which the years of the "thaw" brought to light, were the utter inhumanity of the tortures and insults endured by the masses, the mockery made of the lives of children and old people, the humiliation and the enslavement! They are impossible to comprehend or even to imagine.

Years later, when my father was already retired and working on his memoirs (with me helping him as best as I could), we went back again and again to evaluate the period of the Cult of Personality. Father consistently repeated what he had said at the Twentieth Congress: Stalin's services and achievements were great, but no services could justify his crimes. And in those days I agreed with him. How could I not? After all, I had been raised by my father, and he was inextricably linked to his times, to the tragic realities of the Stalin era. Only today do we understand with painful clarity that the achievements of those years were possible not thanks to, but *despite* Stalin; that his "services" were mixed with the blood of human suffering on a scale unprecedented in history. Father's evaluation of Stalin so long ago had an involuntary unfinished quality, a fear of that last step to a complete break with Stalinism, such as we have made today. But it is not for me to judge Father for this concession to his own biography. As Ecclesiastes says, "to everything there is a season . . ."

It was then that the letters started.

Sometimes I would find them on my desk at the "scientific research institute," as our restricted design office was called,[2] with a short request attached that I pass them on to Father. I usually

---

[2] From 1958 to 1968, Sergei Khrushchev worked in missile design for the Soviet Defense Industry.

did, although, to be honest, I read their contents first. (I did not inspect them out of a desire to see what somebody else had written—it was just that the growing stream of letters included some that openly vilified my father. After all, it was not only victims who were writing to him, but also henchmen. And, since the letters came to me first, I thought it my right to shield him from reexperiencing events that had been difficult enough for him as it was.)

Sometimes, too, when I was sitting in for his assistants, I would read Father summaries of the mail that arrived addressed to him at the Central Committee. And on other occasions, one of my friends would take me to visit former "enemies of the people," who had returned home literally the day before.

The flow of information that came crashing down on me disturbed my thoughts, completely unsettled me, played havoc with my everyday life. But never mind about me—an accidental bystander. My father, too, was clearly shaken by the scope of the tragedy that had been uncovered. But he was always unbending in everything—in the good and, unfortunately, in the bad. That was just his nature.

We never discussed those letters, or the fates of the people whose stories they brought to light—everything was clear enough without any discussion. But if, with the stubbornness of a puppy, I did try to impress my opinion on him, he always firmly said, "Stay out of it. It's none of your business." And that was that.

But still!

Still, even if some things were done wrong in those days, even if everyone did not get justice at that moment, or someone did not get heard; still I and—I hope—my children are proud to bear my father's name: KHRUSHCHEV.

I remember how, at Father's funeral—even that sad procedure was characterized, thanks to someone's ill will, as an "anti-Soviet spectacle"—suddenly a woman whom I hardly knew climbed wearily to the top of the pile of earth that had been dug out of the grave. She talked for a long time and not very coherently, now and then wiping away tears which belied her dry, businesslike manner of speech. She said that in the thirties she had worked with Father, but then had disappeared into the islands of the notorious Gulag Archipelago. At the end, in the Russian tradition, she addressed my late father directly: "Nikita Sergeyevich, you brought me and thousands of others out of that hell, and for that we will always be grateful to you and remember you. . . ."

The history of our country is the tragedy of entire peoples. It is a bitter, even a black one, full of suffering and fear. Indeed, even the *science* of history is no less dark, for to this day it has been a tradition of the Party leadership to hide the real course of events. Today, we have the chance to fill in the "blank spots" in history, to tell the real truth about the Stalin terror, the struggle against the opposition in the Bolshevik Party, the horrible consequences of forced collectivization and Stalin's repressions, which took away millions of my fellow citizens' lives. My father was the first to talk about any of it.

However, we still have much to discover, especially about things that have happened more recently: about events from the beginning of the Great Patriotic War right up through—of course— the stagnation period. Discovering *those* truths, it turns out, is even harder, because many of the people who made that history and falsified it, on their own or at some order-giver's behest, are still alive and still in office. And until we can look at the history of the country throughout this century, we will not truly be able to comprehend recent events.

When Father was removed from office, and throughout the many years since, I've sometimes heard about his mistakes. Well, what can I say? It is said that the only person who makes no mistakes is somebody who does nothing at all. As for father . . . he was not a saint. But even today—nearly twenty years after his death—it still seems to me that the good he did outweighed everything else. . . .

Sergei Nikitich KHRUSHCHEV
Letter to *Ogonyok* written especially for inclusion in this book
December 1989

THE "LITTLE GAMES"
OF NIKITA SERGEYEVICH

I probably will find no supporters in your magazine, but knowing that you recognize other points of view, I have decided to express my opinion.

It seems to me that one example of the way we race today from one extreme to the other is that we have started to make Nikita Khrushchev into an idealized hero, despite the fact that his guilt for taking agriculture in this country to the state it's in now is enormous; I would even say he played the key role! It is just amazing. Even Stalin, with his barbaric, monstrous methods, did not succeed in killing off the Russian village—although he certainly tried his best, going so far as physically to exterminate hundreds of thousands of peasants. But then Nikita Sergeyevich played his little games, and within some five to seven years, the Russian village was dead and buried. I'm not saying that Khrushchev deliberately set out to accomplish this; but all of his actions, especially in view of his persistence with them, literally killed any desire in the peasants to work with the soil and feed the nation.

Remember these events: personal plots of land[1] were reduced in size; the peasants were prohibited from mowing hay for their own cattle; the "Virgin Lands" program[2] was implemented, which stripped all the other areas bare. And then there was the forcible introduction of corn right up to Archangel; the ban on letting fertile land lie fallow and on crop rotation; and the introduction of guaranteed payments for labor to each collective farm, regardless of how much it actually produced. All of this led to what we have now: peasants left their villages in droves, and now, where the villages used to be, there are empty huts. The land is overgrown with weeds, and huge tracts of land have been taken out of circulation. There is only virgin soil where people had lived since time imme-

---

[1] Plots, of a specified limited size, where peasants on *kolkhozes* (collective farms) are permitted to raise food or animals for their own use or sale.

[2] A scheme to increase grain production by ploughing and sowing vast acreage of fertile, but arid, soil—much of it in Siberia. In order to accomplish this task, thousands of farm workers, students, and supervisors were transferred from areas already under cultivation.

morial and where tilling the soil was always a certainty, not a risky thing.

No, I give Khrushchev his due in debunking Stalin's Cult of Personality, a task which, unfortunately, he did not complete. But I cannot forgive him for the destruction of agriculture, or, for that matter, for his persecution of the intelligentsia (remember Pasternak, and the poets, filmmakers and artists of the sixties). Never!

V. VILIN
Construction engineer
Sochi
Published January 1989

LAMBS (AND COWS) TO THE SLAUGHTER

I read the letter by V. Vilin (*Ogonyok* issue no. 2 of 1989) and have come to the conclusion that he failed to mention Nikita Khrushchev's main miscalculation in agriculture, for which we are still having to pay to this day, thanks to the "stagnation period."

The problem began when the secretary of the Ryazan *Oblast* Committee had the wonderful idea of eliminating private cattle farming. They bought up all the cows from the population, but soon found that—since there had been barely enough food to keep the *sovkhoz* and *kolkhoz* cows alive in the first place—a wholesale thinning out of the herds would now be necessary. The short-term result of all this was that Ryazan was inundated with meat and flooded with milk. Khrushchev awarded the *Oblast* Committee secretary the Order of Lenin and the Hero of Labor gold star, and the Ryazan experience began to be implemented everywhere. Thus, all around the Soviet Union, more than two million cows (I don't remember the exact figure) went to the slaughter.

In addition, while visiting the Central Asian republics, Khrushchev became familiar with local sheep farming and came to the conclusion that there was no reason to feed sheep in the north in wintertime, where fodder was in short supply. So all the *kolkhoz* sheep farms were ordered closed, and the sheep were sent to Central Asia. The little lambs lived through the summer there, but in the winter they all died because they didn't know how to find fodder under the snow. About ten or even fifteen million head died. You can find the exact numbers in the newspapers of the time.

A year later, the Ryazan secretary put a bullet through his brain. Shortly after that, Khrushchev was asked to retire. I vividly remember all these events, because they were closely related to the status of my pocketbook and my stomach.

> Igor Sergeyevich NEVSKY
> Radio technician, retired
> 12 May 1989
> Zaraisk
> Unpublished

A MONUMENT FOR KHRUSHCHEV?

On the fourteenth of July, 1989, Nikita Adzhubei, the grandson of Khrushchev, appeared on the television program "Vzglyad" ["Glance"] and expressed the opinion that since Khrushchev, during the period of his reign, had been an outstanding political leader, he now deserved a monument. With all due respect to Comrade Adzhubei, the current trend is to build monuments to the victims of repression. Societies have been formed in our country to build a monument to the victims of Stalinist repression. So wouldn't it be better to erect a monument to the victims of Khrushchev's *repression?* Not only people, but even domestic animals, were victims— specifically cows. In fact, by Khrushchev's order, herds of cows were destroyed in rural areas across the country—in Russia, and in all the republics except for the Baltic republics.

There, at that time, intelligent people were in the leadership, and not people like the secretary of our Communist Party here in Novosibirsk. In the Baltic republics, in spite of Khrushchev orders, they left the cows in the fields untouched. (They've told us this in recent years to explain why the population of the Baltic republics has adequate meat and milk products, and the rest of us don't.) Indeed, when I was in Vilnius[1] on business, I sent packages back to Novosibirsk containing condensed milk and three different kinds of canned meat hash. From the time of Khrushchev to the present day, the majority of the population in Siberia have known such products only in their dreams.

So what is there to say about Khrushchev's service, when he destroyed all agriculture and husbandry and when, until the moment he was chased out in October 1964, even bread couldn't be found in the stores? This country was misled to such an extent that to this day we get ration cards for one kilogram of sausage and 400 grams of butter.

And as for politics, he showed all his leadership skills in the United Nations when he banged his shoe on the table, for which our country was reprimanded so severely that we are still being judged by it to this day.

No, Comrade Adzhubei, Khrushchev deserves not a monument, but the wrath of the whole Soviet people.

I. V. ROSLYAKOV
Novosibirsk
Received by *Ogonyok* August 1989
Unpublished

THE HERO OF MALAYA ZEMLYA

Malaya Zemlya, which means "the Small Land," was the scene of a World War II battle in which Leonid Brezhnev, then a military officer, took part. Over the years, as Brezhnev climbed toward the pinnacle of power, the importance of the battle, and of Brezhnev's role in it, steadily "grew." Finally, in 1978, a short (forty-eight-page) memoir was published, allegedly written by the General Secretary himself, which served to glorify

---

[1] The capital of Lithuania.

Brezhnev's exploits at the front. Titled simply Malaya Zemlya, *it earned the first-time author the Lenin Prize for Literature.*

No one would dispute what *Malaya Zemlya* actually was, a place where our soldiers fought with the Nazi forces with no thought for their lives. And as a veteran of the Great Patriotic War, I bow my gray head to those who will lie forever on that small patch of land and to those who, to our great fortune, stayed alive.

But I can't understand why this book that I have in front of me had to be published. To honor the soldiers who fought at Malaya Zemlya? Nothing of the kind! The purpose of the publication was to glorify Brezhnev and to support his cult of personality. And to that end, all the resources of the mass media and propaganda— newspapers, radio, television, lectures—were used on a daily basis. It was all done so unconscionably, with such contempt for the opinion of the populace, that in the end reading the papers and watching television with all of those photos of Brezhnev started to

Malaya Zemlya and its prizewinning author, as he appeared, appropriately air-brushed and medal-bedecked, on the book's frontispiece.

make people disgusted with just about any information that came from the top. Every day, all you heard was "Malaya Zemlya," "Malaya Zemlya!" It was as if those great battles outside Moscow and Stalingrad and in Kursk had never occurred.

I suggest that the text of *Malaya Zemlya* be rewritten so that its real heroes come to life. I think the book in its present form should not be kept in libraries or museums of the Great Patriotic War, because everybody knows that Brezhnev never wrote it, and consequently never was a great writer. It's incomprehensible how he could have been awarded the Lenin Prize for this work. How could he have become a member of the Writers' Union when in his day-to-day life he couldn't even say hello to his colleagues without a crib sheet?

F. A. SNEGIREV
War invalid, pensioner
Kiev
Published January 1988

THE LENINIST MEDICAL SOBERING-UP STATION

There was a local radio report about a raid conducted by the motor vehicle inspection agency. An agency inspector said, "The detainee was transported to the Leninist Medical Sobering-up Station." Now really. I can't tell you how ridiculous that sounds. *Rabotnitsa* [*Female Worker*], in its report on sloppy workers, cited the full name of the "V. I. Lenin Zlataustovsky Machine Factory." So that's what Lenin's name has come to, being on the Board of Honor of Sloppy Workers!

On the one hand, we emphasize the greatness of the man, yet on the other we are constantly mentioning the name flippantly and taking it in vain. Such misuse is promoted by the fact that so many streets, collective farms and organizations, etc., have been given the name "Lenin."

Indeed, all of the organizations in the Lenin district *automatically* become "Leninist": we have Leninist trade unions, Leninist associations, etc. Isn't it obvious that things have gone too far?

> B. I. FOMIN
> Veteran of the Party, war and labor
> Penza
> Published April 1988

"PLENTY OF DEAD ENDS"

I don't support the idea of reburying the remains of people who are guilty of crimes against the Soviet people. I say the dead should be left where they are, including those who are buried at the Kremlin Wall. But their tombstones should be marked with the words "Guilty of bloody crimes against the nation and humanity."

Also, streets in Moscow need to be renamed. After all, there are plenty of dead-end streets there. They should be named "Stalin Dead End" or "Brezhnev Dead End." Such names would serve as a memorial and at the same time be symbolic.

By obliterating part of our nation's history from our memory, we may pave the way for even bigger mistakes.

> A. S. KARPOV
> Scientific research worker
> Published September 1988

"THE PARTY OF THE FUTURE"

On Tsilkovsky Prospekt, in our city, there is a gigantic billboard. Against the background of a hammer and sickle, it reads: "We are the Party of the future, and the future belongs to the young." Five or six years ago, there was a signature under those words: "L. I. Brezhnev." But when the Brezhnev times were over, a new signature appeared on that same billboard: "Lenin." Well, who really is the author of the slogan? In my opinion, it could hardly be called appropriate for our times—we've spent so much time talking and thinking about the future that we've allowed the present to slip through our fingers.

Other such slogans have been engraved in stone, so to speak, for all eternity. For more than twenty years, on the facade of one of the five-story buildings on Victory Prospekt you have been able to read these words, which everyone knows only too well: "Today's Soviet generation will live under Communism!" Another twenty to thirty years will pass, and another generation of people will appear. But as long as that building still stands, the slogan will remain.

And what about that old warhorse of a slogan expropriated from the French Revolution: "Happiness, Equality, Fraternity"? What ever happened to "Liberty"?

Yu. ZNAMENSKY
Veteran of the Great Patriotic War
Member of the CPSU since 1947
Published October 1989

SMALL FIRES

Dear Editors:

Thanks to *glasnost,* the mass media have told us a great deal about the past. We learned about the persecution of talented people, who either were victims of repressions or were forced to emigrate abroad, but still remained patriots of their country. We found out a lot about the genocide carried out by the "Father of All Peoples," about the significant mistakes made before and during the Great Patriotic War, and the truth about the Afghanistan war. We learned about environmental problems, although sometimes too late (the Chernobyl tragedy, for example); we learned the truth about the poisoning of our food, etc., etc. How could the mood of the people be good after all that?

M. S. Gorbachev, whenever he meets with the people, always asks this question first: "How is your mood, comrades?" And everybody always answers in chorus: "Good." All that's missing is a "hooray."

It seems to me that people who really want the best for our country could not talk that way. How am I supposed to be in a good mood if I find out that my grandfather was a victim of the repressions and died and was then posthumously rehabilitated; if my father ended up a disabled veteran of the Great Patriotic War; if my children can't get competent medical care; if they eat dirty food and breathe polluted air; if I am an assistant professor and my working hours are twice as long as those of my Bulgarian colleagues, but my salary lower; if after work I have to stand in line all the time for everything, but I still have to remember that I am a woman, too. If M. S. Gorbachev can be critical of himself ("Yes, there were and will be mistakes under *perestroika;* you can't avoid them"), why must we deceive ourselves? We go to absolutely absurd lengths with our lies. A peasant woman is asked (on the TV program "Glance"), "What kinds of groceries do they sell in your stores?" Answer: "Bread; it'd be nice to have a little sugar." "And do you think you are living well?" Answer: "Yes." This raises the question: if we are living well, if our mood is good, what more do we want?

This is what made me write to you. It is no accident that M. S. Gorbachev always asks his question about the people's mood first. Any psychologist will tell you that the people's mood is the engine of progress. It's good that the door to the past has been opened. Thank you to the government for taking this step and to the journalists who wrote the truth. But, unfortunately, after reading and seeing all these things, normal people can't be in a good mood. I think that even Mikhail Sergeyevich's mood isn't always good, because there still are plenty of obstacles in *perestroika*'s path. But he has faith, and that faith should be transmitted to the people. And, it seems to me, one of the most important tasks for the press now is to do all it can to change people's mood for the better, so that "small fires" of hope for the future will ignite.

To accomplish this, I think less time should be spent on the *past:* much is already clear, journalists are already beginning to repeat themselves. More emphasis should be placed on those new buds—those which are offering something fresh and progressive— so that people will at least have the hope that in the future their grandchildren will be better off. Of course, it will be tough going for you journalists on this road; we Russians have one bad quality—

saying no at first to everything new or progressive. But still I think this is the tack that the press should take.

One of the most courageous peoples on earth, one of the most talented peoples on earth, should live better. We have earned that right!

L. A. MATOKHNYUK
Kiev
Received by *Ogonyok* May 15, 1989
Unpublished

GLOSSARY

Adamovich, Ales. A noted Byelorussian writer and antinuclear activist, and a member of the Congress of People's Deputies.

Andreyeva, Nina. A rigidly pro-Stalinist teacher of chemistry at the Leningrad Council Institute of Technology, whose letter, "I Cannot Compromise My Principles," sent tremors through the ranks of the adherents of *perestroika* when it was published in *Sovetskaya Rossiya* in March 1988. At first, it was feared that the publication of Andreyeva's letter indicated that conservatives were regaining the upper hand in the Party. But in early April, an editorial in *Pravda* strongly condemning Andreyeva's ideas helped restore the confidence of the reformers.

apparat. The Soviet political apparatus; its individual members are known as *apparatchiki*.

Argumenty i Fakty (Arguments and Facts). A progressive Soviet weekly whose circulation is reportedly the largest of any newspaper in the world—twenty-two million. In October 1989, its editor, Vladislav A. Starkov, was ordered by Communist Party ideology chief Vadim A. Medvedev to resign, reportedly for running the results of a readers' poll showing that the most popular deputies in the Supreme Soviet included several of Gorbachev's most severe critics. Starkov refused to comply.

Armenian Soviet Socialist Republic. A constituent republic of the USSR, sharing common borders with Iran, Georgia and Azerbaijan. Its capital city is Yerevan.

Azerbaijan Soviet Socialist Republic. A constituent republic of the Soviet Union, bordering on Iran, Armenia and the Caspian Sea. Its capital is Baku.

Baku. The capital of the Republic of Azerbaijan, and the scene of major anti-Armenian unrest.

Beria, Lavrenti Pavlovich. The head of Stalin's secret police.

blat. Russian slang for the universal system of using influence, connections, favors and bribes to get what one needs.

Bolsheviks. The revolutionary party that rose to power with the Russian Revolution of 1917.

Brezhnev, Leonid (1906–1982). First Secretary of the Communist Party from 1964 until his death. This era is now often referred to as the Period of Stagnation.

Byelorussia. A constituent republic of the USSR, bordering on Poland, to which it once belonged. The name means "White Russia." The capital of Byelorussia is Minsk.

Central Committee. The chief policy-making and administrative body of the Communist Party of the Soviet Union. Nominally, its members are elected by, and responsible to, the Party Congresses.

Chebrikov, V. M. The former head of the KGB under Gorbachev, replaced in 1989 by Vladimir A. Kryuchkov.

Cheka. The original name of the KGB.

complaint book. A book, supposedly available on request at all public service establishments, in which customers can write complaints and suggestions.

Congress of People's Deputies. The upper house of the newly constituted bicameral national legislature created as part of a package of reforms announced by Gorbachev in 1988. The Congress consists of 2,250 members, 1,500 of whom are elected at local, regional and republic levels. The other 750 Deputies are preselected from the Communist Party, trade unions and other official organizations. The Deputies convened for the first time in the Kremlin's Palace of Congresses in May 1989.

cooperatives. A limited form of free enterprise permitted by the Law on Individual Labor Activity, a Gorbachev-era statute, under which groups or individuals may join together voluntarily to form, run and profit from their own businesses. Gavriil Popov notes that these cooperatives are now the center of great controversy. "The issue," he writes, "is not so much the cooperatives themselves—the percentage of new cooperatives in the economy is extremely small—as the fact that they symbolize an alternative system of administrative socialism. High hopes rest on them for the very reason that they are not subject to state control. In practice, however, cooperatives have thus far only partly succeeded in becoming instruments of *perestroika*. In many cases, they have not so much begun to overcome the *shortcomings* of the command economy as they have reaped *benefits* from it (for example, by illegally buying up shortage goods in state stores and reselling them at a profit)."

cosmopolitan. A label of disparagement that came into vogue during the 1930s. It was used to imply an undesirable interest in, or loyalty to, external, as opposed to Russian, influences. Often, although not always, the word was used as a euphemism referring to the Jews.

Crimean Tatars. An ethnic group accused by Stalin of collaborating with the Nazis, and deported by him to live—under terrible conditions—in Kazakhstan. After four decades of struggle, Crimean Tatars were granted legal permission to return to their homeland. However, housing shortages and registration requirements continue to make such moves virtually impossible.

dacha. A country house or villa.

Daniel, Yuli, and Andrei Sinyavsky. Soviet writers who, in the first of a continuing series of showcase trials, were convicted in 1966 of having published "anti-Soviet" works abroad. They spent eight years in a labor camp.

Denikin, General Anton I. (1872–1947). A leading commander of the White Army during the Civil War that followed the Bolshevik Revolution.

Druzhinniki. Volunteer auxiliary police, identifiable by their red armbands.

Dyushambe. The capital of the Soviet Republic of Tadzhikistan. Also **Dusanbe.**

Estonia. The northernmost of the three Baltic republics, annexed by the Soviet Union in 1940, after the conclusion of the Molotov-Ribbentrop Pact. Like its neighbors, Latvia and Lithuania, Estonia is the center of a strong independence movement. Its capital city is Tallinn.

Fergana. A city in the Republic of Uzbekistan. On June 3–4, 1989, mobs of Uzbeks, avenging an insult made by a Meskhetian Turk to an Uzbek woman peddling fruit in the nearby town of Kuvasai, killed forty Meskhetians and ransacked hundreds of Meskhetian homes and businesses. At least ten Uzbeks also perished during the rioting. Later the same week, when Uzbek youths tried to storm a refugee camp that had been set up for the Meskhetians, five Uzbeks were killed by Soviet troops.

Georgian Soviet Socialist Republic. A constituent republic of the USSR, bounded on the east by Azerbaijan, on the south by Armenia, on the north by the peaks of the Caucasus Mountains and on the west by the Black Sea. Its capital city is Tbilisi.

"Glance" ("Vzglyad"). A popular late-night, public-affairs-oriented television program, broadcast by Soviet Central Television.

glasnost. The policy of "greater openness" in Soviet society, promoted and implemented by Mikhail Gorbachev.

Gorbachev, Mikhail Sergeyevich (1931–   ). The President of the USSR, and, since March 1985, the General Secretary of the Soviet Communist Party.

Gori. A city in central Georgia. The birthplace of Stalin, and the home of the Stalin State Museum.

Great Patriotic War. Common Soviet name for World War II. Also called the Great Fatherland War.

Grigorenko, Major General Pyotr G. An honored officer from the faculty of the Soviet War Academy who was denounced as insane, fired from his job and stripped of his citizenship after he went to Tashkent in 1969 in an attempt to aid eleven Crimean Tatars who were on trial there. He died abroad.

Gromyko, Andrei Andreyevich (1909–1989). Appointed Foreign Minister of the USSR by Nikita Khrushchev in 1957, Gromyko was politically adroit enough to hold on to the office until 1985, when Mikhail Gorbachev replaced him with the younger, and more progressive, Eduard Shevardnadze. Gromyko was then given the highly prestigious, but largely ceremonial, post of Soviet President. When Gromyko died in July 1989, Gorbachev was conspicuously absent from his funeral.

Gushchin, Lev. The deputy editor-in-chief of *Ogonyok*.

hard currency. Foreign currency that—unlike the ruble—is convertible.

informal groups. Since the state has traditionally permitted the existence of only one formal party, other political organizations—operating outside the official state and Communist Party machinery—have become known as "informal groups."

Ingush. A predominantly Muslim people native to the Northern Caucasus Mountains. The Ingush were, for all practical purposes, eliminated as an ethnic unit by Stalin's repressions during World War II.

international front. A movement organized to defend the interests of the non-indigenous population of the USSR's increasingly nationalistic constituent republics. Most typically, such groups represent native Russians living and working in areas where they are the ethnic minority.

internationalist soldiers. A term frequently used to describe the troops who fought in Afghanistan.

Izvestia. The official newspaper of the Presidium of the Supreme Soviet. The name means "news."

Kazakhstan. A constituent of the USSR, situated northeast of the Caspian Sea. Its capital is Alma-Ata.

KGB. The Soviet secret police, literally the "Committee of State Security" (*Komitet Gosudarstvennoi Bezopasnosti*).

Kharkov. A large city in the Eastern Ukraine.

Khrushchev, Nikita Sergeyevich (1894–1971). Former First Secretary of the Soviet Communist Party (1953–1964) and Premier of the Soviet Union (1958–1964).

Kiev. A major city, on the Dnieper River; the capital of the Ukrainian Soviet Socialist Republic.

kolkhoz. A collective farm. Gavriil Popov writes: "A *kolkhoz* is a cooperative venture among peasants in which both the land and the means of production are taken away from them; the overwhelming majority of their work with the land is done collectively. The only individual property retained by the peasants is the small plots of land next to their houses. A *sovkhoz,* or state-owned collective farm, is also operated collectively, but it does not belong to the workers on it, but to the state. For all practical purposes, the difference between a *kolkhoz* and a *sovkhoz* has been negligible for many years."

Komsomol. The "Young Communist League," open to youths sixteen years old and up.

kopeck. A Soviet unit of currency, equal to 1/100 ruble.

Korotich, Vitaly Alekseyevich. The editor-in-chief of *Ogonyok,* and a member of the Congress of People's Deputies.

krai. A Soviet administrative region, larger than an *oblast.*

Kryuchkov, Vladimir A. The Chairman of the KGB since 1989. In July 1989, after an unprecedented hearing in the Supreme Soviet, he became the first KGB Chairman to be officially confirmed by an elected legislature.

kulaks. Independent peasant small landholders whom Stalin, as part of his policy of forced collectivization, ordered "liquidated as a class." The result was massive repression, bloodshed and chaos.

Kurile Islands. A chain of small islands extending from northern Japan to the southern tip of the Kamchatka Peninsula.

Kuzbass. An abbreviation, commonly used in everyday speech, for the Kuznetsky Basin, the Soviet Union's richest coal-mining region. Located in the Kemerovo *oblast* of Siberia, the Kuzbass was a major center of strike activity during the summer of 1989.

Latvia. A constituent republic of the USSR, located between Estonia and Lithuania, on the Baltic Sea. Its capital city is Riga. On March 14, 1990, three days after the Lithuanian parliament voted to secede from the Soviet Union, Latvian members of the Congress of People's Deputies requested negotiations with Mikhail Gorbachev on the subject of Latvian independence.

Ligachev, Yegor K. A hard-line conservative member of the Politburo; appointed Secretary of Agriculture in 1988.

Likhachev, Dimitri S. One of the Soviet Union's most distinguished scholars; also well known as a political activist. In 1989, he was elected to the Congress of People's Deputies, and became allied with such progressive legislators as Boris Yeltsin, Gavriil Popov and Vitaly Korotich.

Lithuania. A constituent republic of the USSR whose legislature formally declared, on March 11, 1990, that it was seceding from the Soviet Union, touching off an escalating war of nerves with Moscow. Located south of Latvia, on the Baltic Sea, Lithuania had been an independent state until 1940, when it was annexed by Stalin after the conclusion of the Molotov-Ribbentrop Pact between the USSR and Nazi Germany. Lithuania's capital city is Vilnius.

Lysenko, Trofim D. In the late 1940s, Lysenko, whom historian Donald W. Treadgold described as a "poorly educated plant breeder," became the chief ideologist for Stalin's agricultural program. Lysenko, who believed that heredity is not based on genes and chromosomes, and that acquired characteristics can be passed on from generation to generation, imposed his views on Soviet genetics and agricultural policy. Biologists and agronomists who disagreed with him were arrested and, in some cases, liquidated. Many feel that neither Soviet science nor agriculture has yet entirely recovered.

mafia. Gavriil Popov explains: "The 'mafia,' as it is everywhere, is organized crime. But the concept of crime in a country where prices are set by the state, where it is impossible to buy anything you need in a normal way, is a peculiar one. The 'black market' is 'black' to a great extent only because there is no free, normal market." (See **underworld economy**.)

Malaya Zemlya (*The Small Land*). A minor World War II battle in which Leonid Brezhnev apparently took part. In 1978, a book of the same name was published, allegedly written by Brezhnev himself. The work, which glorified the battle and Brezhnev's role in it, earned for its first-time author the coveted Lenin Prize for Literature, an event which still provides amusement for cynics in the Soviet literary community.

March 26, 1989. The date on which first-round elections were held for the new Congress of People's Deputies.

market. After meeting governmental quotas, growers are allowed to sell surplus produce in special markets. Prices here are usually much higher than in the state stores.

Masonry. Since Stalinist times there has been a conviction in some circles that Soviet Communism is threatened by an international conspiracy of Freemasons.

Memory Society. See **Pamyat**.

Mensheviks. Early socialists, more moderate than the Bolsheviks, who advocated cooperation with bourgeois parties.

Minsk. The capital of the Byelorussian SSR. On October 30, 1988, a demonstration on behalf of the victims of Stalinism in Minsk was violently dispersed by the police. A subsequent article about this episode in *Ogonyok* sparked a major controversy about what constitutes "appropriate" press coverage.

Moldavian Soviet Socialist Republic. A constituent republic of the USSR, created in 1940 when the former autonomous republic of Moldavia was merged with Bessarabia, newly incorporated into the Soviet Union after the completion of the Molotov-Ribbentrop Pact. The capital city is Kishinev.

Molotov-Ribbentrop Pact. This treaty, which shocked the world when the Soviets and Nazis concluded it on August 23, 1939, was ostensibly a straightforward pledge of nonaggression. But it also contained a secret protocol partitioning much of Eastern Europe. Under the terms of this agreement, Finland, Estonia, Latvia and Bessarabia were allotted to the USSR.

Mordovia. The Mordovian Autonomous SSR—also known as Mordvinia—is an administrative division of the Russian Republic. It is located in the mid-Volga River region.

Moscow News. A progressive Soviet newspaper.

Nagorno-Karabakh. A mountainous "autonomous *oblast*" in the predominantly Muslim Soviet Republic of Azerbaijan. Part of Armenia until 1923, Nagorno-Karabakh's population is still 90 percent Armenian and Christian. In February 1988, massive demonstrations calling for "reunification" between the *oblast* and Armenia touched off the ever-escalating chain of violence that, by the end of 1989, had brought Armenia and Azerbaijan to the brink of interrepublic war.

Nakhichevan. An autonomous *oblast* on the Iranian border. It is part of Azerbaijan, but is separated from the rest of that republic by a narrow strip of Armenian territory. On December 31, 1989, Azerbaijani mobs attacked Soviet border stations in the *oblast*. Amid reports that Iranians were supplying arms to the Azerbaijanis, Gorbachev, on January 22, sealed the Iran-Nakhichevan border.

Nash Sovremennik (Our Contemporary). The monthly magazine of the Russian Writers' Union, noted for its advocacy of right-wing Russian nationalist ideals.

national front. A movement championing the interests of people of a given nationality—most typically, the indigenous population of one of the Soviet Union's constituent republics.

NKVD. The secret police of the Soviet Union from 1935 until 1943, when the agency was split into two commissariats and renamed the MGB. In 1954, the KGB was separated out from the MGB, with control of security police, border guards and selected military units.

nomenklatura. The vast hierarchy of officials appointed by the Communist Party and the government.

obkom. A regional party committee. (The term is an abbreviation for *oblastnoi komitet*.)

oblast. A Soviet administrative region, comparable to a province. It is made up of several *raions*.

Odessa. A port city on the Black Sea, in the southern Ukraine.

Okudzhava, Bulat. A famous Russian ballader and poet.

Pamyat (Memory). An ultranationalist organization whose stated purpose is the care and restoration of buildings and other artifacts of antique Russian culture. In reality, it is a virulently antisemitic paramilitary organization, many of whose members sport black T-shirts and Nazi-style greatcoats.

Party Congress. A national meeting of Communist Party officials.

payment book. A book containing coupons which accompany bill payments.

perestroika. Mikhail Gorbachev's policy of "restructuring" the economy and society.

Period of the Cult. The era of Stalin's reign, often referred to obliquely as the "Cult of Personality."

Period of Stagnation. A phrase used to describe Leonid Brezhnev's reign as First Secretary of the Soviet Communist Party, 1964–1982.

personal plots. Pieces of land, of a specified limited size, where peasants on *kolkhozes* are permitted to raise food or animals for their own use or sale.

Pioneer camps. Communist youth camps which millions of Soviet children attend every summer.

Pioneers. A Communist children's organization, comparable to the Boy Scouts and Girl Scouts.

Politburo. The highest decision-making body of the Soviet Communist Party.

Popov, Gavriil. A noted Soviet economist, editor of the magazine *Voprosy Ekonomiki* (*Questions of Economics*), and an outspokenly progressive members of the Congress of People's Deputies. In 1990, he was elected Representative of the Moscow Council of Workers, arguably the most powerful position in the city government.

Pravda. The official newspaper of the Soviet Communist Party. Its name means "Truth."

Presidium. The executive council of the Supreme Soviet, consisting of one member from each of the USSR's constituent republics and other Supreme Soviet officials.

raion. A Soviet administrative region, smaller than an *oblast;* or an administrative unit or district within a city.

registration system. All Soviet citizens must be "registered" in the place where they reside. One cannot move until one has obtained a new residence permit.

residence permit. See **registration system.**

Riga. A seaport on the Gulf of Riga (an arm of the Baltic Sea); the capital of Latvia.

RSFSR. Abbreviation for the Russian Soviet Federated Socialist Republic, the largest constituent republic of the Soviet Union.

ruble. The basic unit of Soviet currency. One hundred kopecks equal one ruble.

Rukh. A Ukrainian nationalist organization.

"rule of the grandfathers." The practice, common among second-year soldiers in the Soviet Army, of terrorizing, and in some cases virtually enslaving, new recruits. Until recently, military authorities insisted that the "rule of the grandfathers" was an invention of the press.

Russian Soviet Federated Socialist Republic. The largest constituent republic of the USSR, comprising more than 75 percent of the Soviet Union's total area. The capital city of the RSFSR is Moscow.

Ryazan *oblast.* An agricultural and industrial center in the Russian Republic, southeast of Moscow.

Sajudis. The Lithuanian nationalist organization whose victory in parliamentary elections in February 1990 set the stage for Lithuania's March 11, 1990 declaration of independence from the USSR.

Sakharov, Andrei Dimitryevich (1921–1989). A Lenin and State Prize-winning physicist and the "father" of the Soviet hydrogen bomb, Sakharov devoted the second half of his life to fighting for human rights, inside and outside the Soviet Union. In 1975, he was awarded the Nobel Peace Prize; five years later, the Brezhnev regime exiled him to the city of Gorky. Rehabilitated under *perestroika,* Sakharov was elected to the Congress of People's Deputies, where he played an activist role until his death, of a heart attack, in December 1989.

"secret speech." Nikita Khrushchev's speech before a closed session of the Twentieth Party Congress on the evening of February 24, 1956, at which he presented an itemized list of "crimes" committed by Stalin and called upon the Party to eradicate the "Cult of Personality." The full contents of Khrushchev's speech were not published in the Soviet Union until April 1989.

Shevardnadze, Eduard. The foreign minister of the USSR since 1985, when Mikhail Gorbachev appointed him to replace Andrei Gromyko.

Sinyavsky, Andrei. Dissident Soviet author. See **Daniel, Yuli.**

"socialism in one country." Stalin's theory that Communism could be built in the Soviet Union alone, even if revolution in the rest of the world failed to keep pace. This slogan became Stalin's rallying cry in his ideological struggle with Trotsky.

sovkhoz. A state farm, owned and run by the government. See *kolkhoz.*

soviets. "Local soviets" are councils with specific local administrative powers. In the early days after the Bolshevik Revolution, the local soviets were elected by workers, peasants and soldiers. The local soviets would in turn elect members of regional soviets, and so forth, in an ever-ascending hierarchy of soviets leading up to the Supreme Soviet, the legislature of the USSR. The electoral reforms instituted by Mikhail Gorbachev in 1988 enable citizens to vote directly for People's Deputies of the Soviet Union, who then choose the members of the Supreme Soviet from among their membership.

special camps. A common epithet for the labor camps of the Stalin era.

special stores. State-owned and run stores in which only specified categories of VIPs are allowed to shop. The merchandise available in special stores is invariably of higher quality than that to be found in the ordinary state stores, and goods which are in short supply are far more likely to be available there.

SSR. The abbreviation for Soviet Socialist Republic.

Stalin, Joseph V. (born Iosif Vissarionovich Dzhugashvili) (1879–1953). Former Secretary General of the Communist Party (1922–1953) and Premier of the Soviet Union (1941–1953).

state store. A store owned and run by the state and open to the general public, at which merchandise is sold, for rubles, at the official state price mandated by the central planners.

Strugatsky brothers (Arkady and Boris). A best-selling team of fantasy and science-fiction authors whose specialty is allegorical satire.

Suleimenov, Olzhas. A noted Kazakh poet, and a progressive member of Congress of People's Deputies and the Supreme Soviet of the USSR.

Sumgait. A Caspian port city in the Republic of Azerbaijan, approximately twenty miles northwest of Baku. On February 28, 1988, it was the scene of massive disorders, during which crowds of Shi'ite Muslim Azerbaijanis reportedly beat, raped and killed members of the city's Christian ethnic Armenian minority on sight. The official death toll from the incident was thirty-two, but Armenian nationalists insist that the number killed was at least ten times higher. Eight Soviet Army soldiers also allegedly died as they attempted to restore order, but this figure was not confirmed by state sources.

Supreme Soviet. The lower house of the Soviet Union's bicameral national legislature, and the country's standing parliamentary body. Under constitutional changes adopted in 1988, its 542 members are selected from—and chosen by—the 2,250 deputies of the People's Congress, the legislature's upper house.

Suslov, Mikhail A. (1902–1982). A senior member of the Politburo under Khrushchev and Brezhnev. For years the Communist Party's leading ideologist, Suslov is reported to have organized the coalition that toppled Khrushchev from power, and was one of the chief architects of the concept that Western concerns about human rights were nothing more than a vehicle for ideological sabotage.

Tadzhikistan. A constituent republic of the USSR, bordering on three foreign countries—Afghanistan, India and China. Its capital is Dyushambe.

Tallinn. A Baltic seaport, the capital of Estonia.

Tashkent. A city in Soviet Central Asia. The capital of the Republic of Uzbekistan.

Tbilisi. The capital of the Soviet Republic of Georgia. On April 9, 1989, Soviet Army troops broke up a massive but peaceful nationalist demonstration there, using clubs, sharpened shovels and poison gas against unarmed civilians. Eighteen people were killed, most of them women, and dozens more were wounded.

Ukraine. One of the constituent republics of the USSR, located in the southwest European portion of the country. Its official name is the Ukrainian Soviet Socialist Republic, and its capital is Kiev. In July 1990, the Supreme Soviet of the Ukraine passed a resolution declaring that the laws of the republic would henceforth take precedence over those of the USSR—an important move toward secession.

underworld economy. Gavriil Popov writes: "In our country, the principal manifestation of the underworld economy is what the West calls normal, everyday business: buying and reselling to make a profit. Such activities become part of the 'underworld' because they operate outside official, nonmarket channels for distributing goods, and outside the system of state prices. The success of such activities is no accident: they flourish because of shortages that force the buyer to overpay the underworld economy for goods that are hard to get the official way. Indeed, it was such shortages that created the stimulus for the underworld economy to spring up in the first place.

"Another major activity of the underworld economy is the illicit production, from state raw materials and using state equipment, of goods that are in great demand.

"Yet another is administrators' selling 'permissions' to the general public. Our country's endless maze of bureaucratic regulations offers the opportunity to trade power for bribes, to profit from one's right to allow something or not.

"Of course, we also have the 'classical' forms of 'underworld' activity, from drugs to racketeering. But, on the whole, our underworld economy is the inevitable result of the nonmarket nature of our economy, and of universal state-ification and bureaucratization."

Uzbekistan. A constituent republic of the USSR, located in the southern portion of Central Asia. Its capital is Tashkent.

Vilnius. The capital city of Lithuania.

"virgin lands." A scheme, implemented in the mid-1950s by Nikita Khrushchev, to increase grain production by ploughing and sowing vast acreage of fertile, but arid, soil—much of it in Siberia. In order to accomplish this task, thousands of farm workers, students and supervisors were transferred from areas already under cultivation. The net results were little short of disastrous.

Volgograd. A Soviet city, formerly called Stalingrad.

"Vremya" ("Time"). Soviet Central Television's nightly news program, at nine every evening.

Vysotsky, Vladimir. A very popular Soviet singer, poet and actor.

"Vzglyad." See **"Glance."**

"Word From the Reader, A." *Ogonyok*'s weekly letters column.

Yeltsin, Boris. For several years the most outspoken antiestablishment member of the Supreme Soviet and the Central Committee, he has constantly demanded that Gorbachev speed up the course of reform. Also a member of the Politburo until 1988, when Gorbachev ousted him. In May 1990, Yeltsin was elected President of the Russian Republic; in July, he shocked the XXVIIIth Communist Party Congress by abruptly announcing his resignation from the Party.

Yerevan. The capital of the Soviet Republic of Armenia. In February 1988, there were huge nationalist demonstrations here in support of the demands of ethnic Armenians in Nagorno-Karabakh that their region be reunited with Armenia.

Yevtushenko, Yevgeny. Arguably the Soviet Union's most famous poet, he was in the vanguard of anti-Stalinist reform during the Khrushchev era. In 1989, Yevtushenko was elected to the Congress of People's Deputies, where he immediately allied himself with the forces pushing for reform.

Yumashev, Valentin. Editor of the *Ogonyok* letters column.

zakuski. Russian-style hors d'oeuvres.

INDEX

ABOUT THE EDITORS

Christopher Cerf's twenty-five-year career as an author, editor, composer and producer has ranged from trade book publishing (he spent eight years as a senior editor at Random House), to education (he founded the "Sesame Street" Book and Record Division and served as its editor-in-chief for seven years), to political satire (he conceived and co-edited the landmark parody, *Not the New York Times*). Since 1972, he has been an Emmy- and Grammy-winning contributor of music and lyrics to "Sesame Street." His most recent book project, Marlo Thomas and Friends' "Free to Be . . . a Family," which he edited and packaged, reached number one on *The New York Times* nonfiction best-seller list two weeks after its publication. Cerf spent much of 1988 shuttling between Moscow and New York in his role as co-executive producer of the television version of "Free to Be . . . a Family." This program, the first prime-time network special ever jointly produced—and broadcast—in the U.S. and USSR, also earned Cerf an Emmy Award.

Marina Albee is co-founder and president of Belka International, Inc., a company headquartered in New York and Moscow which specializes in American and Soviet co-ventures—most of them involving the media. An honors scholar at the University of Vermont, Ms. Albee, who speaks fluent Russian, did her postgraduate work at Columbia University's Harriman Institute. Among her clients during the past two years have been ABC Television, Abbeville Press, MTV, the Discovery Channel and CBS Records. Ms. Albee has also served as a coordinating producer of "Capital to Capital," a series of television specials in which members of the United States Congress and the Supreme Soviet debate the major issues facing their two countries over a live satellite hookup; and of "Free to Be . . . a Family," the joint Soviet-American network TV special, on which she collaborated with Mr. Cerf.